SECRET
VICTORY

LIAM NOLAN & JOHN E. NOLAN

SECRET VICTORY

Ireland and the War at Sea
1914–1918

MERCIER PRESS
IRISH PUBLISHER – IRISH STORY

MERCIER PRESS
Cork
www.mercierpress.ie

Trade enquiries to CMD,
55a Spruce Avenue, Stillorgan Industrial Park,
Blackrock, County Dublin

© Liam Nolan & John E. Nolan, 2009

ISBN: 978 1 85635 621 3

10 9 8 7 6 5 4 3 2 1

A CIP record for this title is available from the British Library

Mercier Press receives financial assistance from the Arts
Council/An Chomhairle Ealaíon

Printed and bound in the EU.

CONTENTS

INTRODUCTION

Queenstown (renamed Cobh in 1922) played an immensely important role in the First World War, but has to a large extent been written out of that war's history. The 17 June 1919 edition of *The Times* (London) said, 'the part that Queenstown played during the Great War is not generally known, by reason of the very necessary veil of secrecy that was drawn over its work …'

This book is not a history of the First World War, but of an extremely important part of it. From 1914 to 1918 Queenstown was the base for, at first, a miscellaneous fleet of British armed trawlers, drifters, tugs, Q-ships, submarines, motorboats, armed yachts, sloops and, ultimately, a large force of American destroyers.

From May 1917 until the end of the war, these American destroyers operated out of, and were controlled from, Queenstown. The principal tasks of the naval forces based in Queenstown were (a) the protection from U-boats of merchant shipping coming in through and going out through the Western Approaches, and (b) clearing the deadly minefields laid by the Germans around the coast of Ireland.

In overall operational command of these naval forces from July 1915 until the end of the war was a brilliant and sometimes cantankerous Royal Navy admiral named Sir Lewis Bayly. He was an autocrat, but an outstanding leader. That an Anglo-American force was commanded by a British officer was an astonishing development in naval cooperation.

The First World War eclipsed all previous wars. H. G. Wells called it 'The War that will end War.' An orgy of bloodshed and butchery, it caused the deaths of almost twenty million people. Over six-and-a-half million of those were civilians, and they included passengers and crews on ships that were sunk by gunfire, torpedo or mine.

The 1914–1918 war at sea received only a fraction of the press coverage of the land battles. The enormous casualty figures in Europe were mainly responsible for that. Less understandable was the diminution of the *importance* of the maritime war. And yet Lloyd George, in his memoirs, said, 'The sea front was as essential to victory as the Western or any other front', and that it was impossible rightly to judge the wisdom or otherwise of the general campaign without understanding thoroughly how the command of the sea would affect the military situation.

'The war at sea,' as historian Martin Gilbert has said, 'was in many ways the forgotten war.' And yet, as Jonathan Raban wrote in his Introduction in the *The Oxford Book of the Sea*: 'The sea shaped and defined the nation. It was the terrain on which the Englishman's major wars had been fought, his road to the markets of the world, his route to Empire …'

The Central Powers – the wartime alliance of Germany, Austria-Hungary, Turkey and Bulgaria – came very close to defeating the Allies. (Britain, France and Russia were originally referred to as the Entente Powers, but the name Allies was adopted when more nations joined the alliance.) The terrifying success of the German U-boat campaign against merchant shipping, particularly in the Western Approaches, almost strangled Britain. Such strangulation would of course have forced surrender. The converging sea-lanes that formed the Western Approaches were the world's most crowded highway of commercial shipping.

By the spring of 1917, German submarines had sunk millions of tons of merchant shipping (in 1941 President Roosevelt would call them 'the rattlesnakes of the Atlantic'). Germany's Chief of the Naval Staff, Admiral Henning von Holtzendorff, had earlier stated that an unrestricted submarine campaign would force a peace before 1 August 1917. They were on target to compelling Britain to surrender before the year ended. Admiral Lord Jellicoe, First Sea Lord of the Admiralty, feared that capitulation was all but inevitable.

But early in May 1917 America intervened, by sending warships to Queenstown. It was the first ever intervention by the United States into European affairs. If it had been delayed by even a few weeks, the Allies would almost certainly have been defeated. 'The freedom of the seas,' Woodrow Wilson had told the United States Senate in January, 'is the *sine qua non* of peace, equality and cooperation.'

Initially a division of six destroyers crossed the Atlantic to Queenstown. Many others soon followed them, with the United States Navy operating primarily in support of the Royal Navy. The complexion of the war at sea changed, with the addition of American naval power helping to tip the scales of victory against the U-boats.

The roles played by Queenstown and its harbour have been largely ignored. This book is intended to restore a balanced perspective by fleshing out the story of what was known officially as the Queenstown Command. It is not a dry recitation of dates, statistics, battles, names and ranks. Nor is it just a story in the distant past. It isn't abstract. It humanises a part of the history of Queenstown and its harbour, covering especially a crucial period of the First World War, and does so by bringing long-dead people and events back to life.

It tells of the British and American officers and ratings who crewed the ships and boats stationed in Queenstown. It embraces the story of the 1915 sinking of the liner *Lusitania* off the coast of County Cork.

In particular it focuses on the two extraordinary admirals who influenced and dominated the Queenstown Command. The Commander-in-Chief of the Western Approaches, Admiral Sir Lewis Bayly, KCB, KCMG, CVO, lived in, and operated from, Admiralty House in Queenstown. That building is now a monastery for Benedictine nuns. Admiral William S. Sims, the charismatic pro-British commander, United States Naval Forces Operating in

Europe, had his headquarters in London, but was a frequent visitor to Queenstown where he stayed at Admiralty House.

Powerful and influential in the 1914-1918 era were the peace campaigning and neutrality fixated American president, Woodrow Wilson, and his Secretary of the Navy, Josephus Daniels. Two other Americans whose work also impacted on the town were the courageous and humanitarian American consul in Queenstown, Wesley Frost, who was shabbily treated and humiliated, and the American Ambassador to the Court of St James, Walter Hines Page, marginalised by his president for telling the truth. These are just some of the people who are brought to life here in a manner that banishes the remoteness of history.

Studs Terkel wrote in 1984 that 'the disremembrance of World War Two is as disturbingly profound as the forgettery of the Great Depression ...' Exactly the same claim could legitimately be made about the First World War and the role played by Queenstown/Cobh in the winning of that war. It is hoped that this book will go some way towards correcting the imbalance.

1

THE TOWN THAT CHANGED ITS NAME

Although the main focus of this book is the war at sea between 1914 and 1918, and the pivotal role played by Cork Harbour and the town known as Queenstown, it is important to get a grasp of that town's history in order to understand the place and its people.

The name of the town when Queen Victoria sailed into Cork Harbour on the royal yacht *Victoria and Albert* in August 1849 was Cove. By the time she left at the end of her short visit, it was Queenstown. It is built on the south-facing slope of a hill on the ocean side of Great Island, the biggest island in the harbour. Great Island covers an area of approximately 13,000 acres and is roughly 7 miles in length and 4 miles wide.

Halfway through the eighteenth century a tiny village with a population of only sixteen persons stood where the present town now spreads out along the waterfront and up the terraced hills. Before the American War of Independence, someone had described it as consisting of 'little more than the mud cabins of a few fishermen'.

In 1750, the historian Doctor Smith described it as 'a village … inhabited by seamen and revenue officers.' Two years later John Wesley, the founder of Methodism, said there was nothing to be bought in Cove – 'neither fish nor flesh, nor butter, nor cheese'. Shortly before the end of the eighteenth century a tourist named Holmes spoke of Cove as 'a wretched, dirty place …'

Between 1798 and 1853 that 'wretched, dirty place' was their last sight of Ireland for the 30,000 men and 9,000 women banished forever as convicts and sent overseas in ghastly prison ships. The same applied to the 4,000 orphan girls taken out of the country's terrible workhouses in the period between Victoria's 1848 visit and the year 1850, and sent as servants to Australia.

In 1805 an English travel writer named John Carr wrote of the harbour that it was 'perfectly safe and capable of affording complete protection to the whole navy of England from every wind that blows. Ships from England, bound to all parts of the West-Indies, put in here; and in one year, in pacific times, no less than two thousand vessels have floated upon its bosom'.

Lewis' *Topographical Dictionary* said, 'So recently as 1786 it [Cove] was a small village consisting of a few scattered houses inhabited by the tidewaiters [customs officers who boarded and inspected incoming ships] and pilots of Cork, and some miserable cabins occupied by fishermen.' But by 1837, according to Lewis, it was 'a large and handsome town, comprising nine large and several smaller streets.' This increase in its population he attributed to 'its convenient situation for the shipping in Cork Harbour in which, during the French war, 600 sail of merchant vessels have been at anchor at one time, and 400 sail have left the harbour under convoy in one day.'

The wooden ships of that era with their flat bottoms, very full hulls, and rounded bows, which pushed, rather than cut, through the water, were slow lumbering vessels which sailed at only a few miles an hour. The great fleets, Lewis said, 'always lay immediately in front of the present town, and many of them within half a cable's length [about 100 yards] of the shore.' In 1840 Anna Maria and Samuel Carter Hall, wrote: 'Cove is almost always clean – a fall of rain carrying its impurities into the Atlantic.'

Because the prevailing winds on the south coast of Ireland are from the south and south-west, sailing ships found the entrance to the big natural harbour easy to negotiate. Sir Francis Drake, pursued by ships of a squadron of the Spanish Armada, sailed in between the headlands, then turned sharply to the west, passed Curragbinny, and continued upstream for about a mile-and-a-quarter to a sheltered anchorage. That spot is still known as Drake's Pool. The bewildered Spaniards stayed in the harbour for several days, searching for Drake, even sending boats up the river to Cork. Eventually abandoning their search, they concluded, it was said, that Drake and his ship 'could have disappeared only through the power of magic'.

Two years before Queen Victoria's 1849 visit to the harbour, the *Cork Examiner* ran a story that told of 'the acute distress that exists in this town'. The distress was aggravated 'in a degree unprecedented, by the want of habitations for the multitude of poor attracted there from the country … ' It told of rooms 'and other small tenements' so crowded that, in them, disease was rampant among the very poor.

Those were the Famine years. Famine, a dictionary tells us, means 'extreme scarcity of food'. Yet there was little scarcity of food in Ireland – except as far as the poor were concerned and there were millions of poor. The Famine years lasted from 1845 (when the potato crop, the staple food of the country, ended as rotten pulp) to 1849. Over two million Irish people in Ireland depended wholly on the potato for survival. The killer fungus that destroyed the crop came to Europe from North America. It struck in England, too, in 1845, but, as Robert Kee said, 'unlike Ireland, [in England] even the poorest could afford food other than the potato'.

In Ireland up to a million-and-a-half of the population died of starvation, or of hunger-related fevers and diseases such as dysentery, cholera, typhus and relapsing fever.

Most of the Irish who died in Ireland during the Famine years were from the agricultural labouring class. Karl Marx was to comment: 'The Irish Famine of 1846 killed more than 1,000,000 people, but it killed poor devils only.' The deaths took place over a five-year period.

In 1846 the first deaths from starvation were reported – from

Macroom and Castlehaven in County Cork, and from Ballycastle in County Galway. In February of 1847 the Soup Kitchen Act (the Temporary Relief of Destitute Persons (Ireland) Act was its real name) became law. But there weren't nearly enough soup kitchens, and the diluted 'stirabout' made from maize, rice and oats that they doled out was of little or no nutritional value.

A soup kitchen was set up on one of Cove's quays. Homeless people moved into large empty casks that were lying on their sides, and occupied them, the only shelter available to them. Some of the casks had up to four or five children and their mother 'wedged and packed together, the young tenants half suffocated and struggling and fighting in their prison.'

Hundreds of thousands of starving, disease-ridden people scraped together the money for their fares and sailed away from Ireland in conditions that often were worse than those they were escaping from. They travelled in utmost squalor on unseaworthy ships, their meagre belongings crammed into a basket, or tied up in a sheet. All they got in return for the fare was a place to lie down in the four-to-a-bunk, mixed-sexed, unventilated, unheated, unfurnished and unlighted spaces known as the 'tween decks. Groups of people had to share a bucket in which to urinate and defecate. There was no privacy. The atrocious smell from the buckets was overpowering. Mixed into the overall stench was the stink of crowded, unwashed humanity. Most of the food they received was rotten. And rats ran everywhere.

Over 17,000 Irish emigrants died in the coffin ships on the Atlantic crossings. Corpses were routinely thrown overboard. Leaking, rotting ships disappeared, sank with the loss of everyone on board. Between 1845 and 1851 almost fifty emigrant ships foundered. But still the Irish fled from their native land, 1.8 million of them to North America alone.

Queen Victoria (who had given a £2,000 contribution to a famine relief charity) sailed in between the forts at the entrance to Cork Harbour on Thursday 2 August, 1849. She had had an uncomfortable voyage, but she saw, she claimed, 'many bonfires on the hills, and the lights and rockets that were set off from the different steamers'. She was struck by the immensity of the harbour.

At eight o'clock on the oppressively humid Friday morning the people of the town heard gunfire as Royal Navy ships at anchor in the harbour fired salvos of salutes to the monarch. Later on, senior naval officers, a general, and a couple of peers of the realm paid their respects to Her Majesty.

At two o'clock that afternoon the Queen was taken around the harbour in the *Fairy*, which then tied up at the pier where Victoria stepped ashore. There was the usual bowing, curtseying, saluting, and spouting of formal addresses of welcome – after which the town had its name changed yet again. Its original name had been Ballyvaloon, but a British vice-admiral named Malcolm had changed it to The Cove of Cork, and subsequently to just plain Cove. That had remained its name until the 3 August 1849. On that day Bartholomew Verling, a White Point resident who acted as the local consul for Spain and was listed among the town's 'Nobility and Gentry', begged Queen Victoria to give her blessing to the new name change – 'after which,' she wrote, 'to give the people the satisfaction of calling the place Queenstown, in honour of it being the first spot on which I set foot upon Irish ground, I stepped on shore amidst the roar of cannon … and the enthusiastic shouts of the people.'

Following the giving of such 'satisfaction' to the people, Her Majesty went on board the *Fairy* again, and the royal party went up the River Lee, across Lough Mahon and into Cork where there was a repeat of the welcoming performance.

Long before Queen Victoria's visit, there had been a Royal Navy presence in Cork Harbour. Big and safe, with deep-water anchorages, it was an ideal location for merchant ships to assemble. They sailed from there in convoys to countries overseas. Men-of-war of the Royal Navy protected those groups of ships from privateers, pirates and the warships of other nations. By the end of the eighteenth century arrangements were well under way to make the harbour a major naval base. In 1743, on the instructions of the already mentioned Vice-Admiral Malcolm, a fort, or battery, was built at Cuskinny, east of the town and facing straight out to sea.

Malcolm's initial arrival in the harbour had caught the attention of at least one balladeer who wrote:

You're welcome, you're welcome,
Vice-Admiral Malcolm,
To anchor your squadron at Cove;
And moreover the stronger
Your force, and the longer
Your stay,
The more welcome, by jove!

Cork Harbour was more extensive, more accessible and safer than Kinsale, which was a cruiser base. Kinsale's arsenal was transferred to Spike Island in Cork Harbour. A mile due south of Cove, the island shielded the harbour from the worst of the storms sweeping in from the Atlantic. Cove itself became the station of a port admiral, an officer who served as the shore commander, in charge of supplying, refitting and maintaining the naval ships that used the port.

A huge victualling yard for the Royal Navy was established on Haulbowline Island, which the English had first begun to fortify in 1602. Convicts from the harsh prison on Spike Island carried out the labouring work on the six massive grey stone storehouses and on the Royal Naval Hospital. These men were marched across each day via a wooden causeway specially constructed to link the two islands. Workshops, mast houses, wharfage, stables, and living accommodation, together with a barracks, were also built on Haulbowline. The establishment was completed in 1822 and was officially named the Royal Alexandra yard.

The small (three acres) Rocky Island south of Haulbowline was excavated to a depth of almost 30 feet, and two magazines were constructed. Together they could hold 25,000 barrels of gunpowder.

Spike's artillery barracks was bombproof. A fort had been built on the island in the mid eighteenth century. Fort Carlisle, on the eastern side of the harbour entrance, had been built in 1596, and Fort Camden, on the western headland, was built in 1803. There were also Martello towers at Ringaskiddy, on Great Island, and on Haulbowline. The harbour was thus strongly protected against attacks from the sea.

The town of Cove, with its steeply terraced houses, enjoyed what was described as a health-giving climate. The country's first ever steam-powered boat, the *City of Cork,* a passenger vessel, was built up the river at Passage West in 1815. She worked the Cork-Cove-Cork route, each one-way journey taking about two hours.

By 1830, Cove had become a noted health resort. But the Admiralty downgraded Cork Harbour as a naval base, withdrawing its port admiral. It was 1846 before another was stationed there. The place became a backwater as far as the British Admiralty was concerned, a place to which they attached little importance. No ambitious career officer wanted to be stationed there. Cove and its mighty harbour were virtually ignored in official circles in London and beyond, becoming a place of no consequence or standing.

But one man who was determined to try to turn back the tide of neglect was John Francis Maguire, Member of Parliament for Cork, and founder of the newspaper the *Cork Examiner.* He brought up the question of Cork Harbour in the House of Commons in 1857, citing the undertaking made by a former British government to raise the status of the harbour as a naval base to the equivalent of Portsmouth and other similar bases in Britain.

The promise, when it had been made in 1800, had been used as an inducement to get the Act of Union passed. The promise, as with so many other political 'promises', had never been fulfilled. Maguire wouldn't let go and pressed, argued, harassed, campaigned, made a nuisance of himself, becoming a sorely irritating embarrassment to the government. He kept up his campaign for seven years, and eventually his persistence paid off. In 1864 the British government set up a select committee to deal with the matter of Cork Harbour, and Maguire was appointed a member.

The committee prepared and delivered its report with a set of proposals, and in 1865 a sum of £300,000 was allocated for the completion of a nine-acre dockyard on Haulbowline. It would be completed, government sources said, within five years. Work on the project began in 1865, and once again convicts from Spike Island gaol initially supplied the bulk of the manual labour. But the work force had to be supplemented by locally recruited men.

John Francis Maguire died in 1872, fifteen years before the dockyard on Haulbowline was finished. By then the population of Cove/Queenstown had grown to over 10,000.

In September 1884, *Harper's New Monthly Magazine*, a prestigious American publication, featured an article called 'A Run Ashore at Queenstown', written by a well-regarded author and feature writer, William H. Rideing. He called Queenstown 'a place of meeting and farewell' and said, 'Queenstown Harbour is not unlike that of New York. As the Narrows protect the latter, Roche's Point and its opposite headland are so close together that they shut out the storms ... and keep the water within it smooth when that outside is raging. The circular bay, with its islands and hilly shores, is also a duplicate of what may be seen in the neighbourhood of Staten Island.' He wrote that on a clear and placid summer day 'Queenstown Harbour is as beautiful as anything that can be imagined'.

The town he described as being 'at the head of the bay, in an almost straight line from the Point' and it was 'built in terraces, one above the other, on a wooded and heathery bluff.' The higher terraces were principally dwellings, 'and the higher they are, the better is the class to which they belong. On the ridge above all the others are two or three houses which may be called palaces without extravagance of phrase.' (One of those 'palaces' was undoubtedly Admiralty House; another is likely to have been the mansion, which in time became the residence of the Catholic bishop of Cloyne, and was thenceforth known in the town as The Bishop's Palace.)

Mr Rideing observed that in Queenstown 'the lines of caste and rank are drawn with English precision'. The harbour was 'made for by many ships consigned to order, or, in other words, sent here that the choice of a port of delivery may be governed by the conditions of the market ... ' Having stated that the 'salubrity' of the town's climate brought a small number of invalid visitors to it, 'especially consumptives and sufferers from nervous debility', he claimed that 'the dominant person in this little society is the admiral of the port, and not to know him is to be unknown – at least in fashionable eyes.' An obsolete old warship was moored in the harbour, according to Rideing, and its principal use was as a vessel on which the admiral could fly his flag, 'and the harmless old frigate is maintained with a crew of two hundred or more men, to fulfil a tradition'. He asserted that when one of the 'enormous armoured ships or a great white transport comes into the harbour to carry troops away from *this inactive little station* to the Cape or India ... the captain in full uniform enters a boat which bears him away to the admiral to report – *and the admiral receives him with satisfying blandness* [italics added]'. The functions of the admiral were, according Rideing, *'almost entirely ornamental, and around him clusters an acquiescent little court* [italics added]'.

Mr Rideing labelled Queenstown 'dull', and said that to an active temperament the torpor of its ways 'soon become execrable.' And he said that after the passengers of the ocean steamers rippled the surface for a few hours, 'the moment they are gone, the place relapses into its usual and oppressive quietude.' He wrote that long before the tender came in from Roche's Point, 'a voluble rabble of hawkers, beggars, and carmen gathers on the quays'. There was, 'an unblushing fluency of lying, flattery and humbug ...'

If Royal Navy interest and activity in Cork Harbour had waned, merchant shipping activity mushroomed. Before the invention of wireless telegraphy, nearly all the ships approaching Britain from overseas with cargoes of grain, sugar, timber and the like, had to call at Queenstown to find out where they were to go. 'Queenstown for orders' was one of the most common entries in the log books of merchant ships. Queenstown acquired a rail link and railway station (opened in 1860, the year after the Cunard company first opened an office in the town), a deep water quay, hotels, guesthouses, shipping agencies, and port offices.

Cork Harbour became a major port for cross channel trade, as well as for trade with Europe, the Mediterranean, North and South America, and the Far East. The port was a hive of coastal shipping, and it became the main departure port for hundreds of thousands of Irish men and women driven out by famine, disease, and grinding poverty, heading to countries where they hoped to find a better life. The transatlantic shipping lines did a roaring trade in the sale of passages to men, women and children set on emigrating to Canada and the United States.

When the Americans closed their Ellis Island Immigrant Reception Station in New York, and insisted that those who intended to enter the USA had to (a) have a hot bath and (b) undergo a certificated medical examination immediately before leaving their country of departure, Queenstown also acquired a delousing station. It was situated on the Baths Quay on the site where formerly had stood the town's public hot and cold seawater baths.

Thus developed the fishing village of Ballyvaloon/Cove, the 'wretched and dirty place'/Queenstown, to become the most important port in the 1914–1918 World War.

2

'THE BOILING CAULDRON OF WAR'

Between 1–4 August 1914, Germany declared war on three countries: Russia, France and neutral Belgium. Technically Germany recognised Belgium's neutrality. But the Germans had a plan – the Schlieffen Plan – which their former Chief of the General Staff, Count Alfred von Schlieffen, had worked on for twelve years up to 1905, and they intended adhering to it. They aimed to march rapidly through Belgium and encircle the French army.

They counted on taking Paris within six weeks, and forcing France to surrender. The German request for free passage through Belgium (it was really a twelve hour ultimatum) was delivered to the Belgian Foreign Minister, M. Davignon, by the German Ambassador at Brussels, Herr von Below Saleske, on 2 August. The request stated that Germany had in view 'no act of hostility against Belgium'. But it also contained the threat: 'Should Belgium oppose the German troops, and, in particular, should she throw difficulties in the way of their march by a resistance of the fortresses on the Meuse, or by destroying railways, roads, tunnels, or similar works, Germany will, to her regret, be compelled to consider Belgium an enemy.'

Belgium rejected the request for free passage, refusing to allow her neutrality to be violated. The note conveying the refusal was handed to von Below Saleske on the morning of 3 August 1914. It pointed out that Belgium had 'always been faithful to her international obligations' and that 'the attack upon her independence with which the German government threatens her, constitutes a flagrant violation of international law'. Germany was told that the Belgian government was 'firmly resolved to repel, by all means in their power, every attack upon their rights'.

On the afternoon of Wednesday, 4 August, a clear quiet day, the Germans invaded Belgium. The first to cross the border were cavalry troops carrying 12-foot lances, pistols, rifles, and old-fashioned sabres. After them came the ranks of grey uniformed infantry, and behind the infantry came the artillery. As the troops marched into Belgium, they were singing *Deutschland über Alles*. The Germans had 60,000 troops in their spearhead. 'You will be home,' the Kaiser had told his departing troops, 'before the leaves have fallen from the trees.'

The Prussian Karl Marie von Clausewitz (1780–1831), sometime director of the General War School in Berlin, had written: 'Whoever uses force, without any consideration and without sparing blood, has sooner or later the advantage ... It is a vain and erroneous tendency to wish to neglect the element of brutality in war merely because we dislike it.' He also said that war was 'the continuation of politics through other means', and that it was 'merely a situation in which great numbers of men or of ships fought one another'. He was recognised as one of the most outstanding writers about war – his major treatise, *Vom Kriege* (On War), has had a lasting impact worldwide on strategic studies. He was idolised by the German military.

As far as Belgium was concerned, the Germans showed no inclination at all to 'neglect the element of brutality'. But 'brave little Belgium', as the country came to be called, put up a fierce resistance before being overcome, and though facing overpowering odds, shot and killed as many of the invaders as possible in the attempt to halt the avalanche of enemy troops pouring in.

What followed became known as the 'rape of Belgium'. On the first day of invasion, the Germans began shooting priests and other civilians. Six Belgian hostages were shot at Warsage, and the village of Battice was burned to the ground. It was the beginning of a three-week campaign of massacres, looting and destruction.

The list of Belgian towns where massacres of civilians were carried out is a roll call of horror and shame – Andenne, Dinant, Seilles, Tamine. In Andenne, 211 civilians were killed; at Tamine, 384. Anyone at Tamine who didn't die immediately on being shot was bayoneted where she or he fell. In the medieval town of Dinant on the River Meuse, German execution squads rounded up 612 people, including children and women, took them into the town square, and shot them.

Between 6 and 12 August 1914, 550 troop trains crossed the Rhine from Germany every day. They carried a total of over a million soldiers. On 25 August the university city of Louvain was attacked by 10,000 German troops. They set fire to buildings and entire streets, burned a priceless collection of nearly 250,000 books, including a collection of ancient manuscripts. They killed 209 civilians, among them a number of Catholic priests. They gutted the university and other public buildings, and forcibly 'evacuated' the town's population of 42,000 people.

Germany's chancellor, Theobald von Bethmann-Hollweg, told a crowded Reichstag: 'Our invasion of Belgium is contrary to international law, but the wrong … that we are committing we will make good as soon as our military goal has been achieved.'

There was a cynical attempt to justify the German army's use of terror by claiming that it was a legitimate extension of warfare, intended to induce rapid civilian submission. The same claim would be made by the Allies in the Second World War in the attempted justification of the carpet bombing of such non-military targets as Dresden, one of the most beautiful of all German cities. No one was tried as a war criminal for the destruction of Louvain, just as no one was tried as a war criminal after the Second World War for the destruction of Dresden, or Hiroshima, or Nagasaki and other non-military targets

Germany's reason for wanting to go *through* Belgium was because they felt that the French frontier next to Germany was too strongly fortified to allow a quick knockout blow. France, relying on Belgium's neutrality, had neglected to fortify her frontier with Belgium. Therefore, the Germans reasoned, entry into France would be easy. Pulitzer Prize winner (for *The Guns of August*) Barbara W. Tuchman, later wrote that the violation by Germany of Belgium's guaranteed neutrality 'established the image of bully in the public mind'.

On 3 August 1914, Britain's Foreign Secretary, Sir Edward Grey (described by the American writer S. L. A. Marshall as 'the gentle dreamer who knew nothing of armies') stood up in the House of Commons and addressed the assembly. He spoke for almost an hour. Borrowing from a speech by Gladstone, he asked, 'Could this country stand by and witness the direst crime that ever stained the pages of history, and thus become participators in the crime?' He was listened to in silence, but when he finished the members rose to their feet, cheering.

Also on 3 August Francis Townson Clarke was arrested in Queenstown as an alleged spy for the Germans. The police, when they searched his room, found sketches he had made of Cork Harbour. The sketches showed Carlisle Fort, Roche's Point and a battleship. Clarke was remanded in custody.

The next day, Britain, through its ambassador in Germany, Sir Edward Goschen, delivered an ultimatum to Germany: halt the invasion of Belgium, or Britain would be at war by midnight. Goschen presented the ultimatum personally to the chancellor, Bethmann-Hollweg. In his report of the meeting, Goschen said, 'I found the Chancellor very agitated. His Excellency at once began a harangue, which lasted for about twenty minutes. He said that the step taken by His Majesty's Government was terrible to a degree. Just for a word – "neutrality" – a word which in wartime had so often been disregarded, just for a scrap of paper Great Britain was going to make war on a kindred nation which desired nothing better than to be friends with her.'

That 'scrap of paper' Bethmann-Hollweg referred to so contemptuously was the formal 1839 Treaty of London, which guaranteed

Belgium's neutrality. Bethmann-Hollweg's choice of phrase would be used as propaganda against Germany for years afterwards.

The Germans ignored Britain's ultimatum, the deadline passed, and Britain carried out its threat and declared war on Germany. And so Field Marshal Sir John French (an 'uncertain and timid leader' according to one reference book) led 90,000 soldiers of the British Expeditionary Force (BEF) across the channel between the 12–20 of August. The soldiers had no idea that they were facing slaughter.

An anonymous writer of barrack-room ballads and rough verse almost immediately got to work when it was learned that one of the German generals was named von Kluck. To the tune of a popular song of the time, 'The Girl I Left Behind Me', the soldiers sang:

Oh, we don't give a fuck
For old von Kluck
An' all his fuckin' army!

Another version was:

The Crown Prince he's gone barmy
Poor Kaiser Bill is feeling ill
And we don't care a fuck
For old von Kluck
And all his bleedin' great army.

Sir Edward Grey, in a different context, was more elegant in his choice of language. He said of the war, 'The lamps are going out all over Europe; we shall not see them lit again in our lifetime.' Later he would say that in 1914, 'Europe had arrived at a point in which every country except Germany was afraid of the present, and Germany was afraid of the future'.

At a meeting of the Queenstown Regatta committee the members unanimously adopted the resolution: 'That in view of the ominous happenings which have intervened since our previous meetings, the proposed regatta and fireworks of the season be abandoned until a happier future.' It was decided to send a copy of the resolution to Vice-Admiral Sir C. H. Coke, the president of the committee.

On the morning of 5 August the *Cork Examiner* ran a short item about that evening's scheduled recital in Queenstown by the band of the Rifle Brigade. It was to be given in the bandstand of the promenade. The programme included music by Wagner, Tchaikovsky, Puccini, Greig and Rossini, and the conductor was to be Mr Richard T. Stevens. The news item mentioned that this might be the last time for quite a while that the Rifle Brigade's band would be heard in public performance.

On the same day the British cable ship *Telconia*, using a grapnel, raised from the seabed Germany's telegraphic cable which ran from the German-Dutch frontier down the English Channel to France, Spain, Africa and the Americas. The ship severed the cable, isolating Germany from the outside world. Unable to communicate by cablegram, Germany had to depend on radio transmissions and, if possible, the use of neutral countries' cable links.

Around Britain, fourteen wireless intercept stations were manned by operators who, wearing headphones, painstakingly searched the radio bands for messages being transmitted by the enemy. They picked up the orders transmitted from Germany's 200 kW transmitting station at Nauen telling all German merchant ships either to return to Germany immediately, or to head for ports in neutral countries. Those particular orders were transmitted in clear, non-coded language, but other messages were encoded to protect them from unauthorised persons. The airwaves were alive with radio messages flowing between the fleets and ships at sea, and their land-based command headquarters.

Winston Churchill, the First Lord of the Admiralty, was quick to realise the intelligence potential of the top-secret coded messages that began to pour into the Admiralty, so a new code-breaking department was set up in Room 40 at the old Admiralty building in London's

Whitehall, and a team of cryptanalysts was recruited. Through a combination of brilliance, hard and painstaking work, and luck, the team broke the significant German codes.

'The nations,' Sir Edward Grey said, 'slithered over the brink into the boiling cauldron of war.' That war turned into the most murderous struggle in history. Bigger armies than ever before set about killing each other with new weapons – poison gas, machine guns, and tanks.

The war at sea saw the introduction of submarines. (The German word for submarine was *Unterseeboot*. In English it was shortened to U-boat.) Back in 1902 Rear-Admiral Sir Arthur Wilson, a winner of the Victoria Cross, had labelled submarines 'underhand, unfair and damned un-English'. He said that they would never be any use in war! But in January of 1914 the greatest British admiral since Nelson, Lord Jackie Fisher, wrote a memorandum on the submarine, which he sent to Prime Minister Asquith. It turned out to be prophetic, for Fisher wrote that the coming of the submarine 'means that the whole foundation of our traditional naval strategy … has been broken down … this submarine menace is a truly terrible one for British commerce and Great Britain.' He predicted unrestricted U-boat war being waged by the Germans.

When Winston Churchill received a copy of the memorandum, he was dismissive, discounting the admiral's prediction. He didn't believe that unrestricted U-boat war 'would ever be done by a civilised power.' But another distinguished old sea dog, Admiral Sir Percy Scott, the Royal Navy's greatest authority on naval gunnery, chose the Letters Page of the *The Times* to express the view that 'all war is, of course, barbarous, but in war the purpose of the enemy is to crush his foe. To arrive at this he will attack where his foe is most vulnerable. Our most vulnerable point is our food and oil supply. The submarine has introduced a new method of attacking these supplies. Will feelings of humanity restrain our enemy from using it?'

The answer would turn out to be an unequivocal No.

On 2 August 1914, the Germans, in a note marked 'Very Confidential', had made clear that they were going to enter Belgian territory. Their stated reason: 'Reliable information has been received by the German Government to the effect that French forces intend to march on the line of the Meuse by Givet and Namur. This information leaves no doubt as to the intention of France to march through Belgian territory against Germany.'

3

THE WAR AT SEA

On 25 July 1914, with war in Europe seemingly inevitable, Britain's Foreign Secretary, Sir Edward Grey, had proposed the setting up of a peace conference in which France, Italy, Britain and Germany would participate. The proposal was declined by Germany.

At the time, Britain's authority over the seas was unquestioned. She had many more of the heavier ships of war than the Germans. The statistics told the story – Britain had 177 heavy ships; Germany had eighty-seven. Britain also had sixty-five submarines (some accounts place the figure at seventy-four); Germany had only twenty-four out of its thirty-three ready for duty.

On Tuesday 28 July 1914 Winston Churchill, the impetuous and opinionated young First Lord of the Admiralty, ordered Britain's Grand Fleet, complete with all its reservists, not to disperse, but to sail to its War Stations – Scapa Flow (a 50 square mile stretch of water in the Orkneys) and Cromarty, up in the far north of Scotland. The fleet, with full crews at war strength, had just a day or two previously completed a test mobilisation and manoeuvres at Portland on the coast of Dorset.

If Churchill had not issued his order, the fleet's various components parts would have headed for their home ports, with the reservists being paid off within a few days. Instead, the fleets steamed at speed during the hours of darkness along the English Channel, through Dover Straits, and up the east coast of England and Scotland, the battle cruisers to Cromarty and the battleships to Scapa Flow. (Both, incidentally, were undefended anchorages with virtually no base facilities.) The procession of warships was 18 miles long. All external lights on the ships were extinguished. Once they reached their northern anchorages, the warships were refuelled, and placed on a war footing.

Churchill had become First Lord of the Admiralty in 1911. His appointment dismayed senior naval officers at the Admiralty. They were experienced men who valued their status, their seniority, and the traditions of the service. They considered the brash and truculent Churchill to be an arrogant, abrasive upstart. Some of them despised him. At one stage the entire Board of Admiralty threatened to resign in reaction to his ill-mannered behaviour, his highhandedness and his peremptoriness.

To the *National Review* he was 'a self-advertising mountebank' and 'a political gambler of the worst type'. *The Spectator* viewed his appointment as 'appalling', said that he didn't possess the dignity, the loyalty, the good sense or the steadfastness required, and that he 'must always be living in the limelight, and there is no fault more damning in an administrator'.

Prime Minister Asquith's view of him was that he had 'a pictorial mind brimming with ideas [and] is in tearing spirits at the prospect of a war, which to me shows a lack of imagination.' Asquith considered him to be 'very bellicose', and 'longing for a sea fight ...'

Nevertheless, Churchill, convinced that Britain was on the brink of war with Germany, had, in cahoots with Prince Louis Mountbatten, the First Sea Lord of the Admiralty, decided to keep the fleet together to maintain mastery of the trade routes. It was through these routes that the island nation transported the supplies on which it depended for existence.

It was one of Churchill's imperatives that the Grand Fleet should be ready to take on the German navy in the event of a full scale sea battle developing. There was, too, the issue of protecting Britain against any attempts at invasion. And lurking at the back of Churchill's and the Admiralty's minds was a fear of the relatively new weapons, the submarine and its torpedoes.

A one-time controller of the Royal Navy, Admiral Sir Arthur Wilson, had, in 1901, ordered that any captured crews of submarines should be hanged as pirates. He was the man who said that submarines were 'underhand, unfair, and damned un-English'. In June 1913, retired Admiral of the Fleet Lord Fisher called submarine warfare 'an altogether barbarous method of warfare'.

The Imperial German navy had only about twenty operational U-boats at the outbreak of war. Their forward base was Heligoland, on a small (1,800 yards long, 650 yards wide) rocky island off the mouths of the Rivers Elbe and Weser. It was known as the Red Rock of the North Sea, and had been ceded to Germany by Britain in 1890 in exchange for Zanzibar. In overall command of the U-boats was *Korvettenkapitan* (Commander) Hermann Bauer. His title was *Führer der Unterseeboote*, shortened to *FdU*.

Britain's Grand Fleet (made up of capital ships, cruisers and destroyers), under the command of Admiral Sir John Jellicoe, was anchored at Scapa Flow in the Orkney Islands. Bauer was aware that it was the most powerful navy in the world.

On 4 August 1914, the position of Commander-in-Chief of the Fleet (nearly thirty dreadnoughts and battle cruisers, plus squadrons of ordinary cruisers and flotillas of destroyers) had been given to fifty-four-year-old Jellicoe, the son of a master mariner. Jellicoe had a brilliant mind and an exceptional brain. He was a superb seaman and an outstanding ship handler, and all ranks in the Grand Fleet came to love and admire him. Quiet and gentlemanly, he had for a long time been Admiral Sir John (Jackie) Fisher's first choice to lead the Grand Fleet in the event of war. Fisher, the man responsible for the building of the first all-big-gun battleship, HMS *Dreadnought*, and known in Britain as 'the greatest British admiral since Nelson', had characterised Jellicoe in 1904 as 'one of the five best brains in the navy under the rank of admiral.'

To deal with the threat of the British navy Bauer had come up with the idea of sending U-boats to attack the British warships as they rode at anchor. It required his boats having to penetrate the huge enclosed anchorage. That would take great courage and determination, and could easily end up as a disastrous mission.

Bauer was under the impression that Scapa Flow was as elaborately defended as the German bases. It wasn't, not at that stage. It had no booms, no mines, no nets – facts that continually worried Jellicoe, so much so that he took the Grand Fleet temporarily to Loch Ewe on Scotland's north-west coast, and to Lough Swilly on Ireland's north coast.

On 6 August 1914 Bauer sent ten U-boats out on patrol into the North Sea. They were ordered to make a sweep, in line abreast, 350 miles up the middle of the North Sea, with a distance of 7 miles between each boat. Their mission: to seek and sink British warships. Around midday on 8 August one of the U-boats, U-15, came across three dreadnoughts, launched a torpedo at one of them, missed, and suffered the frustration of watching the three battleships getting away unscathed and at speed.

At a quarter to four in the morning of the following day, the light cruiser HMS *Birmingham* found U-15 on the surface. Depth charges hadn't yet been invented, so there was no way of attacking a submerged submarine. But this one was hove to, and sounds of hammering could be heard coming from inside her. The *Birmingham* turned, intent on coming in on a ramming run. She struck the submarine a glancing blow on the stern, came about, and returned at full speed, smashing into the U-boat, slicing her in two. The submarine sank with all hands. There were no survivors.

One U-boat captain, *Kapitanleutnant* (Lieutenant-Commander) Baron von und zu Peckelsham, said later that where there were no survivors from a submarine that was sunk, the men on board her 'drowned like rats in a trap, with some perhaps left to die of slow suffocation. I could imagine how some might even now be alive in the strong torpedo compartments, lying in the darkness, hopeless, waiting for the air to thicken and finally smother them.'

Another one of the ten U-boats sent out by Bauer on 6 August, U-13, was lost without trace, destroyed in a minefield. Two others developed engine problems and had to return to base. Not a single enemy ship was sunk. The U-boats' first patrol was a total failure.

But a month later, on a calm, sunny 5 September, came the kind of spectacular success that the service desperately needed to boost wavering morale. SM U-21, captained by Otto Hersing, travelled up the Firth of Forth, almost as far as the bridge, before turning and heading back towards the open sea. Suddenly Hersing got lucky. Into range, off May Island, came the flotilla-leader of the Forth destroyer patrol, HMS *Pathfinder*, commanded by Captain F. Martin-Leake. Hersing fired just one torpedo at her. It struck, and exploded, and within five minutes the *Pathfinder* was gone from the surface of the sea. Her magazine had exploded. She took 259 of her crew down with her. Captain Martin-Leake, though injured, survived. He was picked up unconscious, clinging to a piece of flotsam.

HMS *Pathfinder* was thus the first warship to be sunk by a German U-boat, and Hersing became a national hero in his own country. Martin-Leake went on to command the cruiser HMS *Achilles*. He spent a period at Queenstown as flag captain. 'Everyone loved the little commodore', Admiral Bayly said in later years. Martin-Leake eventually became an admiral.

At sunset on 1 August 1914 the U-boat U-9 had been on the surface, its captain, *Kapitanleutnant* Otto Weddigen (32), and his *Erster Wachoffizier* (First Watch Officer), Johannes Spiess, standing alongside each other in the conning tower. Weddigen had turned to Spiess and said, 'Spiess, look how red the sky is. The whole world seems to be bathed in blood. Mark my words – England will declare war on us.' He was right.

Early on the morning of 22 September, Weddigen, still in U-9, an obsolescent, small U-boat, spotted three elderly Bacchante-Class Royal Navy cruisers. It was 6.10 a.m. The cruisers were on patrol 18 miles north-west of the Hook of Holland and were steaming in a straight line. They had no destroyer escorts. The 12,000-ton four-funnelled old cruisers were the HMS *Aboukir*, the HMS *Cressy*, and the HMS *Hogue*. In smooth water and bright sunshine Weddigen steered his U-boat on an interception course.

A month earlier, Commodore Roger Keyes, the officer in command at Harwich, had pleaded, 'For heaven's sake, take those Bacchantes away!' He said that the Germans were aware that the three old warships were in the area, 'and if [the Germans] send out a suitable force, God help those cruisers!'

Weddigen began his attack by targeting the *Aboukir*. U-9 was 12 feet under the surface when, just before 6.30 a.m., Weddigen ordered the first torpedo to be fired. It struck the warship on her starboard side. 'There was a fountain of water,' Weddigen reported, 'a burst of smoke, a flash of fire, and part of the cruiser rose in the air. Then I heard a roar, and felt reverberations sent through the water by the detonation. She had been broken apart, and sank in a few minutes … Her crew were brave, and even with death staring them in the face kept to their posts.'

The *Cressy* and the *Hogue* came about and approached the stricken *Aboukir* to pull survivors out of the water, moving straight into the line of fire. Weddigen lined up on the *Hogue*, and fired a single torpedo at her. Again the aim was accurate. The torpedo struck close to the cruiser's aft magazine, which exploded. Following the explosion, men on the *Hogue* saw a periscope (U-9's) about 300 yards off the ship's port bow. Weddigen said that the *Hogue* 'lay wounded and helpless on the surface before she heaved, half turned over, and sank.'

Next, from a distance of between 500 and 600 yards, he fired two torpedoes at the *Cressy*. One of them struck the ship on the starboard side just before the after-bridge; the second hit the cruiser under the No. 5 boiler room. It was now about 7.15 a.m. The men on the *Cressy* started throwing overboard tables, chairs, lengths of wood, hammocks and towing-targets, anything that would float and might save lives if clung to in the water. The cruiser began to sink by the head and 'careened far over,' Weddigen reported, 'but all the while her men stayed at the guns looking for their invisible foe. They were brave and true to their country's sea traditions. Then she eventually suffered a boiler explosion, and completely turned turtle. With her keel uppermost she floated until the air got out from under her, and then she sank with a loud sound, as if from a creature in pain.' It was 7.55 a.m.

The effect on U-9's *Erster Wachoffizier* Spiess was reflected in his account of what he called 'a horrifying scene'. He said, 'We in the conning tower tried to suppress the terrible impression of drowning men fighting for their lives in the wreckage, clinging on to capsized lifeboats ...'

'Having done my appointed work,' Weddigen said, 'I set my course for home.'

The trawler *Coriander* came to the aid of the survivors. She picked up 156 officers and men. The Dutch vessels *Titan* and *Flora* also helped with the rescue work. A total of 1,460 men died in the sinking of the three cruisers.

When U-9 returned to base, the Kaiser personally presented the Iron Cross, First Class and Second Class, to Weddigen. Every member of the crew was awarded the Iron Cross, Second Class, and permission was given for the boat to use a representation of the decoration as its symbol on the conning tower.

Weddigen and his crew didn't survive the war. In the month after he had sunk the *Aboukir, Cressy* and *Hogue*, he sank another British cruiser, the 7,350-ton HMS *Hawke*, and in February 1915 sank four merchant vessels. He was given command of U-29, and on 18 March 1915 his luck ran out when HMS *Dreadnought* rammed and sank the U-boat. There were no survivors.

Up to this the U-boat war against British vessels was confined to warships. But that was about to change. And, as an eventual result,

Queenstown would become the single most important port in the sea war.

E. Keble Chatterton, a former RNVR lieutenant-commander-turned-author, wrote in 1934 that long after Britain declared war on Germany, it was something of a shock to many people when they were reminded that Queenstown 'still possessed one considerable link in that it continued to be a base of the Royal Navy: not in the same category as Portsmouth or Devonport, yet at least it was a second-class depot such as existed across St George's Channel at Pembroke.'

Almost immediately on the outbreak of war, a decision was taken by Britain to impose a naval blockade on Germany, to halt the flow of trade by sea routes into and out of that country. Those sea routes to Germany's short North Sea coast passed through both British home waters, and across the North Sea. Scapa Flow in the northerly Orkney Islands controlled the passage between Norway and the north of Britain. The 270 miles of sea that separated Scotland from Norway were patrolled by the Royal Navy.

Blockade was a harsh draconian device, banned by the Declaration of London in 1908, an agreement signed by most of the world's major sea powers. Significantly, Britain (a nation for which the sea had been a lifeline for three centuries) never ratified the Declaration. And so it was that the long-range blockade, brought about by patrolling the whole North Sea, and closing the Straits of Dover, was technically illegal.

British officials used a convenient euphemism for the word 'blockade' – they termed it 'economic warfare'. But blockade it assuredly was, and it soon became a matter of international controversy because it struck, by indirect attack, not only at Germany's civilian population (the 'hunger blockade' some Germans called it), but also at the free flow of neutral commerce.

The concept of freedom of the seas was raised again and again, and sharp disagreements were voiced and hotly debated. For long periods from the eighteenth century to early in the twentieth century, Britain, through its Royal Navy, held command of the sea (the Germans termed it *Beherrschung der Meere)*. This dominance allowed its merchant ships and naval vessels to move around at will, moving supplies and troops to wherever it wanted them to go. This was why, during the Napoleonic Wars, Britain was able to blockade France, and able to blockade the United States during the war of 1812. When Ralph Waldo Emerson crossed the Atlantic in 1832, he noted that the English regarded the seas of the world as their exclusive colonial possession.

With the First World War under way, the United States, caught between the two belligerents (Britain and Germany), protested against the violations of its neutral rights and the destruction of the doctrine of the freedom of the seas. Subjects of contention between neutrals and belligerents included the right to seize neutral property and persons who were aboard an enemy ship, the mining of sea-lanes, and the exclusion of neutral vessels from enemy ports by blockade.

Freedom of the seas was a principle first established by the Romans, and the doctrine held that ships of any nation could travel unmolested through international waters. The idea gave to all nations unrestricted use of the seas for naval and commercial navigation in times of peace. In 1609 the Dutch jurist and one of the founders of international law, Hugo Grotius, defined the seas as being, like the air, limitless and therefore common to all people.

As long ago as September 1776, the US Congress adopted a committee's proposals relating to neutral commerce in wartime. It was the first official American statement on freedom of the seas. In 1783, John Adams, the second president of the USA, said, 'The United States of America have propagated far and wide in Europe the ideas of liberty of navigation and commerce. The powers of Europe, however, cannot agree as yet in adopting them to their full extent.'

Early in the First World War President Woodrow Wilson compared the British to thieves and the Germans to murderers, inasmuch as the British, he said, seized property, whereas the Germans took lives which were lost forever. As the *US History Encyclopedia* says: 'While the United States strongly took the position that neutral ships should be allowed to carry goods for belligerents in times of war, other nations enforced rules of contraband (mostly defined as military stores) and blockade.'

Sir Edward Grey was concerned to get the maximum blockade that could be enforced without a rupture with the United States. By November 1914 the whole of the North Sea had been virtually, though not completely, closed off. It should be remembered that Denmark, Norway, Sweden and Holland were neutral.

In February 1916, a special Ministry of Blockade was set up in Britain with Lord Robert Cecil at the helm as the first Minister of Blockade. He, as a devout Christian, found his duties and responsibilities distressing, because the aim was to starve the German people. In 1919 the Germans claimed that the blockade had caused malnutrition, which resulted in the deaths of 763,000 people, and that it had raised child mortality by 50 per cent and women's mortality by 51 per cent.

As early as the day after Britain declared war on Germany, the Germans started to lay mines by surface vessels off Britain's coast. The SS *Konigen Luis* dropped 180 of these floating bombs into the sea off Southwold, the east Suffolk seaside resort south-south-west of Lowestoft. Three weeks later 200 mines were laid by the *Nautilus* off the Humber estuary. Heavy British shipping losses from vessels striking mines were sustained almost from the beginning. But it wasn't until 20 October 1914 that the SS *Glitra* became the first merchantman to be sunk by a submarine, although she was neither torpedoed nor shelled. It happened off the coast of Norway when the ship, carrying coal, oil and iron plates, was spotted by U-17. The U-boat captain manoeuvred his submarine alongside the tramp steamer and sent a boarding party to inspect her cargo. They ordered the *Glitra*'s crew to abandon ship, and gave them ten minutes to get clear. When the ship's lifeboats pulled away, the boarding party opened the valves in the ship's bottom (her sea cocks) allowing the water to flood in. The *Glitra* sank 14 miles off Norway's coast. The Germans on the surfaced U-boat, and the steamship's crew in the lifeboats, looked on. When the ship disappeared, the U-boat captain, Feldkirchner, towed the lifeboats closer to the coast.

It had all been done strictly according to the internationally recognised prize rules, but six days later came the first attack on a ship without any warning given. That the French vessel *Amiral Ganteaume* didn't sink when torpedoed by U-24 off Cape Gris Nez became almost irrelevant when considered in the context of its being an attack-without-warning. The ship had 2,500 Belgian refugees on board, and 40 of them lost their lives. A nearby steamer rescued the remainder. The stricken vessel was towed into Boulogne.

The first ship to be sunk off the coast of Ireland was the merchantman SS *Manchester Commerce*. She went down on 26 October 1914 off the coast of Donegal, sunk by a mine. Her master and thirteen other members of her crew perished, and news of the sinking was withheld until well after the war. The mine that sank the *Manchester Commerce* was part of a minefield that a German armed merchant cruiser, SS *Berlin*, had laid midway through October, close to and north of Tory Island. The British had not known of the minefield's existence.

At the time, because work was under way at Scapa Flow to try to make it secure against attack, part of Britain's Grand Fleet (including the Second Battle Squadron) was temporarily stationed in Lough Swilly. Two days after the *Manchester Commerce*'s destruction, the Second Battle Squadron was at sea to carry out target practice when suddenly the new (1913) super-dreadnought battleship HMS *Audacious* struck a mine further south in the same Tory Island minefield in which the merchant ship had gone down.

The White Star liner *Olympic*, outward bound from Liverpool, was in the vicinity. Seeing the *Audacious'* plight, the liner's master brought his ship close to the stricken warship and, even though the sea was rough, he began a brave attempt to tow the warship to Lough Swilly.

The admiral commanding the squadron took the remaining ships of the squadron out of danger by steaming north immediately. But a fleet collier (the *Thornhill*) and the light cruiser HMS *Liverpool* were ordered to stand by to render assistance and pick up survivors.

Meanwhile, the officer commanding the First Battle Squadron, Vice-Admiral Bayly, asked to be allowed to go out to the badly damaged (but still afloat) *Audacious*, to assess the chances of salvaging her and to see what he could do. When he reached her and went on board, he found that the ship had lost her steam and was dead in the water. With heavy seas running, three hawsers from the three ships close by, all parted. The battleship's stern began to sink lower in the water and it became obvious that successfully towing her into Lough Swilly was going to be virtually impossible. Other efforts were made and abandoned only when it was clear that she was likely to capsize soon and sink.

Most of the ship's company were ordered by her captain to leave her before it got dark, and they were transferred to the light cruiser. The last man to leave the ship, cleaving to tradition, was her captain, Captain Dampier, RN. The second-last man to leave her was Vice-Admiral Bayly. They went on board the light cruiser HMS *Liverpool*, and had barely finished eating dinner when there was a tremendous explosion on the *Audacious*. She had capsized, and her magazine had exploded.

That minefield *had* to be found, and swept. It took the British until 20 December to locate it, and when they did, they found that it consisted of 200 mines running in a north-east to south-west direction. Requisitioned trawlers and ordinary excursion paddle-steamers were assigned to the job of sweeping up and destroying the mines. It was slow and hazardous work, made all the more dangerous by the filthy weather the ships had to deal with on so many days and nights. By the end of April 1915 they had swept up forty-three mines, but it took them until July to complete the job.

Between 5 August and the end of December 1914, the Germans laid a total of just over 1,000 mines in five different areas along the east coast of England as well as the minefield off Tory Island. Those mines sank forty-two merchant ships – a rate of one ship for every twenty-four mines.

What with mines and, possibly, U-boats to contend with, the Admiralty decided to set up a base at Larne in County Antrim to which more than eighty steam net-drifters and armed patrols were sent to carry out antisubmarine operations. Their area measured 30 miles by 22 miles. The rough seas and generally inclement weather in that part of the ocean severely hampered the effectiveness of the drifters, small, slow (9 knots maximum) vessels. Kingstown (Dún Laoghaire) became an auxiliary naval base from which armed trawlers patrolled the Irish Sea, and Milford Haven and Liverpool were also pressed into use.

On 23 November 1914, a U-boat, U-18, got into Scapa Flow through the Hoxa entrance. She slipped in daringly by following directly in the wake of a steamer. It couldn't have been simpler, but instead of a fleet of battleships at anchor, all that the U-boat commander, von Hennig, saw was a virtually empty expanse of water – the Grand Fleet was out in the North Sea on exercises.

Having successfully got into the Flow, von Hennig now had to get out. Unfortunately for him and his crew, the armed trawler *Dorothy Gray* and the destroyer *Garry* had other ideas. Both of them rammed the submarine. In trying to escape from them, U-18 was caught in a rip tide that forced her onto the rocks of the Skerries where her crew scuttled her. It took until February 1915 for antisubmarine defences to be put in place at Scapa Flow, Hoy Sound, Switha and Hoxa.

By the end of 1914, U-boats had sunk ten merchant ships, totalling over 20,000 tons, and eight secondary warships. The Germans had lost five U-boats.

The development that caused the greatest concern to the Admiralty was that U-boats began to travel further and further west from their home bases. In January 1915 Hersing (the same Hersing who had sunk HMS *Pathfinder* the previous September) managed to pass through the Dover Straits on the surface at night in U-21. The British had put protective antisubmarine nets in place, but they proved to be useless, as they didn't stretch the full way across the channel. Added to this, they could be ripped open by the saw-like devices which the Germans mounted on the bows of their U-boats for just that purpose. Hersing took his U-21 along the full length of the English Channel, and then turned north up the Irish Sea. Off the Mersey he sank three British steamers. The serious implications for Britain could not be ignored.

At around the same time as Hersing ended this highly successful patrol and returned to his home base at Wilhelmshaven, Germany announced that as from 18 February 1915 the waters around Britain and Ireland would be deemed to be a war zone. Any merchant ship, neutral or otherwise, caught in it, was liable to be sunk. This would be Germany's answer to the Royal Navy's blockade – a counter blockade, but by U-boats, as advocated by Admiral von Pohl, chief of the naval staff, back in the first week of November 1914.

Liddell Hart, in his *History of the First World War*, made the pithy observation that when the attack on sea-borne commerce was exercised against Britain herself in a novel form and by a new weapon – the submarine – 'it was human, if illogical, that she should decry it as an atrocity.'

U-boats sank ships off Cape Gris Nez, Calais and Le Havre. The 15,000-ton battleship, HMS *Formidable*, was torpedoed and sunk off Portland Bill in the war's first underwater night attack by a U-boat.

An alarming burst of sinkings took place in the Irish Sea in February and March, with ships being sunk off the Isle of Man, Point Lynas in Anglesey, the Liverpool Bar, Ilfracombe and County Down. On 14 March 1915, a major shock to the Admiralty occurred when a U-boat attacked the steamer, SS *Atlanta*, 12 miles south of Inishturk

Island off the west coast of Ireland. On the 28 March a U-boat began to operate off Ireland's south-east coast for the first time and U-28 (*Kapitanleutnant* Georg-Gunther Freiherr von Forstner) sank the Elder Dempster liner SS *Falaba* within sight of the Coningbeg lightship. Over 100 people died.

The message was brutally clear: the U-boats were able to travel far to the west, could reach and would operate in the Atlantic. But the Atlantic Ocean encompassed 32 million square miles, and that immensity of waters posed enormous challenges for submarines trying to locate ships – and for antisubmarine vessels trying to locate U-boats as radar had not yet been invented.

On the same day in 1914 (4 August) that Britain declared war on the German Empire, America's President Woodrow Wilson proclaimed the USA's neutrality, to which he was puritanically attached. As Barbara W. Tuchman said in *The Guns of August*, he saw in the war an opportunity for greatness on the world stage.

4

THE PRESIDENT
AND THE AMBASSADOR

The president of the United States in 1914, Thomas Woodrow Wilson, was a bespectacled, slender, long-faced, grey-haired man with a first-rate intellect. He was his country's twenty-eighth president, and was a conservative Democrat. His take on the word 'conservative' was wry rather than profound. 'A conservative,' he said, 'is a man who sits and thinks, mostly sits.'

Wilson's ancestry was Scots-Irish – his grandparents had emigrated from County Tyrone. The president, whose father was a Presbyterian clergyman, grew up in an academic household, studied law, was admitted to the bar in 1881. 'I used to be a lawyer,' he would say in another attempt at humour, 'but now I am a reformed character'. He earned a PhD, (an academic distinction held by no other US president before or since), and taught at Princeton University for over a decade. Indeed he was elected president of Princeton.

He detested war, and when he received news of the outbreak of hostilities in Europe, he found it hard to believe. He considered vigilant neutrality to be in America's best interests and was, as Barbara Tuchman said, 'rigidly attached to neutrality'. Wilson hoped that a neutral United States might serve as a mediator, and he offered mediation. No one took it up. 'The United States must be neutral in fact as well as in name during these days that are to try men's souls,' he said. 'We must be impartial in thought as well as in action.'

Wilson entered politics in 1910 when he was elected Governor of New Jersey. From then on he dropped the Thomas from his name, and called himself plain Woodrow Wilson. He loved power but didn't like sharing it, even though in a private letter to a woman friend written in 1913 he held that 'power consists in one's capacity to link his will with the purpose of others, to lead by reason and a gift of cooperation'. He bitterly resented any criticism of his political decisions. He was proud, obstinate, and opinionated. 'Dour' and 'cold' were words often used in descriptions of him. Widely read, he was recognised as a fine orator.

Wilson appointed William Jennings Bryan as Secretary of State, and had Bryan's full support. Bryan, like his president, scrupulously favoured neutrality. It was a policy that reflected the general view of the American public at the beginning of the war when the prevailing attitude in the USA was one of relief and self-congratulation that 'the war in Europe has nothing to do with us'. Bryan differed from Wilson only in that he (Bryan) was against the granting of loans to Britain and France.

People from the far west of the USA, and in particular the farmers, didn't feel any affiliation with Europe, and ethnic groups, such as Irish and Eastern European immigrants, had grievances against some of the Allied powers. An Indiana newspaper, the *Plain Dealer*, said: 'We never appreciated so keenly as now the foresight of our fathers in emigrating from Europe.' The anti-intervention bloc believed in isolation.

Despite the fact that his own ancestry was Scots-Irish, Wilson, when he was a prolific academic and popular historian, had a jaundiced view of what he called 'hyphenated Americans'. He was referring to German-Americans, Polish-Americans, Italian-Americans, and Irish-Americans. He was suspicious of hyphenated Americans' dual loyalties, saying, 'any man who carries a hyphen about with him carries a dagger that he is ready to plunge into the vitals of this Republic whenever he gets ready.' His views moderated over time, and when he became president he extended the hand of friendship towards these same hyphenated Americans. Indeed an Irish-American Catholic lawyer from Jersey City, Joseph Patrick Tumulty, became Wilson's private secretary, and *de facto* assistant president.

Two days after Britain declared war on Germany, Wilson's wife of thirty years died from kidney disease. Deeply affected by her death, the president was close to collapse. On Sunday 9 August the American Ambassador in London, Walter Hines Page, wrote Woodrow Wilson a letter that began:

'Dear Mr President,
God save us! What a week it has been! …'

British Foreign Secretary Sir Edward Grey and Ambassador Page had become firm friends. They shared similar interests and enthusiasms, and when they met, which was often, they nearly always shed observance of stuffy official diplomatic protocol and behaviour, and just sat and talked man-to-man. Both of them loathed war, and they had closely similar beliefs about justice and fairness. The two men were knowledgeable about and devoted to the poetry of Wordsworth; they read the same kind of books, and shared a deep affection for birds, hedgerows, trees, and nature in general. Grey's opinion of Page was that the American was just about the finest example he had come across of the value of character in a public man.

On 4 August 1914 Grey had asked Page to come and see him at the foreign office. The American ambassador arrived at three o'clock in the afternoon and found Grey gloomy and subdued. The foreign secretary spoke of Belgium's neutrality being violated by Germany – neutrality that was assured by a treaty to which Germany had been a signatory.

'England would be forever contemptible if it should sit by and see this treaty violated …' Grey said to Page. 'I have therefore asked you to come, to tell you that this morning we sent an ultimatum to Germany …' He asked Page to explain the situation to President Wilson, and said he hoped the United States would be neutral. Page left the foreign office with, he later revealed, 'a sort of stunned sense of the impending ruin of half the world'.

In his 9 August letter to President Wilson, Page said that he would never forget how Grey had wept in telling about the ultimatum, and that he (Page) would never forget, 'the King as he declaimed at me for half-an-hour and threw up his hands and said, "My God, Mr Page, what else could we do?"'

Page ended that letter with these words: 'Now, when all this half of the world will suffer the unspeakable brutalisation of war, we shall preserve our moral strength, our political powers, and our ideals. God save us!'

Walter Hines Page was a cultured southerner, born in North Carolina, opinionated, used to expressing his views forcefully and elegantly, in writing as well as in conversation. In 1900 Page became one of the founders of a publishing house – Doubleday, Page and Company. Among the books the company published were those of Woodrow Wilson.

Page was a tall, homely looking, widely read and scholarly man, an incessant and humorous talker who liked to relate anecdotes and quote aphorisms. It was while Woodrow Wilson was president of Princeton University that Walter Page first picked him out as a possible future president of the United States. He supported and befriended Wilson, and when Wilson was eventually elected his country's president in 1912, Page, at the age of fifty-eight, was appointed ambassador to Britain. It was a reward for loyalty and support.

Walter Page wasn't wealthy, and being ambassador to the Court of St James was a draining financial experience. He arrived in London in the spring of 1913, and soon developed close personal relationships with many high officials, notably Foreign Secretary Grey. A prolific letter-writer, Page sent streams of letters, written in his precise, neat handwriting, back to Washington. Some, giving detailed descriptions of Britain and the British, he sent direct to the president. Some he sent to Colonel Edward Mandell House, the president's closest foreign policy adviser.

House, a Texan, wasn't really a colonel at all. His was an honorary title, bestowed upon him by James T. Hogg, whose political campaign he'd managed in 1892. But House had formed a warm friendship with Woodrow Wilson in 1911. They shared similar political and moral values, and by the time the war started, he was Wilson's most trusted confidant. House read Ambassador Page's letters aloud to the president who apparently enjoyed hearing them. But as the war in Europe grew more bloody and ferocious, with the casualty numbers growing to hundreds of thousands, and then millions, and the German U-boats taking a frightful toll of shipping and lives in the Western Approaches, criticism of Wilson and the American nation for holding back from entering the war, grew and intensified in Britain. The conscientious and principled Page reflected this criticism in his letters.

The ambassador remained steadfastly loyal to the president and refused to join the critics. But because part of an ambassador's duties is to report what is being said about his country, Page continued to do just that, even when it meant passing on views that were vitriolic. Wilson, introspective, highly strung and complicated, and given to self-questioning, became increasingly irritated by his ambassador's letters. The president disliked and felt aggrieved by anyone in his circle who dared to criticise him, however well-founded the criticism might be. If anyone continued to censure, or find fault with Wilson's views, or passed on the criticism of others, Wilson had no compunction about coldly excluding him from the inner circle, which is what he eventually did to Ambassador Page. The years of support given to Wilson by Page, the lengthy first-name friendship, came to count for nothing. Page began to be looked upon, and spoken about, in Washington as just an irritating extreme Anglophile.

The anti-American sentiments in Britain grew more vocal and virulent following the sinking of the passenger liner *Lusitania* off the Old Head of Kinsale on 7 May 1915.

5

VERDICT: MURDER

Once the fog burned off and the liner emerged into sunshine at around 11.00 a.m. on Friday morning 7 May 1915, it looked like the start of a perfect day – no wind, the sea surface like glass, the sky a glorious blue. Mrs Belle Saunders Naish (49) from Kansas City, a Second Class passenger, said later, 'A lovelier day could not be imagined'.

An Irishwoman, Mrs Rose Howley, exclaimed when she saw the coast, 'Look at the green hills. God save Ireland!' A group of people standing at the rail beside Mrs Howley began to sing 'The West's Awake'. They followed it with 'God Save Ireland'.

The ship's master was Captain William (Bill) Turner, a stocky, taciturn fifty-eight-year-old Liverpudlian, who had run away to sea as a boy. By 1915 he was one of the Cunard company's most experienced captains, having joined them in 1878 as a third officer. When the 30-metre-high lighthouse on the tip of the Old Head of Kinsale became clearly visible, he felt a surge of relief because when he'd come on the bridge at eight o'clock, visibility was down to thirty yards. The ship had run into thick fog before dawn, and her raucous foghorn had been continually shattering the stillness of the morning. Turner ordered the ship's speed to be increased from 15 to 18 knots.

Some passengers had feared that the roaring blasts of the foghorn would attract any German U-boats that might be in the area. But Turner always did things by the book. He had already ordered the lifeboats to be swung out, the ship's watertight doors to be closed, and the number of lookouts to be doubled.

On the previous evening the master had received a radio message saying: 'Submarines active south coast of Ireland.' He'd requested a repeat, and got exactly the same message again. He subsequently received a message from the Admiralty which said, 'To all British ships: Take Liverpool pilot at bar and avoid headlands. Pass harbours at full speed. Steer mid channel course. Submarines off Fastnet.' Around 4 to 4½ miles off the south-west corner of Ireland, west of Cape Clear in County Cork, the Fastnet lighthouse, a huge (54 metres high) granite tower on the jagged Fastnet Rock, was the landfall light for all ships inward bound from the west.

At one stage in his career Turner had served on a sailing ship, the *Queen of the Nations*, which was captained by his father. In 1915 he was no stranger to U-boat warfare. Earlier that year he had been master of the *Transylvania* when she'd been diverted to Queenstown to await destroyer escort, because U-boats were operating off the south coast. Now, however, on this beautiful May morning, with the Old Head of Kinsale lighthouse at last in full view (it is a bold headland with steep cliffs, the lighthouse standing like a warning finger on its southern extremity), Turner's deck officers would be able to take the four point bearing fix he'd ordered to establish the *Lusitania*'s exact position. The process, he knew, would take the best part of an hour.

The *Lusitania* was a 30,396-ton, 787-feet-long, 87-feet-6-inches-wide, quadruple screw, express passenger liner, with four funnels. Designed in 1902 by Leonard Peskett, she was shown in the first drawings with only three funnels. Built in John Brown's yard at Clydebank, the *Lusitania* was launched in June 1906, and was the first ship larger than 30,000 tons gross. Over four million rivets were used in her construction, each one individually hammered into place. At the time she was launched, she was the biggest ship in the world. She was delivered to the Cunard company on 26 August 1907. A crowd of 200,000 lined the shore on 7 September 1907 to watch her begin her maiden voyage – from Liverpool to New York, via Queenstown.

In October 1907 she won the Atlantic Blue Riband, crossing

the ocean in four days, nineteen hours and fifty-two minutes, at an average speed of 24 knots. The transatlantic crossing (for Blue Riband purposes) was the distance between Daunt Rock lightship off Cork Harbour, and Sandy Hook Lightship off New York – 2,781 miles. Her log for her first week in September 1908 westbound crossing shows the distance between Liverpool and Queenstown as 228 miles. She left Liverpool landing stage at 6.03 p.m. on Saturday 5 September, and arrived at Queenstown just before a quarter to six the next morning.

An extremely fast giant express liner, she had 76,000 horsepower engines, and burned a thousand tons of coal a day in her furnaces, coal which had to be hand loaded each time she took fuel on board. With her speed, she could easily outstrip any U-boat. Even after her No. 4 boiler room was shut down in November 1914 to conserve fuel, she was still capable of 21 knots.

Captain Turner had first been given command of her in November 1908 when her then master, Captain James Watt, retired. So by May 1915 he was familiar with her and her performance capabilities. Indeed at the end of her very last westbound crossing, he himself, without the aid of tugs, had berthed this 787-foot behemoth at Pier 54 in New York.

The *Lusitania* had plenty of lifeboats – twenty-two of the regular clinker-built wooden variety, and an additional twenty-six collapsibles. And, as with all passenger steamers of the Cunard Line, the ship was fitted with 'Marconi's system of wireless telegraphy'.

In the six days immediately following the liner's 1 May departure from New York, twenty-two ships had been sunk in the war zone by German U-boats. Nobody on the liner knew that. On the day she sailed out of New York, an advertisement had appeared in ten American morning newspapers (seven in New York, one in Boston and two in Philadelphia). It contained a blunt warning:

NOTICE!

TRAVELLERS intending to embark on the Atlantic voyage are

reminded that a state of war exists between Germany and her allies and Great Britain and her allies; that the zone of war includes the waters adjacent to the British Isles; that, in accordance with formal notice given by the Imperial German Government, vessels flying the flag of Great Britain, or of any of her allies, are liable to destruction in those waters, and that travellers sailing in the war zone on ships of Great Britain or her allies do so at their own risk.

IMPERIAL GERMAN EMBASSY
WASHINGTON, D.C., APRIL 22, 1915

Copies of the advertisement, which was framed in black, were handed to embarking passengers on the quayside at Cunard's Pier 54 at the bottom of New York's 14th Street where the *Lusitania* was berthed. The passengers who boarded her chose to ignore the alert.

U-20, one of three U-boats boats ordered to the Irish Sea and Bristol Channel in April 1915 by the officer commanding Germany's U-boats, *Korvettenkapitan* Herman Bauer, had four torpedo tubes – two bow and two aft – and carried a total of seven torpedoes. She also had a 3.5 inch deck gun. Her two eight-cylinder diesel engines gave her a flat-out speed on the surface of just under 15 knots. When submerged, her top speed was 9 knots, but she could keep that up for only an hour before having to surface to charge her batteries.

She sailed from Emden on 30 April 1915. Her captain was a Berliner – *Kapitanleutnant* Walther Schweiger, aged thirty. In February he had attacked the hospital ship *Asturias,* saying afterwards that he did so because the ship was sailing from England and therefore, by his reasoning, could not, would not, have been carrying wounded. He wasn't one of the more humane U-boat captains.

Schweiger, three other officers, and thirty-one crewmen were crammed into the U-boat's machinery-and-weapon-packed hull, which was 210 feet long. By the time U-20 spotted the huge liner on 7 May, Schweiger had already, on 5 May, sunk by gunfire a 132-ton schooner, the *Earl of Latham*, south-south-west of the Old Head of Kinsale. He had also unsuccessfully attacked the *Cayo Romano* off Queenstown on the same evening, and on 6 May had sunk by torpedo the two 6,000-ton cargo ships *Candidate* and *Centurion* off the Waterford coast, south of the Coningbeg lightship.

When the *Cayo Romano* arrived in Queenstown, she reported the details of the attack made on her. Queenstown in turn notified the Admiralty in London. Therefore London knew there was a U-boat operating in the path of the incoming *Lusitania*.

Schweiger was on the bridge on the conning tower of his U-boat when the liner was first sighted between 10 and 13 miles away to starboard. A lookout drew his attention to the giveaway smoke from the ship's funnels. No one on U-20 realised then that the vessel they were looking at through binoculars was the *Lusitania*. Her orange Cunard funnels had been painted black in February to help to disguise her identity. On sighting the liner, Schweiger gave the order to dive. It was twenty minutes past one in the afternoon of 7 May.

Schweiger had three torpedoes left. He was required by standing orders to keep two for possible use during the return trip back to base. At 1.40 p.m., because of a change of course to starboard by the liner, Schweiger realised that the ship was steaming in a path that would bring her within torpedo range. The liner's tonnage was forty-six times that of the U-boat. She was three-and-three-quarter times longer, could travel more than one-and-a-half times faster, and had a crew that was twenty-four times the size of the U-boat's crew.

At ten minutes past two the *Lusitania* and U-20 were only 700 metres apart. The liner coming through the calm water was almost dead ahead of U-20, and was in the perfect position for Schweiger to make a bow shot.

The G-type torpedo, set to run at 9 feet below the surface, blasted from the torpedo tube and sped towards the *Lusitania*. On the liner, the starboard lookout on the forecastle head, an eighteen-year-old boy named Leslie Morton, spotted the track of the torpedo when it was about 500 yards away, could see it coming directly towards the ship. He put his megaphone to his mouth and shouted to the bridge, 'Torpedoes coming on the starboard side!'

The torpedo was only 200 yards from the *Lusitania* when the crow's nest lookout, Thomas Quinn, caught sight of it. Captain Turner had just returned to the bridge from his day cabin when the torpedo struck.

The *Lusitania*'s five piece orchestra – John William Hemingway, Edward Drakeford, Charles W. Cameron, Handel Hawkins, and Edwin Carr-Jones – were halfway through Johann Strauss' sweeping waltz 'The Blue Danube'.

Marconi Wireless Operator Bob Leith, aged twenty-nine, the senior of the ship's two operators, was in the after dining saloon on D deck, just about to start his lunch when suddenly he felt a shock and heard an explosion. He didn't know what it was and thought it was most likely a boiler bursting. He tore out of the dining saloon, then along the boat deck to the wireless cabin where David McCormick, the junior wireless operator, was on duty. Leith immediately began sending an SOS message, with the letters MFA (the ship's call sign) at the end of it. A deck officer rushed into the wireless cabin and gave him the ship's position, which Leith included in all his transmissions from then on. But it was only minutes before power failed. Leith switched to emergency power and kept on transmitting.

The SOS was picked up and acknowledged by a land-based station on the coast. It was also picked up by at least two freighters and a tanker. They changed course and headed towards the *Lusitania*'s position.

Leslie Morton, the young lookout who had been the first to see the torpedo streaking towards the *Lusitania*, was blown off his feet when it struck and exploded. He got up and ran as fast as he could towards the ship's lifeboats. Amidst all the confusion, he began helping with guiding and shepherding the passengers into the boats, acting with a maturity and presence of mind remarkable for his age. He stayed doing it until, if he wanted to live, he had no other option but to jump into the sea.

Even then he did his utmost to save people all round him from drowning. He and another seaman swam to one of the collapsible boats floating nearby, and between them they managed to tear off its canvas cover. There were terrified people on all sides, floundering in the water. Morton and his companion pushed and heaved to get as many of them as possible on board the collapsible. For their actions and courage, the two seamen were awarded medals.

Schweiger watched the *Lusitania* through his periscope. In his log he recorded that the ship was struck on the starboard side 'close abaft the bridge', and that the impact explosion was followed by a second, the ship coming to a stop, listing heavily to starboard, the bow going down.

The *Lusitania*'s forward movement ended when her bow struck the seabed. Nearly 800 feet long, she had been steaming in an area in which she had approximately 300 feet of water beneath her keel.

Her list to starboard increased, and Schweiger thought she was about to capsize. He also thought he saw evidence of 'considerable panic' on board the liner.

Other ships that he had torpedoed remained floating for a considerable time after being struck, and on a few occasions had had to be finished off by either a second torpedo or by gunfire. He was amazed at how quickly the *Lusitania* was sinking.

Because of the heavy list to starboard, it was impossible for the liner's port side lifeboats to be launched successfully, and several of them (each weighed five tons), when lowered to the deck and their snubbing chains released, crashed inboard, smashing against the ship's superstructure, crushing, killing and maiming people who were either in or near them. Some of the boats on the port side were just let go, and they went slamming and bouncing down the ship's side, their planking ripped to splinters by the protruding rivet heads on the hull.

On the starboard side, some of the lifeboats suddenly tipped into vertical position, bow down or stern down, dumping their occupants screaming into the water.

According to his log, Schweiger decided to 'dive to 24 metres and proceed out to sea. Also I could not have fired a second torpedo into this mass of people struggling to save their lives.' He came up to periscope depth again about fifty minutes later to take another look. 'In the distance astern, a number of lifeboats,' he wrote. 'Of the *Lusitania* nothing more can be seen ... Wreck lies in 90 metres of water.'

At periscope depth, Schweiger could see some of what was happening on the surface, but could hear nothing of it. There were many dying screams on the afternoon air.

The *Lusitania* sank at 2.28 in the afternoon. Only six of her twenty-two regular lifeboats were successfully launched.

On 8 September Schweiger would torpedo another liner, the 11,000-ton *Hesperian*, 80 miles south-west of the Fastnet. On that ship another thirty-two lives were lost. The Queenstown-based sloop *Sunflower* rescued several hundred survivors and landed them at Queenstown.

Not far from Courtmacsherry Lifeboat House at Barry's Point, the lifeboat's coxswain, Tom Keohane, was on watch, looking seaward. He witnessed what happened when the *Lusitania* was torpedoed. The warning rocket summoning the crew was fired, and the men came running. They launched the boat around three o'clock, and immediately began rowing with desperate urgency. The lifeboat had no engine, the oars were heavy, but since there wasn't a breath of wind, there was no point in raising the sail. They knew that, even pulling as hard as they could over the calm sea, it would take them until around six o'clock to cover the 14 miles to where any survivors might be.

There were no survivors at the scene when, close to total exhaustion, they eventually arrived. There were just corpses floating in the tide. The lifeboat didn't get back to Courtmacsherry until around one o'clock in the morning, having been towed part of the way by a drifter.

The two freighters and the tanker which, on hearing the *Lusitania*'s SOS calls, had altered course to come to the rescue of survivors, turned away when a lookout reported that he had seen a torpedo. The three merchantmen concentrated on leaving the area as fast as they could.

About 3 miles from the spot where Schweiger's torpedo ripped a hole in the *Lusitania*'s side, the crew of the Isle of Man fishing boat *Wanderer* (a 20-ton two-masted lugger out of Peel), watched in horror as the liner's bows went down rapidly. They could see that she was sinking at an alarming speed. The *Wanderer* had come down the Irish Sea in search of mackerel. Her voyage had already yielded a catch of over 800 fish, and there were more to be had, but Skipper William Ball and his six-man crew, when they saw what was happening to the liner, realised that they now had an urgent new priority. Ball brought the *Wanderer* about and steered towards the sinking ship.

The Isle of Man boat was among the first rescue craft to reach the scene. Indeed Ball said that for two hours theirs was the only rescue craft there. As they got closer, they could hear the screams of people in the water, and could see floating corpses. The sea was littered with debris, pieces of furniture, cargo, and live and dead people of all ages – women, men, children and infants. The temperature of the water was 55 degrees Fahrenheit. They saw a few lifeboats with white-faced scared people in them.

The crew of the *Wanderer* began transferring survivors from the lifeboats onto the fish-scales-slippery deck of their small craft. When it became too dangerous to take any more on board – they already had 160, and their fishing boat was in danger of sinking – the skipper decided to head for Queenstown, towing two lifeboats behind them. The condition of some of the survivors, Ball said later, was indescribable.

On the way towards Cork Harbour, the *Wanderer* was met by one of the old tenders whose normal duty was to ferry passengers to and from the liners calling at Queenstown. This was the paddle steamer *Flying Fish*, commanded by Captain Thomas Brierely. The 160 survivors the *Wanderer* had on board were transferred to the *Flying Fish* and were subsequently landed 25 miles up the coast at Queenstown.

The armed trawler *Heron*, which had been on patrol between Kinsale and Ballycotton, lifted five corpses out of the tide and took them into Kinsale. Another trawler, the *Bluebell*, rescued Captain Turner. He had been in the water for almost three hours. He said that during that time he had seen seagulls massing and diving on helpless people in the water, and pecking their eyes out. Turner, together with another of the *Lusitania*'s officers and some passengers, was taken to Queenstown by the *Bluebell*.

The Kinsale coroner, solicitor John J. Horgan, acted quickly, carrying out his official duties to the letter. Under no circumstances would he allow bodies that had been brought ashore within his jurisdiction to be removed before he had carried out those duties. He convened an inquest to be held in the town's Old Market House, and empanelled a jury of twelve local fishermen and shopkeepers.

The inquest was formally opened on Saturday 8 May, the day after the liner was sunk. Among those Horgan subpoenaed to attend was the *Lusitania*'s master, Captain Turner. Horgan went to Queenstown himself and served the subpoena *ad testificandam* (which requires a person to give evidence) on Captain Turner. The solicitor, a Sinn Féin supporter, was afraid that the British authorities might attempt to stop Turner testifying.

Captain Turner arrived at the resumed inquest on the Monday morning wearing an ill-fitting and old-looking suit and 'suffering', as Horgan said, 'from the strain of his experience'. The *Lusitania*'s master was not legally represented. Also in attendance was District Inspector Wansborough of the Royal Irish Constabulary. Captain Turner answered fully the questions put to him, except in two instances. The first was when he was asked what was the nature of the wireless messages he had received about the presence of submarines off the Irish coast. His answer was: 'I respectfully refer you to the Admiralty, sir, about the answering of that question.'

The second instance was when he was asked if he was at liberty to tell the inquest what the special instructions were that he had received. He said, 'No, sir.'

When the coroner asked him if the U-boat had given the *Lusitania* any warning before firing the torpedo, Captain Turner answered, 'None whatever, sir … ' It was a quarter-past-two by his watch when the explosion occurred, he said. His watch stopped at 2.36. He said he spent between two and three hours in the water before he was rescued. All around him in the sea were dead bodies. He saw no one who was alive.

Coroner Horgan said he believed that Captain Turner had remained on the bridge all the time.

'Yes, sir,' Turner replied, 'and she went down from under me.'

At the conclusion of Captain Turner's evidence, the coroner said, 'We all sympathise with you, Captain, and the Cunard Company, in the terrible crime that was committed against your vessel, and I also desire to express our appreciation of the great courage you showed – it was worthy of the traditions of the service to which you belong. We realise the deep feeling you must have in the matter.'

Turner bowed his head and wept. Horgan then thanked him for his attendance at the inquest, to which Turner responded by saying, 'I am very much pleased, sir. I was glad to come and help in any way.'

The jury returned this verdict: 'That the said deceased died from prolonged immersion and exhaustion in the sea 8 miles south south-west of the Old Head of Kinsale on Friday 7 May 1915, owing to the sinking of the RMS *Lusitania* by torpedoes fired without warning from a German submarine. We find that this appalling crime was contrary to international law and the conventions of all civilised nations, and we therefore charge the officers of the submarine and the German Emperor and the Government of Germany, under whose orders they acted, with the crime of wilful and wholesale murder before the tribunal of the civilised world.'

Half an hour after the inquest ended, the crown solicitor for Cork, Harry Wynne – a friend of Horgan's – called to see the coroner. He informed Horgan that he had been instructed by the Admiralty to *stop* the inquest; Captain Turner was *not* to be called to give evidence but was to remain silent until a Board of Trade Enquiry into the liner's sinking was set up.

Wynne of course was too late to influence the inquest in any way. By the time he spoke to Horgan, the inquest was over. Horgan wrote in 1948 that the Admiralty 'were as belated on this occasion as they had been in protecting the *Lusitania* against attack'.

6

FROST AND WAKING NIGHTMARES

The United States consul in Queenstown at the time the *Lusitania* was torpedoed was Wesley Frost, a thirty-year-old married man from Oberlin, Ohio. A consul being an official appointed by a sovereign state to protect its commercial interests and aid its citizens in a foreign place – in other words, to look after people of his own country in the country to which his government appointed him – Wesley Frost took his duties very seriously.

Queenstown was only his second consular post. Prior to arriving in Ireland in 1914, he had for two years been US Consul at Charlottetown, Prince Edward Island, on Canada's east coast. Like Queenstown, Charlottetown was a seaport, and like Queenstown it, too, had been named after a monarch – Queen Charlotte, wife of George III. Wesley Frost referred to Queenstown as a 'beautiful little city clinging against its steep green hillside by the most charming tidal harbour in the world'.

Of his arrival there on 14 May 1914, he wrote, 'The landing was like an arrival into paradise.' He described 'a rose-madder daybreak in the east and a pale-gold moon setting in the west'. And he referred to 'the estuaries and inlets of the most beautiful harbour in the world'. Queenstown he saw as 'rising against the abrupt hillside of the Cove of Cork', and said that in the clear morning light it was 'crowned by the Admiralty House and the fine spires of St Colman's cathedral'. He mentioned that 'the massive rock escarpments under Spy Hill were gorgeous with purple valerian and golden laburnum.'

'This was the place,' he wrote, 'which, little as we could then guess it, within a single turn of the seasons was to plunge into a species of waking-nightmares … It was to be known no longer as the world's most stately harbour, but as "the port of horrors."'

Frosts' consular district embraced the whole of Munster. His was a busy consular post, and he and his small staff worked from a second floor office above O'Reilly's Bar in Queenstown. Their duties included the inspection of emigrants, the invoicing of Irish whiskey, mackerel and tweeds, and the issuance of bills of health to the passenger liners. There was also a great deal of what Frost termed 'consular notarial and legal work'. The consul had to deal with those American tourists who were in southern Ireland to visit places like Killarney, Glengarriff and Blarney, and with Irish-Americans who had 'come on summer pilgrimages to the 'ouhld [*sic*] sod'.

When war broke out in August 1914, it was the trippers and the tourists who produced in the consulate their first foretaste of war work. Many Americans came to the consulate for advice, and to learn in what way the war was likely to affect their personal plans. Some looked for loans which, occasionally, the consulate gave – for example £100 'to a stranded aggregation of Irish-American motion-picture artists who had been staging scenes in the Black Valley'.

Between the end of August 1914 and midway through November 1914, when the British authorities finally closed Queenstown to the arrival and departure of anyone other than British subjects (a development that Frost averred was 'in the highest degree natural, as Queenstown is both a naval and a military centre'), about 6,000 Americans returned to the United States through Cork Harbour.

At that point the consular work at Queenstown took on a different character, concerning itself, according to Frost, with commercial opportunities, German interests, American freight ships, and intensive investigation of the claims of various persons to American citizenship. For a while Frost and his vice-consul dealt with the crews of German merchant ships captured by the British and landed in Queenstown and elsewhere along the coast, and with German sailors taken from neutral ships. All of these Germans were despatched to internment camps within Ireland.

The first evidence he had of the presence of U-boats off Queens-town came when he was walking along the Deep Water Quay into town one dismal morning and saw 'a big freighter with a curiously battered funnel and superstructures'. Royal Irish Constabulary (RIC) constables were carrying 'a burlap gunnysack' down the gangplank. The sack contained 'the dismembered fragments of the late master of the *Anglo-Californian*, and it was followed by the mutilated corpses of eight of his staunch seamen'.

The *Anglo-Californian* was a British horse transport of 7,500 tons and was ferrying 927 horses from Montreal to Avonmouth. From the British port the animals were due to be sent to France, and then up to the Western Front. On 4 July 1915, when the vessel was about 90 miles south-west of Queenstown, she was intercepted by a surfaced U-boat, U-39, which began to shell her. In command of the U-39 was an officer destined to become the second highest-scoring U-boat captain of all time, *Kapitanleutnant* Walter Forstmann. He ended the war having sunk an incredible 150 ships (most of them in the Mediterranean) totalling over 399,000 tons. But he failed to sink the *Anglo-Californian*.

The *Anglo-Californian*'s captain was fifty-nine-year-old Frederick Daniel Parslow. His son, Frederick Parslow jnr, was the ship's second mate. Captain Parslow had no intention of giving up his ship easily and, in an effort to get away from the U-boat, began to steer a zig-zag course. The captain himself was at the wheel. But with the U-boat closing fast and casualties mounting, Parslow was at last about to give the order to abandon ship in an attempt to save lives, when he received a message that patrol vessels from Queenstown were on their way to help.

Forstmann increased the intensity of the gunfire at the *Anglo-Californian*. Captain Parslow found himself having to lie flat on the floor of the bridge next to the wheel and steer from there. His forward view from this position was severely restricted. He had to raise his head every minute or two to peer through the confusion of damage, smoke and flames trying to see where the U-boat was, and if there was any sign of approaching patrol vessels.

With shells from U-39 bursting all around Parslow and the horrendous noise deafening him, suddenly it happened – for one instant his head was in the wrong place at the wrong time, and an incoming shell exploded near him, blowing him to pieces. His son, Frederick jnr, squirmed along the floor of the bridge, crawling through debris and the blood and tissue of his dead father. He took the captain's place next to the wheel and steered the ship just as his father had been doing up to minutes before.

Only when the patrol ships came steaming over the horizon did the U-boat stop firing. Forstmann took his boat down hurriedly and escaped.

The damaged *Anglo-Californian* eventually made it into Cork Harbour and tied up at the Deep Water Quay. Captain Parslow was buried in the Old Church cemetery in Queenstown. He was awarded a posthumous Victoria Cross for Valour, and an image of the decoration was carved on his head stone.

'As the German submarines pushed their forays nearer and nearer,' Wesley Frost recalled, 'and Queenstown became the clearing-house for survivors from their attacks, our streets gained a still further element of diversity in the groups of pathetic human salvage. We could hardly walk down Harbour Row without encountering men or women just saved from the ordeals of exposure and assault.'

Frost began to compile reports on the submarine attacks, and he sent them to the US Secretary of State. In most cases, he took detailed legal testimony. The witnesses were mainly American passengers – journalists, doctors, businessmen, clergymen, authors, officers' wives, nurses, actresses, writers, and what Frost called 'society women'.

But passengers were not the only ones from whom he gathered evidence. He also interviewed ships' officers, engineers, stokers, donkeymen, horse handlers, able seamen and bosuns. He took testimony from survivors at all hours of the day and night, recording evidence from people 'straight from the sea, with the voices of their dead companions still ringing in their ears'. They were examined while the occurrences were fresh and vivid in their minds. The consul conscientiously checked out their stories individually against each other. His main reason for taking officers' affidavits 'lay in the superior knowledge and skill which officers possess as to all technical sea matters; and their testimony also has great value merely as corroborating the American testimony'. With a background of legal training behind him, he took professional pride in conducting his enquiries 'with juridical impartiality'.

The survivors came from torpedoed tramp steamers, tankers, transports, liners, warships, graceful and harmless sailing ships, humble schooners, barques and barkentines, and were brought into Queenstown in all sorts of vessels: Admiralty tugs, trawlers, destroyers, sloops, freighters and fishing smacks. Occasionally ships' lifeboats were rowed right into the town's cambers.

Queenstown wasn't the only place where survivors were landed. Some came ashore in Bantry, others at Bearhaven, Schull, Cahir-civeen. Frost went to those places to take the testimony of the survivors, or travelled to Cork or Mallow to catch the survivors on their way to England. Occasionally the only time he had to write their stories down was as long as it took to get from one railway station in Cork city to another.

Admiralty House sometimes informed the American consulate prior to the arrival of ships carrying survivors, particularly if there was a likelihood that there might be Americans among them. The town's shipping agents were particularly helpful and cooperative in keeping the consulate informed, and in sending any American survivors to the consul to be interviewed.

Dead bodies, too, were brought into Queenstown, or floated into Ballycotton Bay, Courtmacsherry Bay, and up on to Garretstown strand. Frost said, 'We had often occasion to be honestly thankful for the queer, puzzled peacefulness which stamps the faces of the drowned.'

He was a painstaking consul who pushed himself to the limits in carrying out his duties, and he won the admiration of the administration in the USA for the valuable evidence he collected about the way in which the U-boat warfare was being conducted.

The 7 May 1915 was to change Wesley Frost's life forever. That afternoon he was busy in his office, working on a commercial report when, at around half-past two, Vice-Consul Lewis C. Thompson rushed up the stairs and into his office and blurted out that there was a wildfire rumour going around the town that the liner *Lusitania* had been attacked. The two men crossed to the windows, which gave a view of the harbour. Tugs, tenders and trawlers – 'the harbour's mosquito fleet' Frost called them – were streaming down towards the Spit Bank beacon where they turned south and went out past Aghada, Whitegate, Corkbeg and Spike Island, towards Roche's Point.

Frost immediately phoned Admiralty House and asked for Rear-Admiral Sir Charles Coke's secretary, Lieutenant Paymaster Norcocks, RN. 'I hear there is a rumour going around the town that the *Lusitania* has been attacked,' Frost said to the officer.

He could hardly believe his ears when Norcocks said, 'It's *true*, Mr Frost. We fear she is gone.' The stress on the word 'true' gave Frost 'an unforgettable mental shock'.

Norcocks hadn't much information to give him, apart from in-forming him about the ship's SOS message, and that there had been telephone confirmation from watchers at the Old Head of Kinsale that the *Lusitania* had disappeared. The consul spent the next quarter of an hour pacing up and down the office 'adjusting my mind to the fact of the disaster.' He said afterwards, 'I did not believe that the submarines had yet shown any striking power equal to the task of attacking and destroying a ship as huge, well-built and fast as the *Lusitania*.' He phoned the town's Cunard office and spoke to the manager, Jerome Murphy. Murphy confirmed the terrible news.

Among those Frost felt should be informed were the American Secretary of State in Washington, William Jennings Bryan; the US Consul General in London, Robert P. Skinner, and the American Ambassador in London, Walter Hines Page. Frost sent brief telegraph messages to both Page and Skinner. He next instructed Vice-Consul Thompson to go immediately to Kinsale where, Frost felt sure, survivors would be landed because it was the nearest port to where the *Lusitania* had been sunk.

Frost himself went to the local branch of the Munster and Leinster Bank and drew out money to cover any eventuality that might arise. It seemed certain to him that there would be Americans among the dying and the dead, and he would need cash to pay for whatever he might have to do for them.

Around six o'clock that evening he sent a cable about the disaster to Secretary of State William Jennings Bryan – in case neither Ambassador Page nor Consul-General Skinner had done so. From then on Frost reported directly to Washington, with copies going to Ambassador Page and Consul-General Skinner in London.

Speaking to reporters about the torpedoing and sinking of the liner, Franklin D. Roosevelt said, 'this is murder, murder on the high seas. You can quote me on that.'

Admiralty House had heard around a quarter-past two about the *Lusitania* SOS, and the message 'Come at once. Big list. Ten miles south of Old Head Kinsale'. Admiral Coke promptly ordered the cruiser *Juno* to sea, to go to where the liner had been attacked. Just before a quarter to three the signal station at Kinsale sent a message saying, '*Lusitania* sunk'.

When Coke reported the news to the Admiralty in London, Admiral Lord Fisher, the First Sea Lord, ordered the *Juno* to be recalled immediately, even though she was close to where survivors were in the water. Fisher allegedly feared the *Juno* would be sunk, as the *Aboukir,* *Cressy* and *Hogue* had been, if she slowed down and stopped to rescue people.

But smaller boats and ships continued to converge on the Old Head of Kinsale, their crews wondering what horrors they might find – and hoping against hope that they would be in time to pull some survivors from the sea. Among those that went on the rescue mission were the minesweeper *Indian Empire*; the trawlers *Bluebell*, *Brock* and *Bradford*; the inspection vessel *Julia;* the paddle steamer tender *Flying Fish*; the tugs *Stormcock* and *Warrior*; the drifter *Golden Effort*; the three torpedo-boats 050, 052 and 055; the Isle of Man fishing smack *Wanderer;* the Courtmacsherry Lifeboat, and the fishing boats *Daniel O'Connell* and *Elizabeth.* None of them was equipped with wireless and so were unable to send back reports of what they had found, and it was many hours before the craft that had gone out on rescue missions returned.

Meanwhile in Queenstown, people in Westbourne Place and West Beach and East Beach, in Harbour Row and the Holy Ground, and higher up on Roche's Row, Roche's Terrace and Hawthorn Terrace, and on the steep hills like Barrack Street, East Hill, Spy Hill and Top o' the Hill, on King Street and Harbour View, Old Street and Bellevue Terrace, stopped and whispered, and they said things like, 'God between us and all harm', and 'God in heaven, isn't it terrible?' and 'Jesus have mercy on them'. Women put their hands to their mouths as if afraid to utter the terrible things they were thinking and fearing.

Jerome Murphy, the Cunard company's manager in Queenstown, sent a telegram to head office in Liverpool at 3.25 p.m. It wasn't received until 5 p.m., its transmission and delivery held up by the censor. Murphy and his staff then contacted Queenstown's hotels – the Queen's, the Imperial, the Westbourne and the Rob Roy. They also contacted lodging houses. The Cunard staff reserved as many rooms as they could, because they guessed there was going to be a pressing need before the night was out for accommodation for any survivors who might be landed in the town.

The manager of the Queen's Hotel at the time was, ironically, a German who had been naturalised in 1905, and whose wife was English. His name was Otto Humbert, and when news of the sinking of the *Lusitania* reached Queenstown, he had gone into hiding in the hotel's wine cellar, afraid of recriminations.

Barely a couple of weeks later a question about him was raised in Britain's Parliament by Joynson Hicks, MP. Hicks asked the First Lord of the Admiralty if he was aware of Humbert's existence in Queenstown, and if the First Lord would have him removed. The written answer Hicks received claimed that Humbert had been carefully monitored from the start of the war, that so far as was known he was guilty of nothing, but that the matter of his removal from Queenstown would be considered.

When the rumours of the sinking of the *Lusitania* were confirmed, Queenstown settled down to waiting apprehensively. The people in the streets feared the worst. The worst was what they got, and it was more gruesome than anyone could have imagined.

7

THE LIVING AND THE DEAD

RIC District Inspector Armstrong had insisted that the Cunard Wharf and Quay next to Lynch's Quay be closed to the public. Wesley Frost was waiting there when the first of the rescue craft came in at eight o'clock that evening. Towing a line of lifeboats in her wake was the Admiralty tug *Stormcock*. She was one of two tugs (the other was the *Warrior*) that had got away quickly from Queenstown when the news of the sinking of the liner was received.

The *Stormcock* had been involved in an incident with two Kinsale-based fishing craft almost as soon as she arrived at the scene where the living and the dead, and the debris from the torpedoed *Lusitania*, bobbed on the surface. The steam trawler *Daniel O'Connell* and the motor drifter *Elizabeth* had each picked up survivors, and were on their way into Kinsale when the *Stormcock* intercepted them. The tug's master, Commander Shee, imperiously ordered the fishermen to transfer the survivors to the *Stormcock* immediately. The fishermen resented Shee's peremptory manner of addressing them. Who the hell did he think he was? To them he was just a jumped-up gobshite in a brass-button uniform, trying to throw his weight about, an officer in a navy to which they owed no allegiance and no respect. They told him bluntly that Kinsale was their base, was much nearer than Queenstown, and that they fully intended taking the survivors they'd rescued into Kinsale. They said that the people they had hauled out of the sea would be ashore in Kinsale in half an hour at most, much sooner than if they were taken all the way to Queenstown in his tug.

Some of the survivors on the fishing boats told Shee that they didn't want to be transferred to the *Stormcock* – they were afraid that because the tug was bigger than the fishing boats, she would be an easier and a more inviting target for a U-boat. Voices were raised, threats shouted at the fishermen. Shee finally got his own way and the survivors were transferred to the *Stormcock*. But there remained a lot of residual anger among the crews of the *Elizabeth* and the *Daniel O'Connell*. That anger surfaced again during Coroner Horgans' Kinsale inquest. The skipper of the *Elizabeth*, Edward White from Arklow, whose motor drifter had towed lifeboats with eighty survivors aboard them 12 miles and had reached the mouth of Kinsale harbour when intercepted by the *Stormcock*, had bitter words to say about Shee and his hectoring manner; bitter words also about Shee's decision to subject the survivors to the much longer journey to Queenstown.

When Vice-Consul Thompson arrived at Kinsale it was to find that, contrary to what he and Wesley Frost had thought likely, *no* survivors were landed there. So he returned to Queenstown, reaching there at about ten o'clock that night.

The *Stormcock*'s arrival at the pier, followed by the *Indian Empire* carrying 170 survivors, was the start of what Frost later called 'the ghastly procession of these rescue ships as they landed the living and the dead that night under the flaming gas torches along the Queenstown waterfront.'

The arrivals began soon after eight o'clock and continued at close intervals until about eleven o'clock. Ship after ship came out of the darkness, and sometimes two or three could be seen awaiting their turns in the cloudy night to discharge bruised and shuddering women, cripples and half-clothed men, and wide-eyed little children. 'Women caught at our sleeves and begged desperately for word of their husbands,' Frost said, 'and men with choking efforts at matter-of-factness moved ceaselessly from group to group, seeking a lost daughter or sister or even bride … Piles of corpses like cordwood began to appear among the paint-kegs and coils of rope on the shadowy old wharves.'

Those corpses had to be laid out so that they might be identified and given names. Queenstown had never before had to deal with so many dead bodies at the one time, so temporary morgues had to be set up. First there was the shed at the Cunard Pier. The floor space there was quickly filled. With the cooperation of Queenstown's town clerk, James Campbell, part of the Town Hall was then taken over, as well as a disused ship chandlery on Harbour Row in the eastern part of the town.

The London *Times* of 10 May 1917 reported: 'Men and women have been passing down the files of dead all day long seeking relatives and friends who, they feared, were among the missing. Human emotion has at times reached breaking point. … The dead lay as they were found, in the clothing in which they were taken from the water. Their faces still bore the expression with which each one of these cruelly slain men, women and children had met death. For there were several children in the chamber of death.'

The correspondent noted, 'Men broke down when they looked upon a young mother, lying there with her baby folded in her protective arms.' He wrote of seeing twin babies, and of 'a sailor who was found with a body of a little child strapped to his shoulders … Two children who went down together with their arms around each other, were still folded firmly together … Some of the dead,' the *Times* man wrote, 'wore expressions of terror … others were calm and beautiful … There have been heart-rending recognitions …'

In a place whose population was then about 8,000, a town where a single death could cause deep sadness and regret and a sense of desolation, the avalanche of death and gruesome suffering which now enveloped it was overwhelming, numbing and heartbreaking. The town was wet with tears – and there were still the funerals to face.

American Consul Frost wasn't, of course, the only one standing waiting on the pier that night. Cunard's Queenstown manager, Jerome Murphy, was there, and most of the staff. Lieutenant Norcocks had come down the hill from Admiralty House. There were doctors and nurses, members of the RIC, Catholic priests, Church of Ireland clergymen, stretcher-bearers, the local volunteer first-aid corps, and members of Cork's volunteer motor ambulance corps. The town's waterfront streets – West Beach, East Beach and Harbour Row – were thronged with townspeople drawn by compassion, a desire to help, and the morbid curiosity that attracts people to scenes of tragedy.

One of the survivors, Charles Lauriat, later referred in his book *The Lusitania's Last Voyage* to the street 'filled with people ready to do anything in their power to relieve our sufferings'. He said he had never seen 'anything more spontaneous or genuine or more freely given than the Irish hospitality of Queenstown'.

Wesley Frost said, 'Scores of the private residents of Queenstown took survivors into their homes, utterly irrespective of nationality.'

Frost and Vice-Consul Thompson passed the word around that all Americans should report to the consulate the following morning, Saturday. Gathering information about what happened on the *Lusitania* (information he sent to Washington, and to the Board of Trade in London), Frost obtained affidavits from thirty-five American survivors. He asked them to describe in their own words all that they had seen and heard and felt when the ship was torpedoed – eyewitness accounts. (When both the British and Americans subsequently held inquiries into the sinking, not one of the affidavits the American consul had obtained was used.)

Frost was disgusted when he learned that two or three Americans, and a number of other nationals, who had landed 'without injury or exhaustion' straightaway proceeded 'to the best hotel at Cork, and thence on their way to London, without so much as a backward glance or a thought of pity for their companions in the tragedy'.

He wrote about the swift distribution of survivors to various hotels and guesthouses, and the fact that well before midnight the Cunard offices were 'almost empty of the agitated and pitiable refugees who had overflowed them two hours earlier'. He recalled 'the blanket-wrapped or underwear-clad figures ... the bandages and slings, and the hoarse voices and hacking coughs of sufferers from exposure – all these elements of the weird and unforgettable scene vanished away in an incredibly brief space of time, it seemed to us.'

He said that the work of assisting survivors in ascertaining whether or not their relatives or companions on the *Lusitania* had been saved was the most distressing of his duties. The personal visits from bereaved people 'were often poignant to the last degree ... especially when such visits came to be repeated time after time, at intervals of hours or days, with increasing hopelessness and grief as the absence of news became tantamount to certainty of death.'

There were certain cases which he was convinced would remain in his mind for the rest of his life. One involved a businessman who travelled from London to try to find out what happened to his wife and their two small sons. 'Not a particle of information was ever forthcoming even as to their having been seen after the ship was struck, to say nothing of their deaths, or the recovery of their bodies,' Frost remembered. 'And the tragic spectacle of that father and husband, whose entire life had been wrapped up in his family, haunted the consulate for a fortnight.'

Some of the American corpses had to be embalmed to preserve them from decay. Queenstown had no embalmer. In Cork they found a surgeon who was prepared to undertake the task. He and his assistants arrived in Queenstown on the Sunday morning. An improvised operating room was set up at the rear of the Cunard offices, and the surgeon and his colleagues started what turned out to be five hard days work.

Frost said he would never forget the sight that confronted him on the second of his two visits to what he called the work-room – 'the body on the embalmer's slab of a beautiful American girl who was scarcely ten days a bride ... She lay like a statue typifying assassinated innocence.' There were innumerable gruesome sights and incidents.

People who had survived the sinking of the liner were reluctant to visit the dimly lit improvised morgues to help with the identification of bodies. Inside the dingy death houses the predominant sounds were the whispers and the sobbing of relatives looking for their missing dead.

'I saw five or six drowned women with drowned babies in their arms,' Frost recalled. 'And the corpse of one mother who had a dead infant clasped to each of the cold breasts which had so recently been their warm nestling-places ... we contracted a temporary horror of any recumbent body, and especially of sleeping children, after a few days among these tiers of corpses.'

One night several weeks after the *Lusitania* was sunk, Frost, holding a lighted match, went into a bedroom at his home and 'came unexpectedly upon the sleeping form of my own little daughter. I give you my word, I recoiled as though I had found a serpent. That innocent figure had thrust me back automatically into the presence of those poor livid little midget-corpses at which we had looked down so often among the *Lusitania* dead.'

According to Frost, beginning on the Monday afternoon, the Cunard company spared nothing in its efforts to salvage the dead bodies still floating at the scene of the sinking, or washed ashore along the coast. American relatives who had never received any news of their lost ones, Frost said, 'may rest assured that the bodies sank forever in deep water in the ocean, or at least can never have reached the eye of man'.

The bodies of one married couple, Mr and Mrs Keser, were found on beaches 120 miles apart. Corpses were washed ashore at Castlegregory and Ballybunion in County Kerry, and further up the west coast in County Galway. The Cunard company offered £5 for every body found; London solicitors for the Vanderbilt family offered a reward of £1,000 for the recovery of the body of Alfred Vanderbilt.

The corpses that were found relatively soon after the sinking were lifelike. 'The bodies recovered later on,' Frost said, 'perhaps had a still more powerful effect upon the observer because of their revolting condition … The rigidity relaxed into an inebriate flabbiness, and the features broke down into a preposterously animal-like repulsiveness … The faces registered every shading of the grotesque and hideous. The lips and noses were eaten away by sea-birds, and eyes gouged out … It was almost a relief when the faces became indistinguishable as such … Towards the last, the flesh was wholly gone from the grinning skulls, the trunks were bloated and distended with gases, and the limbs were partially eaten away or bitten clean off by sea-creatures, so that stumps of raw bone were left projecting.'

Consul Frost placed more importance on the needs of others than on his own. In the wake of the *Lusitania* disaster, he continued, through steely resolve, to do at Queenstown what he felt was right. He exercised his moral courage for the sake of other people.

In the end, what the *Lusitania* called to Wesley Frost's mind was 'scores and hundreds of corpses of men and women and little folks – some rotting in pools of blood in unnamed deal coffins, some staring wearily up past me from the damp floor of the old Town Hall, and some lying with vile disfigurements in shreds of clothing soaking with the salt ocean. But always corpses. That is what the *Lusitania* means to me – corpses.'

Wesley Frost's name was remembered for years in Queenstown with admiration for the compassion he had shown, and the selfless way he had drawn on his essential decency in looking after the living and the dead.

8

REQUIESCANT IN PACE

When the *Lusitania* left New York there were 1,962 people on board
– 694 crew, 1,265 passengers, and three stowaways. Only 764 people
survived – 474 passengers and 290 crew. The stowaways were among
the nearly 1,200 who perished.

The bodies brought ashore at Queenstown had to be taken from the
piers and coffined. The bodies of known Americans had the Stars and
Stripes draped over them, and were carried on improvised stretchers
along West Beach, past Tyler's shoe shop, the Soldiers' Home and
Sailors' Rest, Delany's Wines & Spirits store and The American
Saloon. Sailors and soldiers saluted, and townspeople, shocked and
silent, stood on the pavements.

It was imperative that the corpses lying in the Cunard shed, the
Town Hall, and the disused chandlery on Harbour Row be buried as
soon as possible. They couldn't be left there indefinitely. Queenstown
hadn't nearly enough coffins. Nor were there nearly enough means of
transport to convey the coffins to the place of burial. The Old Church
cemetery, dating from 1698, was about 2 miles outside the town, up
over the hill and down the far side to where the graveyard nestled
among trees.

Clerks in the Cunard company's Queenstown office began a frantic
search for coffins, hearses, lorries, horses-and-carts, and wagons.
Convinced that many more than the 145 bodies that lay in the morgues
would turn up, Cunard bought hundreds of coffins from sources in
Dublin and Kildare. Not all of what was delivered to the stricken town

were conventional coffins, traditionally shaped and with brass handles – many were just plain oblong deal boxes. And because so many corpses were unidentified, and anyway there wouldn't have been enough time for engraving, the coffin/box lids were numbered with white paint.

It was decided that the *Lusitania* dead would be put into the ground in three mass graves, each measuring 30 feet long and 20 feet wide. They were to be designated A, B and C. Soldiers began digging the rectangular pits on 9 May. Then there was the grim task of lifting the corpses, many of them small children and infants, off the floors of the three make-do morgues, and putting them into the coffins. One survivor said afterwards that the streets of Queenstown reeked with death.

The coffins were left open for as long as possible in case some of the relatives who had begun flooding into the town might identify a loved one, thus giving the body a name, and bringing some kind of closure to the grief-stricken. The burials took place on Monday 10 May, with a special requiem mass beforehand in St Colman's cathedral. Vice-Admiral Coke came down from Admiralty House to be present in the big grey church.

The funeral took almost three hours to pass on that warm May day. Shopkeepers closed their premises, offices were shut, and curtains and blinds were drawn in all the houses. The funeral bell pealed at the cathedral, and the coffins were loaded into hearses, and onto lorries and carts. Soldiers from the Connaught Rangers and the Royal Dublin Fusiliers, and Royal Navy sailors from the moored ships, lined the route from the sea-level morgues along West Beach, East Beach and Harbour Row, up Harbour Hill, past the great doors of St Colman's cathedral. Townspeople came to the footpaths, standing mute and staring, the men with their caps or hats off and clasped in their hands, the women numb and sad, the children looking on quietly. The flags on the ships in the harbour flew at half mast, and the brass band of the Royal Dublin Fusiliers, with muffled drums, played Chopin's 'Funeral March' and the 'Dead March' from Handel's *Saul*.

The horses hauling the three hearses and the carts laboured up the steep climb beyond the cathedral to the top of the town, and then started the winding descent to the graveyard, past the sloping fields where people peered from behind the soldiers, policemen and sailors, and watched the coffins going by.

Those at the graveyard saw Bishop Browne in his vestments and tall mitre, the Catholic priests in white linen surplices over their cassocks; Royal Navy chaplain, Reverend Richard Swann Mason; Archdeacon Daunt of the Church of Ireland; the lord mayor of Cork, Alderman O'Shea, and members of Cork corporation; the Harbour Board; the local Urban District Council; Royal Navy and British army officers, and the ordinary men and women who had made the long slow walk from the town. They saw the three open graves, big pits which had been dug out by soldiers, the long, high banks of earth beside the holes, saw the coffins with their white numbers on the lids. One of the pits was for the Catholics. The coffins were unloaded from the carts, lorries and hearses, and placed side by side in the mass graves – twenty-three in Grave A, fifty-two in Grave B, and seventy in Grave C.

Bishop Browne said the Prayers for the Dead at the Catholics' grave, ending with: 'May their souls and all the souls of the faithful departed, through the mercy of God rest in peace.' Archdeacon Daunt of the Church of Ireland and Reverend Swann Mason said prayers at the other two pits, after which a bugler played 'The Last Post'. A party of servicemen fired a volley over the graves of the *Lusitania* dead, and the people who had come to pay their last respects sang 'Abide With Me'.

Over 800 of the nearly 1,200 victims of the *Lusitania* were never found. On the day following the funerals at Queenstown, Wesley Frost sent a detailed account to Secretary of State Bryan. The consul now expressed his worry that the search for bodies was being wretchedly managed. It seemed to him that both the Admiralty and the Cunard company were attempting to shift the responsibility onto each other.

The Cunard's Queenstown office was faced with trying to dispose of hundreds of coffins which had been bought at £4 each in anticipation of several hundred bodies having to be buried. The final figure had fallen far short of expectations.

9

'TOO PROUD TO FIGHT'

The first news of the torpedoing of the *Lusitania* reached the American embassy in London late in the afternoon of the day on which she was sunk. Colonel House, the president's adviser, and Mrs House were nearing the end of a visit to Britain, and Ambassador Page had arranged a farewell reception and dinner in their honour. It was to be held at the ambassadorial residence, No. 6 Grosvenor Square. By the time news of the *Lusitania* was received, it was too late to cancel the function.

Before arriving at the reception, Colonel House and Sir Edward Grey, the Foreign Secretary, paid a quick visit to Kew Gardens, following which House went by invitation to Buckingham Palace to meet the King.

The first news of the *Lusitania* sinking stated that the liner had been torpedoed, but that all on board had been saved. Bit by horrifying bit, however, the true picture started to emerge – 1,198 dead, including 94 children (35 of them were babies); 128 American citizens among those who lost their lives; the total number of passengers who died, 785; of the liner's crew, 413 died.

It was a sombre gathering that evening to which the ambassador read out each bulletin as it was delivered to him from the chancery. The gloom deepened when they heard about the number of Americans who were victims, and to the gloom was added anger. Surely the United States would now declare war? Page felt certain that America had no other option. Colonel House (who had crossed the Atlantic in the *Lusitania* in January 1915 when her then captain, David Dow, had controversially raised the Stars and Stripes in place of the Red Ensign, thus hiding behind a neutral flag) believed that America's declaration of war would come within a month. He wired the president: 'America has come to the parting of the ways.'

House was anxious to get back to the US as soon as possible. He wanted to be with Wilson when the president declared war. But the USA's declaration of war was still a long way off. Both House and Page were wrong in their forecasts – wrong by two years.

And yet, as Brigadier General S. L. A. Marshall noted, 'America shook with rage. From that day [of the sinking of the *Lusitania*], hatred towards Germany mounted, and public sentiment for an interminable neutrality, or peace at any price, visibly declined. Nothing that Germany could do, by way of official apology, moderation of policy, or offers of compensation … could stem the tide of bitter resentment'.

Britain's *Daily Mail* ran the sensational headline:

British and American babies Murdered by the Kaiser

In Germany, the sinking of the *Lusitania* was headlined in the *Frankfurter Zeitung* on 8 May as 'An Extraordinary Success'. Another German publication characterised it as 'a success of moral significance'. The *New York World* understandably took a very different line. 'Modern history,' the newspaper said, 'affords no such example of a great nation running amok and calling it military necessity.'

And an article in *Le Petit Journal,* Paris, said, the torpedoing of the liner 'will have no other effect than to strengthen humanity in waging a relentless war to the death and to round up the enemy as one rounds up a beast escaped from a menagerie which is flinging itself upon every passer-by'. The *Daily Mail*'s New York correspondent wrote of 'indignation and the bitterest resentment' sweeping over the American continent. He wondered if 'this universal feeling of horror and mingled grief for the innocent victims of the greatest crime in history' would force the American government into a declaration of war.

A few days after the *Lusitania* was sunk, President Wilson made a speech in Philadelphia to several hundred newly naturalised American citizens: 'The example of America must be a special example,' he told them. 'The example of America must be the example not merely of peace because it will not fight, but of peace because peace is the healing and elevating influence of the world, and strife is not. ... There is such a thing as a man being too proud to fight. There is such a thing as a nation being so right that it does not need to convince others by force that it is right.'

Ambassador Page thought that the speech was a tragedy. John Buchan wrote, 'It had an ugly air of cant.' Headline writers all over the world, but particularly in Britain, fastened on to those 'too proud to fight' words. Posters and headlines blazed out: WE ARE TOO PROUD TO FIGHT – WOODROW WILSON. America's president was excoriated. Colonel House was still in London when Wilson's speech hit the headlines. He was shocked when he encountered a sandwich-board man carrying a poster for an afternoon newspaper. In big, hastily written, scrawled capital letters were the words quoted above.

The mood in America changed dramatically as large segments of the population became enraged by reports coming out of Germany that German people were publicly rejoicing at the sinking of the liner, and celebrating what they considered to be a fine achievement by the commander of U-20, Walther Schweiger. Wilson nevertheless stuck to his policy of 'absolute self-control and self-mastery.' And he would hold that line for the next two years. He was obsessed by the idea of becoming peacemaker to the world.

But on 13 May 1915 he sent a note to the American Ambassador in Germany, James Walter Gerard. The note bore the signature of the Secretary of State, William Jennings Bryan, a known pacifist and anti-imperialist. It began with this instruction to the ambassador: 'Please call on the Minister of Foreign Affairs and after reading to him this communication, leave with him a copy.' This was the first *Lusitania* note. It stated that it was 'clearly wise and desirable that the Government of the United States and the Imperial German Government should come to a clear and full understanding as to the grave situation which has resulted.' Having named three other sinkings (one British and two American ships), in which American citizens had lost their lives, the document said that those sinkings, together with the sinking of the *Lusitania,* 'constitute a series of events which the Government of the United States has observed with growing concern, distress, and amazement.'

Spelled out clearly was that the government of the United States 'was loath to believe – it cannot now bring itself to believe – that these acts, so absolutely contrary to the rules, the practices, and the spirit of modern warfare, could have the countenance or sanction of that great [Imperial German] Government.' The note raised the matter of 'methods of [German] retaliation' to the methods adopted by their adversaries in seeking to cut Germany off from all commerce.

Germany's retaliatory policy, Wilson's note said, went 'much beyond the ordinary methods of warfare at sea in the proclamation of a war zone from which they have warned neutral ships to stay away.' The American government could not 'admit the adoption of such measures, or such a warning of danger to operate as in any degree an abbreviation of the rights of American shipmasters or of American citizens bound on lawful errands as passengers on merchant ships of belligerent nationality.'

Then came a warning. The American government would 'hold the Imperial German government to a strict accountability for any infringement of those rights, intentional or incidental.' The tone was equally uncompromising in the passage that said, 'Expressions of regret and offers of reparation in case of the destruction of neutral ships sunk by mistake, while they may satisfy international obligations if no loss of life results, cannot justify or excuse a practice the natural and necessary effect of which is to subject neutral nations and neutral persons to new and immeasurable risks.'

The note was evasively answered. The Germans temporised.

On the same day as Wilson sent his first *Lusitania* note, the London *Daily Mirror* told of German-owned shops in the capital being attacked and pillaged by angry crowds, and Germans being 'very roughly handled.' At Smithfield Market in London, German butchers were set upon and chased away, and a crowd of around 300 people chased a lone German into Holborn. A German barber whose shop was next to Aldgate Station was beaten up, and an Austrian barber was attacked, his shop looted. In another part of London, a German bakery was wrecked, everything of value in it either stolen or destroyed. Further north, in Liverpool, thousands of people took to the streets in anti-German riots, wrecked German shops and dwelling places, and attacked German nationals.

And President Wilson? He sent a stronger note on 9 June. This time the language was so forceful as to cause Secretary of State Bryan to resign as a matter of principle. Bryan said that Wilson's demands on Germany would lead to unnecessary war. Bryan had promised, when he took office in 1913, that there would be no war during his watch. If Wilson could be said to have been fixated on American neutrality, Bryan was totally obsessed with it. Upon Bryan's resignation, Robert Lansing, an international lawyer, was chosen by the president as replacement Secretary of State. Lansing, incidentally, was one of the severest critics of Britain's blockade of shipping, strenuously pointing out that it had a severe impact on US trade.

The president's second *Lusitania* note was, like the first one, also evasively answered, the Germans again temporising.

Wilson protested again on 21 July. He pointed out to the Germans that 'the rights of neutrals in time of war are based upon principle, not upon expediency, and the principles are immutable.' And about the *Lusitania*, he wrote, 'the Government of the United States can not believe that the Imperial Government will refrain from disavowing the wanton act of its naval commander in sinking the *Lusitania,* or from offering reparation for the American lives lost, so far as reparation can be made for a needless destruction of human life by an illegal act.'

Some Germans, according to American Ambassador Gerard in Berlin, 'refer to our notes as things worse than waste paper'. He told Colonel House that the Germans were 'firmly convinced that we can be slapped, insulted and murdered with absolute impunity'.

In a letter to President Wilson, Ambassador Page wrote: 'Ridicule of the administration runs through the programmes of the theatres; it inspires hundreds of cartoons; it is a staple of conversation at private dinners and in the clubs. The most serious class of Englishmen, including the best friends of the United States, feels that the administration's reliance on notes has reduced our Government to a third or fourth-rate power.'

In the days that followed the sinking of the *Lusitania,* Ambassador Page, whose health was in decline, became distant and uncommunicative. He had the appearance of a man in shock and for days he barely spoke. In a letter to his son Arthur he said, 'the vast slaughter goes on and seems just beginning, and the degradation of war goes on week by week; and we live in hope that the United States will come in ... It has all passed far beyond anybody's power to describe. I simply go on day by day into unknown experiences and emotions, seeing nothing before me very clearly, and remembering only dimly what lies behind. I can see only one proper thing: that all the world should fall to and hunt this wild beast down.'

Woodrow Wilson, who had once said he hoped Walter Page's letters would some day be published, because they 'are the best letters I have ever read', underwent a sea change in his attitude towards Page and his letters, and forty years of friendship were dispensed with. 'More British than the British' was how Wilson described him, and the term 'extreme Anglophile' was bandied about freely and used as a condemnatory comment. People wondered, therefore, why Wilson didn't relieve Walter Page of his ambassadorship to Britain; why he didn't sack him. One theory for the failure to do so was his fear of the scandal the sacking would provoke.

Page came close to resigning. Nearly all his communications sent to Washington went unacknowledged. He was coldly and deliberately marginalised. During Bryan's lamented (by Page) incumbency as Secretary of State, Page was unable to send confidential information to the State Department without fearing that the details would be leaked to the press, and would then appear in the newspapers within days. At one point he wrote to Colonel House, 'I shall not send another confidential message to the State Department, it's too dangerous. Time and time again now the Department has leaked. Last week I sent a dispatch and I said in the body of it, "This is confidential and under no condition to be given out or made public, but to be regarded as inviolably secret" [Page's underling]. The very next morning it was telegraphed from Washington to the London newspapers.' Bryan's departure was therefore a matter of considerable relief and pleasure for Ambassador Page. But the ambassador's frustration didn't end with Bryan's departure going. He still had to cope with the misery that can ensue from being isolated and derided.

10

NEW MAN AT QUEENSTOWN

Britain had a general election in May 1915, and on 15 May a new government took over. As with all such events, the change of government brought about changes in appointments. Among these were the appointment of Admiral Sir Henry Jackson as First Sea Lord at the Admiralty (replacing Jackie Fisher), and the appointment of Arthur Balfour as First Lord of the Admiralty (replacing Winston Churchill). Fisher and Churchill were forced to resign with the shadow of the Gallipoli debacle hanging over them.

Among those who regretted Churchill's resignation and wrote to tell him so was Vice-Admiral Sir Charles Coke, writing from Admiralty House, Queenstown. In contrast, the newspapers were virtually unanimous in expressing relief at Churchill's departure, though the *Observer*'s editor, J. L. Garvin, said that Churchill possessed lion-hearted courage, and that no number of enemies could fight down his ability and force. 'His hour of triumph will come,' Garvin wrote. But the naval correspondent of *The Times* said the news that Mr Churchill was leaving the Admiralty 'has been received with a feeling of relief in the Service, both afloat and ashore'.

Admirals Jellicoe, Beatty and the Hon. Sir Stanley Colville were among the senior officers of the Royal Navy who openly expressed satisfaction at Churchill's going. Colville said, 'He was, we all consider, a danger to the Empire.' Jellicoe admitted that for a long time he had distrusted Mr Churchill, 'because he constantly arrogated to himself technical knowledge which, with all his brilliant abilities, I knew he did not possess.' And Beatty said, 'The Navy breathes freer now it is rid of the succubus Winston.'

By July 1915 the torpedoing of the *Lusitania*, and the growing number of merchant ships being sunk by U-boats in the Western Approaches, were uppermost in the minds of Balfour and the lords commissioners of the Admiralty. Although the year was only halfway through, it was already turning into an *annus horribilis* for Britain as far as the sea war was concerned. In the period March 1915 to May 1915 alone, the U-boats had sunk 115 merchant ships – almost 258,000 tons. More than half the 115 ships were sunk without warning, and 22 of the 115 were neutrals.

In February the German government had declared the seas around the British Isles to be a war zone. Germany was intent upon embarking on unrestricted U-boat warfare. *Any* ship found in the war zone was liable to be sunk without warning. The German word for this campaign against merchant shipping was *Handelskrieg*, meaning trade warfare.

It was a retaliatory measure against the blockade that Britain, using her surface fleet to patrol the whole North Sea, had imposed on Germany. Blockade is by definition 'the application of naval supremacy to regulate all shipping activity in a given area'. In the case of the British blockade against Germany, the goal was to halt the flow of trade to and from that country's only coastline. The British termed it 'economic warfare'. One of the blockade's effects was that it threatened the rights of neutral countries to deal with both sides in the conflict. That gave rise to much controversy, and the USA objected strongly to what they considered interference with legal trade.

Germany's counter-blockade using U-boats had the backing of Germany's naval minister, Admiral Alfred von Tirpitz, and the German navy's chief-of-staff, Admiral Hugo von Pohl. The unrestricted U-boat warfare was initially concentrated on shipping in the English Channel, the waters off England's north-east coast, and the southern part of the Irish Sea.

Balfour and the board of Admiralty realised that Queenstown, given its geographical situation, was going to be of crucial strategic importance. But they felt there had to be a change in command. They needed somebody more dynamic and more skilled in naval strategy than the man who was *in situ*, Vice-Admiral Sir George Coke. At the end of July 1915 Coke was ordered to haul down his flag at Queenstown. He retired, and was transferred to the reserve.

But what about his replacement? Who was going to succeed him? Who fitted the bill, fulfilled the requirements of more dynamism and knowledge of naval strategy? The name of the president of the Naval Staff College at Greenwich, Rear-Admiral Sir Lewis Bayly, was raised. He seemed a likely candidate and was impressively endorsed from on high. The First Lord of the Admiralty, Arthur Balfour, summoned Admiral Bayly to a meeting. It was generally accepted that it was the urging of Admirals Jellicoe and Beatty that prompted Balfour. Jellicoe in particular wanted Bayly switched from his job at the Naval Staff College where, Jellicoe thought, Bayly's drive and talents were being wasted, and he felt strongly that Bayly should be given the vital Queenstown command.

So who was this Lewis Bayly? What manner of man was this officer who was born in Woolwich, London, on 28 September 1857? What had his career up to halfway through 1915 been distinguished by?

He was widely recognised in the upper echelons of the navy as an officer of resolute courage and immense driving power. 'A British officer in the grand tradition' was how the American writer Elting Morison described Admiral Sir Lewis Bayly KCB, KCMG and CVO. He said Bayly was 'an admirable seaman with a deep-seated dislike of shore duty; an exacting disciplinarian; a brave man with that dogged determination that sometimes flashes into inspirational recklessness. He was also intelligent.'

He was a student of war and of naval history. He had closely studied the theories of the American Alfred Thayer Mahan, one of the dominant naval writers and an original theorist in his own right. Bayly was familiar with Mahan's dictum on command of the sea, that it was 'the possession of that overpowering power on the sea which drives the enemy's flag from it, or allows it to appear only as a fugitive; and which, by controlling the great common, closes the highway by which commerce moves to and from the enemy's shores'. He had dissected and analysed Mahan's theories and seen how Mahan had extracted from previous events certain strategic principles, and the British admiral respected US naval perspectives.

The American Admiral Sims uncovered in Bayly what he termed 'the genuinely religious nature of the man', and found that the sometimes irascible Bayly was 'at bottom, a generous, kindly and even warm-hearted character' who was deeply read in general literature, history, and science.

'In the Navy our profession is war and how to combat it so that we have every protection against it,' Bayly said. 'Our merchant seamen are necessarily men of peace, and have no protection when trouble comes. Their courage and patience in most difficult situations I have nothing but praise for.'

Throughout his career Bayly always said and did what he thought was right. An extremely serious individual, he was said never to have made friends at first meeting, and overall to have had few genuinely *close* friends. He was an authoritarian, one of whose favourite maxims was: 'Obedience to commands is the very foundation of discipline, and orders are as binding on an admiral as on an able seaman.' He wouldn't tolerate inefficiency or slackness, and throughout the Royal Navy he had a reputation for being strict and hard driving.

One lieutenant-commander recorded that when he heard he was to serve under Admiral Bayly, he 'suffered from a cold shiver. Although I had never met Admiral Bayly, I had heard sufficient from those who had served under him, who never mentioned his name except with awe and reverence ... I wondered how long I should last under his command.' That officer, a sloop captain, went on to serve two-and-a-half years under Bayly and came not only to respect and admire the admiral for his professional ability, but also to love him for his fairness and humanity.

Behind Lewis Bayly's austere expression and brusqueness lay a hidden gentleness and concern. When it came to survivors rescued from torpedoed ships, 'whatever the time of day or night', Elting Morison wrote that Admiral Bayly 'was always there with food and drink and comfort for the exhausted and bewildered men'.

Exhaustion and bewilderment were and are natural effects on those who become victims of war at sea. Many men who escaped from torpedoed tankers had incidents and images burned into their minds which would haunt them for the rest of their lives – like seeing one or more of their colleagues on life rafts being sucked into the burning oil around their ship, the men screaming as they disappeared into sheets of orange flame, or men struggling in the blazing sea that was on fire, seeing men with the skin peeling off their bodies from the flames, or men in lifeboats jumping overboard because half crazed with thirst and hunger, and men losing their minds completely and having to be lashed down to the bottom of a boat before dying the following day. Admiral Bayly listened, silent and compassionate.

He never wasted words. When an American destroyer commander sent him a wireless message saying that a torpedo had just missed his ship, Bayly didn't reply. And when, a short while later, the destroyer captain sent a second wireless message saying: 'Have just been missed by another torpedo', the admiral sent a one-word response: 'Congratulations'.

Bayly had no use for ships that he couldn't send into action immediately. Finding that each of three destroyers sent as reinforcements needed maintenance that would keep them in harbour for perhaps a week, he promptly sent them back whence they came. He didn't want them. The commodore responsible for sending them wired him: 'Sorry my destroyers were not of much use to you.' Bayly responded: 'Why say "much"?'

Jellicoe, Commander-in-Chief of the Grand Fleet and later First

Sea Lord (effectively the Navy Chief-of-Staff), once referred to Bayly as being renowned for being very difficult and said he 'was supposed to have it in for all Americans'. The latter proved to be far from the truth. That rumour probably stemmed from the period Bayly had spent as naval attaché in America, where he had been sent in June 1900. He hadn't wanted to go, but orders were orders.

'The business of a Naval Attaché in those days,' he wrote, 'was really to find out certain things which the country he was accredited to did not wish a foreign nation to know – a very unpleasant position for a naval officer who has not the detective instincts. Not being of a very social nature, I was not anxious to try to get certain information at dinner tables or social gatherings, which I had been told was a method frequently used by those brought up in diplomatic circles. Although there was an idea that the United States Government had no secrets about ships, armaments, etc., the facts were quite the reverse, and information by question and answer was only obtainable about indifferent matters.'

Twenty-one months after arriving in America he received a letter from the British ambassador informing him that the American Secretary of State would be glad if Bayly gave up the duty of naval attaché. Bayly, relieved, returned to England, and was given command of a cruiser.

In 1907, with the rank of second-class commodore, he was put in command of the Royal Navy's destroyers. Those ships were then relatively new, and there was little understanding of how they might be used in flotillas. Commodore Bayly's brief was to find out the best way to use them in the event of war. As well as this, the Admiralty, undecided which of two ports – Harwich and Dover – should be used as the destroyer base, asked him to look into the matter and make a recommendation. He took his destroyers to the two ports, and then unequivocally chose Harwich. His reason was that at Harwich the ships were in still water, whereas at Dover rough seas and wind buffeted them.

For two years, by day and by night, he worked the destroyers hard. On night manoeuvres, regardless of how dark it was, he allowed no lights to be shown. He put the lean, narrow, shallow-draft ships through countless exercises, and he took them north to the big Scapa Flow anchorage in the Orkney Islands. The Admiralty asked him to write a destroyer manual, and this, too, he did. The official historian of the Royal Navy, Sir Julian Corbett, called Bayly 'the father of destroyer tactics and organisation'.

He was sensitive to the conditions under which those who served on destroyers worked, describing the experience as 'living in a ship whose motion is jerky and unexpected, in surroundings that are usually damp'. Years later Bayly said he was convinced that being in command of a destroyer was the finest possible training for a higher command. Serving on a destroyer, he said, taught officers and men resourcefulness, seamanship, self-denial and self-confidence.

Admiral Jellicoe described destroyer work as 'arduous', and he wrote of 'patient and monotonous performance of duty at sea, day and night, in all weathers'. 'All weathers' included gales, dense fog, blinding snowstorms, huge seas. In wartime there were the additional hazards of working in waters that were repeatedly mined, and having to contend with an enemy almost always hidden from view beneath the sea's surface.

At the end of his two years with the destroyers, Bayly was appointed president of the War College and promoted to rear-admiral. He found the two years he spent at the college extremely dull, and was impatient to get back to sea again. In February 1911 he was delighted to be given command of the Battle Cruiser squadron, followed by command of the Home Fleet. He was once more in his element.

There followed a series of appointments with the various fleets, all of which he filled with distinction. No flag officer before him had ever used a smokescreen for a tactical purpose during battle exercises. But Bayly did, and his use of it was so successful that others, including the Germans, subsequently copied it.

In December of 1914, with the war already five months old, he was ordered to leave the Grand Fleet, in which he had been serving under Jellicoe, and become Vice-Admiral Commanding the Channel Fleet. On his departure from the Grand Fleet, Jellicoe sent him three signals that he valued for the rest of his life. The second was the shortest and summed up the essence of all three. It said:

> Before you are out of touch I must once more express my personal and deep sorrow at your departure. I know you will succeed magnificently in whatever lies before you.

Having taken up his new command, Admiral Bayly was ordered, towards the end of December, to take the Fifth Battle squadron (eight battleships and two light cruisers) down the English Channel for firing practice at Portland off the coast of Dorset. Then came a tragic incident for which he unjustifiably took the blame, and which could have blighted his career. He was given an escort of destroyers from Harwich (north-east Essex), but was expressly instructed to send them back as soon as they passed Folkestone in the Straits of Dover, just west of Dover itself. He complied with that order. The departure of the destroyers left the battleships and the two light cruisers of the Fifth Battle Squadron unprotected. Information Bayly received in daily reports indicated that there were *no* enemy submarines in the western half of the English Channel. But U-24 *was* there, and had stalked the battleships and cruisers for most of the day.

The squadron steamed steadily westwards through filthy weather, past Beachy Head, the Isle of Wight, The Needles, St Albans Head and the Bill of Portland, and then across Lyme Bay towards Start Point. Bayly put the ships through several exercises on their way. When darkness came down he ordered all lights extinguished. The ships were steaming at 10 knots. Acting on an Admiralty fleet order, at 7 p.m. Bayly altered course, turning the fleet sixteen points. He did the same at 2 a.m. on the morning of New Year's Day 1915.

At twenty minutes past two there was a tremendous explosion when the last vessel in the line, the 15,000-ton pre-dreadnought battleship HMS *Formidable,* the admiral's flagship, was hit on the port side by a torpedo fired from thirty-three-year-old *Kapitanleutnant* Rudolf 'Rudi' Schneider's U-24. It was a direct hit on the number one port side boiler. The 431-foot ship, commanded by Captain Loxley, began to list heavily to starboard. They were then about 35–37 miles off the Devon coast, or about 20 miles from Start Point. Rain and hail driven by a strong wind, and waves up to 30 feet high, meant that the conditions in the darkness at sea were about as bad as they could be, making the successful launching of lifeboats a near impossibility. Many of the loaded lifeboats were smashed to smithereens, resulting in the deaths of the occupants; other boats reached the water, but were immediately swamped. They sank in the tumultuous seas.

Two open boats, pinnaces, each with seventy men on board, managed to get away from the side of the sinking battleship, but were hammered by waves and gusting winds. Seas poured in over the gunwales, and the frightened men had to bale desperately with anything that would hold water. Three-quarters of an hour after being struck by the first torpedo, the *Formidable* was hit by a second. Flares and rockets from the crippled battleship lit up the darkness at intervals. She stayed afloat until around a quarter to five, but then suddenly lurched and began to sink very quickly.

One account said that immediately following the tremendous lurch that presaged the ship's going down, Captain Loxley shouted, 'Lads, this is the last. All hands for themselves, and may God bless you and guide you to safety!' He was said to have walked then to the front of the battleship's bridge where he lit a cigarette, and stood waiting for the end. He went down with his ship when she capsized in the freezing darkness.

The two light cruisers rescued eighty of the *Formidable*'s crew. Luckily for one of the pinnaces, the Brixham trawler *Provident* reached it just as it was about to sink. The fishing boat saved the seventy occupants.

The second pinnace wasn't so lucky. All through the remaining hours of darkness and into the next day and night, buffeted by roaring seas and freezing wind, the crowded boat inched closer inshore. It was eventually spotted at Lyme, and the alarm was raised. Of the original seventy men in that boat, only forty-eight were alive. During the 22 hours the men had been adrift, fourteen had died and were consigned to the deep.

When the pinnace was brought in, she had six dead bodies on board as well as those who were still alive. Three more men died after landing. Altogether thirty-five officers and 512 other ranks died in the sinking of the *Formidable*. She lies today upside down in 180 feet of water.

According to German Engine Room Artificer Jaud, the U-boat was only about 100 metres from the battleship when Schneider gave the order to fire. From such close range, U-24's torpedo couldn't miss. Jaud said that when U-24 tried to get within firing range of another ship of the squadron and failed, Schneider finally decided to return to the damaged *Formidable* to finish her off with a second torpedo. The battleship had opened fire on the U-boat, which quickly went down 50 metres onto the seabed, and remained on the bottom until Schneider considered it safe to move away.

The U-boat captain told his crew that he hadn't been able to turn away fast enough from the *Formidable*, and had had to pass underneath her, during which U-24 struck the hull of the sinking battleship. When the U-boat surfaced much later in the morning, it was to find that the conning tower hatch was jammed shut. They couldn't open it. Getting out through a different hatchway, they found that the two periscopes had been bent over at right angles, down across the conning tower hatch.

Rudolf Schneider didn't survive the war. In October 1917, by which time he had sunk forty-five ships totalling 126,000 tons, he was swept overboard out of the conning tower of another U-boat, U-87, east of the Shetland Islands. His body was recovered and brought back on board, and he was then buried at sea.

The Admiralty in effect convicted Bayly of negligence over the sinking of the *Formidable*. But it was *they* who had shown a lack of responsibility in failing to provide him with a destroyer screen for the *entire* run down the channel. It was an accepted fact that one of the most important functions of destroyers was to work as screens for fleets against torpedo attack. No warship larger or slower than a light cruiser was considered safe in potentially hostile waters without a destroyer screen. And yet the Admiralty had ordered this squadron's destroyers to be withdrawn when the ships passed Folkestone!

In his memoir, *Pull Together*, Bayly said: 'Next day, when at Portland, I was ordered to haul my flag down.' That order amounted to his disgrace. But, as he revealed, 'I was to remain on full pay! I asked for a court martial, but was refused – I have never known why … However, it is well to remember that in a disciplined force an essential of that discipline is the facing of injustice with a smile. One of my favourite maxims to officers is that success teaches us nothing; failure only teaches.'

With the sinking of the *Formidable* hanging over him, Bayly was appointed president of the Royal Naval Staff College at Greenwich on the south bank of the Thames about 6 miles south-east of London. In the complex of Wren-designed buildings which had once been Greenwich Hospital, Royal Navy officers, as well as officers from other navies, were trained in the naval sciences as well as in the administrative, staff and policy aspects of their profession.

Bayly introduced a novel innovation – using white tape to mark boundaries, he had scale outlines of France, the Dardanelles, and Mesopotamia laid out on the grass lawns. Coloured flags were used to show the positions of the armed forces. The lawn charts were updated every day. The King heard so much about them that he went down to Greenwich to see them for himself. But the charts dealt only with the war on land and Bayly, in the navy from the age of thirteen, was deeply perturbed about what was happening in the war at sea. The German U-boats were causing havoc. Hundreds of thousands of tons of merchant shipping and their precious cargoes and crews were being torpedoed and sunk, and the future for Britain looked bleak.

Almost as soon as Bayly arrived at the July 1915 meeting with Balfour, he was asked if he had any suggestions for dealing with the U-boat menace, and was also asked if he would be prepared to take over command at Queenstown. His said later that he 'took a chart, and pencilled on it the area which I must have command of'. He drew a big circle, which encompassed an area from Ushant to the Sound of Mull. It took in the Western Approaches, all the waters around the coast of Ireland, the Irish Sea, St George's Channel, the Bristol Channel, and the entrance to the English Channel. He told Balfour and the Admiralty that provided he could have command in that circle and they gave him a fast cruiser for his flagship, and as many small craft as could be spared, he would tackle the German submarine campaign 'with my base at Queenstown'.

He also asked to have command over Liverpool, but they stalled on that 'because Liverpool objected to being under anyone stationed in Ireland'.

Bayly estimated that he would need twelve destroyers, and about two dozen of the newly ordered small cruisers called Flower-Class sloops which were under construction – the first two had already been sent north to join the Grand Fleet. They told him that there were no destroyers available – but they promised him sloops.

Admiral Sir George Coke had made repeated requests for destroyers, and had continually been informed that destroyers couldn't be spared because so many were required to protect the Grand Fleet. The commander at Harwich wanted destroyers for the North Sea. The commander at Dover wanted them for the Dover Patrol. Queenstown came well down on the list of priorities regarding the allocation of destroyers. Admiral Jellicoe, who assumed command of the Grand Fleet in July 1914, held that the cruisers *had* to have destroyers in company 'to assist in dealing with the submarines', and that the destroyers should be well in advance of the battle fleet.

Bayly knew that the bulk of the sea-fighting connected with the protection of merchant ships against the U-boats, would be done in *his* area of command – principally in the waters off the south and south-west coast of Ireland, the Western Approaches. That area was already a huge maritime graveyard. He was facing massive problems. The only ships he'd have under his command at the outset would be Coke's 'Gilbert & Sullivan Navy'. But he relished the prospect of being back in the thick of things instead of sitting and fretting at his desk in the Royal Naval Staff College at Greenwich, or out on the lawn adjusting his white-tape outline maps of the land battle zones.

He accepted the Queenstown posting, and they gave him HMS *Adventure*, a ten-year-old, 25 knot, 2,640-ton Scout Cruiser, to be his flagship. She was a four-funnelled job, 395 feet long, and had operated with the 6th Destroyer Flotilla at Dover, and with the 6th Light Cruiser Squadron based on the Humber. Bayly boarded her at Gravesend on 20 July 1915.

On 21 July US President Woodrow Wilson ordered his Secretary of the Navy, Josephus Daniels, and Secretary of War, Lindley M. Garrison, to draft a defence programme.

On the same day, HMS *Adventure*, commanded by Captain George Hyde, steamed in through the 'gate' in the recently installed boom defence of wire nets at the mouth of Cork Harbour, and delivered the fifty-eight-year-old Admiral Bayly to Queenstown where he became, officially, Admiral Commanding Western Approaches. Before disembarking, Bayly told Captain Hyde that he wanted the *Adventure* always to be ready to go to sea at half an hour's notice by day, two hours notice by night. Then he went ashore and up to the house on the hill to take up his new command.

Eight days after Admiral Bayly's arrival in Queenstown, one of the new Acacia-Class sloops, HMS *Sunflower*, rushed to where the 5,273-ton SS *Iberian* had been sunk by U-28, 9 miles south by west from the

Fastnet. Seven men had died. The sloop rescued the survivors, some of whom were badly injured. She also picked up three dead bodies, and took the living and the dead into Queenstown. Bayly, in his green barge, met the sloop as she entered harbour, uttered a brief 'Well done!' to the *Sunflower*'s captain and crew, and then told them to get back to sea as quickly as they could. There were predatory U-boats out there looking for ships to sink, and there were ships aplenty coming and going through the Western Approaches. There was little time for sentiment in the face of urgent necessity.

Four days later the *Midland Queen* was sunk by the same U-boat – this time using her deck gun – 70 miles south-west by west from the Fastnet. A week after that it was the turn of the *Oakwood*, also sunk by gunfire, 45 miles south-south-east from the Old Head of Kinsale.

On 19 August the 15,800-ton White Star liner *Arabic* was sunk 50 miles south by west from the Old Head of Kinsale. She was outward bound for New York with 181 passengers on board, when a torpedo fired from U-24 sent her to the bottom in less than ten minutes. Forty-four people (three of them Americans) died on the ship. In America, the authorities reacted sharply. The U-boat was U-24, commanded by Rudolf Schneider.

On the same day two other vessels were sunk in Admiral Bayly's command area, the SS *New York City*, 44 miles south-south-east from the Fastnet, and the small (277 tons) sailing vessel *St Olaf*. The *St Olaf* was south of Galley Head, and it was gunfire that ripped her wooden hull apart and sent her under.

The sinking of any ship was a matter for concern, regret, and anger to Bayly, but he had a warm affection and respect for wind ships because in his youth in the Royal Navy, on the *Ariadne*, in bare feet, he had climbed the mizzen mast many times and balanced on foot-ropes while lying out on the yards, sending masts and yards up and down, and furling sails when learning to be a seaman. So it was with additional disgust that he had learned of the 5 May sinking by gunfire of the small (132 tons) sailing vessel *Earl of Latham* just a few miles south-west of The Old Head of Kinsale. Now, on his watch, the same fate befell the *St Olaf*, and there would be many more wind ships sunk in his area of command. It spelled the end for the great and graceful tall ships.

In August alone, forty-nine ships of all types and sizes, amounting to 135,000 tons, were sunk.

11

THE HOUSE ON THE HILL

Rear-Admiral Bayly had made an immediate and thorough inspection of the building and grounds as soon as he arrived at Admiralty House on Upper Bond Street. The three-storey building with basement was distinctive and impressive. Each floor had seven windows that afforded perfect views of the harbour. From any of them he could see out over the roofs of the terraced town, over the Belgian blue slate roof of St Colman's cathedral. He was able to look down on Cobh Road, Haulbowline, Spike Island lying like a huge green breakwater a mile due south of the waterfront, and, off to the east, the Spit lighthouse, the inner harbour anchorage, and, across the eastern channel, Aghada. He could also see Whitegate and Corkbeg and, away out beyond Camden and Carlisle forts and at the far end of White Bay, Roche's Point lighthouse.

Admiral Bayly was monarch of almost all he surveyed. As his eyes swept across Haulbowline and its dockyard, he remembered being told that there was an army detachment stationed on the island. He made up his mind to get them to leave – he wanted the entire island to be under his command and control.

The extensive gardens of Admiralty House, most of them sloping down the hill away from the rear of the house, were neat, and impeccably kept. An enthusiastic gardener, who loved growing flowers and vegetables, he was delighted with the grounds of the house. A very fit man who made serious efforts to remain in good physical condition, he noticed with satisfaction that an area had been levelled off and a tennis court installed.

An idea also started forming in Violet Voysey's head as soon as they came to the vegetable garden. She knew instinctively that the vessels under her uncle's command would rescue from the sea as many survivors as they could, and would undoubtedly land them at Queenstown. Clearly there was going to be an urgent need of hot nourishing food to feed them. So it was with more than casual interest that she looked at the vegetable garden.

The admiral had been told that there'd been leakages of information from Queenstown. He would have to maintain (and perhaps install new) strong security measures against the passing on of naval intelligence to the enemy. Having noticed on his way up the harbour the towering mast that rose up from the Admiralty House garden, he saw how easy it would be for signals, semaphored in clear language to ships in the anchorage, to be seen in the town. Anyone with a knowledge of semaphore could read them, and thus pick up valuable information that the enemy would be delighted to receive.

Bayly decided to halt the transmission of signals from Admiralty House direct to the ships. No more would orders be semaphored in clear view. He ordered a cable to be laid from Admiralty House to the waterfront, and from there across to Haulbowline. A new concealed signal station was set up on the island. It was sited in a position from which only the ships in the harbour could see it. From the time the link was completed, orders from Admiralty House were transmitted in code by cable to the Haulbowline signal station, and from there by code to the relevant vessels. The signal station in the garden at Admiralty House ceased to be operative.

The admiral also announced that he would be paying no private social visits to any houses whilst he was at Queenstown, and no social activities, no receptions or dinners for resident or visiting VIPs, would be held at Admiralty House. Only naval commanding officers or dockyard personnel would in future visit the house on the hill on official business. Through these decisions Bayly hoped to curtail the kind of leaks that could arise from loose social gossip. He also decreed that Admiralty House would be 'dry' for the duration of the war. This was in line with the decision made by the King regarding Buckingham Palace. And no one was to be allowed on board any ship in the harbour unless in uniform, or on duty.

As the population of Queenstown was well over 90 per cent Catholic, one of the most influential people in the town was the Catholic Bishop of Cloyne, Most Rev. Dr Robert Browne, who had come to Queenstown in 1894. A native of Charleville, former president of Maynooth, he was well into his seventies when Admiral Bayly arrived at Admiralty House. Bishop Browne was considered by his fellow bishops to be a man of 'indefatigable zeal and perfect taste'. He was to spend forty-one years as Bishop of Cloyne. Queenstown's cathedral was named St Colman's after the saint who had founded the dioceses in the sixth century. The big Dalkey Blue Granite building with its soaring spire dominated the town's skyline.

Bayly held strong Christian beliefs, but he wasn't a Catholic. He enquired about the bishop's name and where the churchman lived, and was told that the Bishop's Palace 'was no distance away – just down the hill and around the corner'. It was within easy walking distance. Bayly walked unaccompanied down Upper Bond Street and around the corner and, arriving at the bishop's residence, said who he was, and asked if he might see Bishop Browne. Instinct and intelligence told the admiral that the bishop would be a useful man to form a friendly relationship with. (He afterwards erroneously referred to Dr Browne as the Bishop of Queenstown.)

The bishop received him courteously, and after the formal exchange of pleasantries, the admiral got down to business. Accustomed to using language plainly and without pretension, he told Dr Browne that it would be a great help if the bishop and he could work harmoniously. As Bishop Browne undoubtedly wielded a great deal of influence in the town and the surrounding area, Bayly would be very grateful for Dr Browne's cooperation. The bishop unhesitatingly promised to cooperate in every way he could. Each man quickly saw admirable qualities in the other, and within a short time the senior naval officer and the senior Catholic cleric became close friends. Bayly later said of Dr Browne that the bishop never failed to help him whenever asked.

The admiral needed an office to work from in Admiralty House, and he ordered a partition to be erected in the spacious drawing-room, dividing that room into two sections. The larger one was the admiral's office; the smaller (one-third the size of the original room) was henceforth the new drawing-room. In a prominent position on the mantelpiece in his office Bayly placed a card which said: 'By the help of God I will keep the balance level.' The bare, cold room was sparsely furnished.

He ordered a timber cover to be made for the top of the house's billiard table. He intended using it as a chart-table using small coloured flags to track the positions of his own ships, and plot the progress of those coming in or going out through the Western Approaches. Because survivors from ships torpedoed and sunk by U-boats were all the time being brought into Queenstown, the admiral let it be known that in the event of any emergency, he would be available at any and all times, day or night.

He had arrived at Queenstown without a flag lieutenant, and it was his niece, Miss Voysey who, at the beginning, helped him every day to move the flags around the charts. The positions of the flags on the charts showed him where his patrol ships were. Violet also helped him to deal with the constant stream of phone calls, telegrams, letters, signals, and complex paper work that went with his job. Paymaster H. R. Russell was eventually assigned to him as his flag lieutenant.

Always sensitive to the strains and exhaustion his hard-worked ship captains were subjected to every day and every night that they were at sea on patrol, and wanting to know as much as possible about their problems and how they tackled them, and what their views were, he began inviting them to Admiralty House for a meal and a chat around the fire. It provided them with an opportunity to unwind and to receive advice and encouragement. And in case any of them wanted to spend the night ashore, the admiral ensured that Number 9 room was always kept in readiness. In this way, Bayly got to know his ship captains, and they got to know him.

From the start of his time at Queenstown he set about establishing strong relationships with the senior officers and officials of the dockyard on Haulbowline. He knew he would be dependent on them to keep things running smoothly as far as ship repairs, construction, marine engine maintenance and general engineering were concerned. The top three men at the dockyard were the engineer officer, Mr Lacey; the naval constructor, Mr J. F. Walker, and the chief store officer, Mr Bennett. Bayly later said that he never had the least anxiety about the ships being prepared – everything worked smoothly. He made schedule alterations and procedural alterations in the way the dockyard worked, and he never hesitated to give praise where and when it was earned.

Through persuasion, or coercion (probably a combination of both) he got the army to leave the part of Haulbowline they occupied and so achieved his aim of having the whole of the island under his command and control. And then, because this was for him a new and complicated command, he settled down to studying the responsibilities and important duties that went with it. Always a stickler for efficiency, he knew that efficiency of the ships and naval establishments under his command would have to be a top priority. The antisubmarine campaign and the protection of sea communications in the vital waters of the area within his command called for all his energy, all his tactical nous, and every vestige of administrative ability he possessed.

He studied the trade routes, the statements made by senior admirals of the German navy, the history and methods employed by the Germans in their U-boat campaign to date, and formulated his own plans and suggestions. He poured over the details in reports that his predecessor, Admiral Coke, had prepared, and realised that such matters as shipping casualties, stranded and damaged merchant ships,

ships in sinking conditions, ships on fire, and ships otherwise in trouble, would bring him into contact with agents, owners, underwriters, and the Salvage Association, all seeking his assistance. And there would always be the human victims of the war at sea – the survivors.

By inclination and training a decisive man, Bayly was accustomed to making up his mind quickly about problems and issues that confronted him. Before leaving London, he had been alerted to the presence of an active Sinn Féin element in Cork, 12 miles up the River Lee. The Sinn Féiners were anti-British and had strong pro-German sympathies. It was made clear to him that he should expect trouble from Sinn Féin activists.

He had no intention of turning Admiralty House into an ivory tower residence. He intended being a hands-on commanding officer, not a remote controller, so he familiarised himself with the town, the harbour and the coastline over which he now had dominion. He hadn't the slightest doubt but that his new job was going to be the most demanding of his entire career, perhaps of his whole life.

12

FISHERMEN OF DEATH

The Admiralty assigned numbers to the Home Waters patrol areas. The English Channel, for instance, had areas that were numbered XI, XII, XIII and XIV respectively. An area off Kingstown/Dún Laoghaire was numbered XVI, and an area off the north-west coast of Ireland was numbered XVIII, and so on.

Knowing that for patrol area No. XXI (base, Queenstown), all Bayly would have at his disposal at the outset was the collection of small slow trawlers, drifters, motor boats and armed yachts that he had inherited from Admiral Coke. But he was sustained by the promise made to him at the Admiralty in London that he would be allocated, and would get, some of the new sloops then under construction.

One estimate of the area in the South-Western Approaches to be covered by what was known as offensive patrolling put the figure at 100,000 square miles. The trawlers were really too slow, too small and too lightly armed for the job of hunting and engaging U-boats.

Admiral Lord Charles Beresford in 1907, when Commander-in-Chief of the Home Fleet, and following a visit he'd made to England's east coast ports, had first advocated the use of Grimsby North Sea steam trawlers in the event of war by the Royal Navy. But he'd been thinking of them in the role of minesweepers. Beresford's argument was that in wartime many steam trawlers would be laid up in port anyway, and would therefore be available for war service. He foresaw the need of providing shipping with adequate protection against mine warfare. Submarines hadn't then yet entered the picture.

In 1911 the Admiralty, foreseeing the dangers to which warships and merchantmen would be exposed if seas strewn with mines could not be quickly cleared, created a new section of the Royal Naval Reserve, the trawler section. It consisted of 142 skippers and 1,136 ratings, all taken from Britain's fishing fleet. Additionally, the Admiralty purchased a number of steam fishing trawlers, and fitted them with minesweeping appliances. Arrangements were made for a large fleet of steam trawlers to be placed at the disposal of the navy if war broke out. When the First World War started, the Admiralty requisitioned these trawlers, eventually taking 800 of them from the Grimsby and Hull fishing fleets alone. Other trawlers were taken from fishing ports such as North Shields, Lowestoft, Fleetwood, Peterhead and Aberdeen.

Tough little vessels ranging between 200 and 300 tons, they were excellent sea-boats, as they had to be for their peacetime work and voyages that took many of them out into the stormy North Sea and as far as fishing grounds in the Arctic. Their peacetime captains came with the trawlers that the Admiralty requisitioned. They were given the newly created rank of skipper, Royal Naval Reserve (trawler section). The rank then appeared in the navy list for the first time. Neither the skippers nor their crews had much knowledge of or regard for Royal Navy rules and regulations and the spit-and-polish that characterised the Navy. The Admiralty got around this by invariably appointing a Royal Naval Reserve (RNR) officer to each trawler.

The trawlers, whose initial minesweeping duties were eventually extended to include patrolling, escorting, and general antisubmarine work, became part of what was called the auxiliary patrol, and they were worked to the limit in all kinds of weather, regardless of the tumult of wind and sea. In severe storms, great mounds of waves pitched and rolled the ships with terrible violence, and seas swept across their decks with unstoppable force.

When he took over from Admiral Coke, Bayly knew that these small ships had no armour plating, no protective bulkheads of the type the warships had. The result was catastrophe when they were attacked by torpedo or gunfire, or struck a mine. Their holds filled with water, and a trawler would sink in mere seconds with the loss of all hands.

From June 1915 on the Germans began using U-boats for minelaying. Cork Harbour became a natural target. Ships steaming through mine-infested waters were always in danger, and the minelayers that came to the seaward approaches to Cork Harbour hoped to inflict casualties among the heavy inwards and outwards traffic. They laid their moored mines in positions that the Germans calculated would make it virtually impossible for ships to pass over without striking one of these underwater weapons. The contact mines were anchored to the seabed by a cable and a heavy weight, with the mines floating just below the surface. They exploded immediately on contact.

These weapons were globular or pear-shaped, about 3 feet in diameter. Each contained 350 lbs of guncotton, trinitrotoluene (TNT) or amatol. The explosive, together with the firing batteries, occupied about half the space available, the remainder being used as an air chamber to give buoyancy to the mine. The upper surface of each mine had five or more 5-inch leaden horns, each horn holding a glass tube containing a chemical mixture. Contact with the hull of a ship fractured a horn and smashed the glass tube. The released liquid then energised the battery, which in turn fired the detonator. The very powerful charges were capable of tearing open enormous holes in the unprotected underwater skin of a surface ship.

U-boat minelayers came repeatedly to the Cork Harbour approaches. It was estimated that by the end of the war they'd made more than thirty visits to lay mines. To sweep the minefields, the mines had first to be found. It was a particularly dangerous job on Ireland's south coast because of the heavy swell and the small tidal range. The task fell initially to the trawler/minesweepers, which were crewed by fishermen. The technique required the trawlers to steam in pairs with a serrated 'sweep' wire trailing in the sea between them as they crawled to and fro, often through howling tempests and driving sleet. Each minesweeping trawler hoisted a black ball at the masthead, and another at either the port or starboard end of the yardarm, to warn other ships which side the trawler was sweeping on.

The skippers and their crews had to put up with the sting of the wind and the lash of the spray driving over the trawlers' bows once the orders, 'Hands to sweeping stations!' followed by, 'Out sweep!' were given. The objective was to cut the mines' mooring cables, causing the liberated mines to shoot to the surface, to be then exploded by rifle-fire. Some mines exploded underwater when dragged into contact with each other during minesweeping operations. An ever-present danger for the minesweepers was that a swept mine could come barrelling out of the depths and strike one of the ships that had swept it. From time to time this happened, and when it did it, it almost always resulted in the shockingly quick end of the ship, and the deaths of most, if not all, of her crew.

E. Hilton Young wrote of the minesweeping trawlermen:

We sift the drifting sea
and blindly grope beneath;
obscure and toilsome we,
the fishermen of death

After the war it was estimated that in 1917 the Germans laid one mine every hour in the waters around Britain. In April of that year the losses among minesweepers was one minesweeper a day for the greater part of the month, according to a Ministry of Information pamphlet, *His Majesty's Minesweepers*, prepared for the Admiralty in 1943.

Bayly had tremendous admiration for the trawler/minesweepers' skippers and crews. On a daily basis he came face to face with their magnificent spirit and determination and, as he acknowledged in a memorandum, 'there were no complaints, they faced any weather, and did wonderful work'.

Two hundred and fourteen minesweepers were lost during the war, an average of one a week. Six of them were from the Queenstown

Command. Of those six, mines sank four. There were only two survivors from the combined crews of the four Queenstown-based minesweepers sunk by the lethal underwater weapons.

The case of the *Morococala* well illustrates the extreme dangers of the work carried out by the trawler/minesweepers. She was a 264-ton steel vessel built in 1915 in Aberdeen. The Admiralty took her over, complete with her skipper, James Duthie, and crew, and appointed a twenty-four-year-old Glaswegian, Lieutenant Alexander Allen, RNR, to her. After she was fitted-out, she was sent to Queenstown in June, a month after she was launched. For two years she carried out patrol and minesweeping duties, and in April 1917 she encountered and fired at a U-boat off the south coast. Admiral Bayly expressed praise for Lieutenant Allen's handling of that particular situation, as well as his regret that the *Morococala* wasn't equipped with a 12-pounder gun, instead of the 6-pounder with which she was armed.

On 18 November, following the discovery of a moored mine off Cork Harbour, eight trawlers were sent out from Queenstown by the Director of Minesweeping for the Coast of Ireland, Commander Heaton. Under the command of Lieutenant Allen, they were assigned to sweep the approaches. The little ships left the sleeping town behind and went out through the greyness of a chilly drizzle with the cloud thickening and getting lower. The minesweepers had first to clear a buoyed channel to enable a convoy of mostly ancient three-island coal burners with tall thin funnels to get out of the harbour safely.

The convoy began to leave the harbour at 11 o'clock on the morning of the 19 November. The long line of ships emerged into the open sea, steaming out between Roche's Point lighthouse and Weaver's Point eight cables west-north-west of it. The ships began to pitch as they met the swell rolling in from the south-west. As they got into some semblance of proper formation, masters and their chief engineers adjusted their ships' revolutions to conform to the laid down speed of the convoy.

Meanwhile the eight trawlers formed pairs. The *Morococala* and the *Indian Empire*, an ex-Grimsby trawler which rescued nearly 200 survivors of the *Lusitania*, set their wire between them and began their sweep. Suddenly there was a thunderous explosion when the two minesweepers were 1½ miles south of the Daunt Rock lightship. The stern of the *Morococala* was immediately enveloped in flames and smoke.

Lieutenant Allen and Signalman William Bellman were seen scrambling onto the top of the trawler's wheelhouse, but another explosion followed quickly, hurling them off the roof into the smoke and flames and clouds of steam and coal dust. They were never seen again. The trawler's stern went underwater, her bow rose vertically, and within a few seconds she was gone. All twelve of those who were on the trawler – Skipper Duthie wasn't on board that day – died. A small scattering of floating debris was all that remained of the ship, scarcely enough timber, as someone said, to make a packing case.

Two days after the *Morococala* went down, Admiral Bayly issued a memorandum addressed to 'The Officers Commanding Armed Trawlers and Drifters on the Coast of Ireland Station':

It is with very great regret that I have learned of the loss of HM Trawler *Morococala*, blown up by a mine. During the two-and-a-half years that I have held this command I have never failed to respect and admire the devotion to duty and the seamanlike ability of the trawlers attached to the coast of Ireland. In spite of tempestuous weather, fogs, mists etc., although usually over-gunned and outranged by the submarines they have engaged with, with few comforts on board and the knowledge that they have no watertight compartments to keep them afloat: yet they are seen day after day to go out to their duties with the one idea – to destroy their country's enemies who ruthlessly prey on helpless ships, showing neither honour, manliness, nor self-respect in their cruel and brutal attacks.

We have lost some of our brother seamen from the dangers of the seas, and some from the violence of the enemy, but the same magnificent spirit continues, and I wish to express to all who serve in the Irish

Trawler Force my wholehearted thanks and pride for what they have done in the past and my faith in their actions in the future.

It may be well said of our Trawler Skippers what was said of one of the first seamen in the world's history:

To tread the path of death he stood prepared.
And what he greatly thought he nobly dared.

Lewis Bayly
Admiral
Commander-in-Chief

The non-availability of destroyers for Queenstown was a sore point with Admiral Bayly, but Admiral Jellicoe, the Commander-in-Chief of the Grand Fleet, consistently, and successfully, argued that it had 'always been held that the Grand Fleet required a total force of one hundred destroyers and ten flotilla leaders for the double purpose of screening the ships from submarine attack when at sea, and countering the enemy's destroyers and attacking his heavy ships with torpedo fire in fleet action'.

A small number of destroyers did, from time to time, engage in trade protection but, Jellicoe said, 'Any further transference ... of destroyers from the Grand Fleet to southern waters for trade protection was a highly dangerous expedient, involving increased risk from submarine attack on the heavy ships *in the event of the fleet proceeding to sea*.' And he added, 'Those who argued then, or who have argued since, that we should have reduced the number of destroyers with the Grand Fleet *will not, I think, meet with any support from those who served in that Fleet* [Italics added].'

Meanwhile in Queenstown, Bayly believed that far greater use should have been made of destroyers for trade protection. All he had was the derisively nicknamed 'Gilbert & Sullivan Navy' he had inherited when he took over the command, plus the new sloops that were eventually sent to him – though he was to say later that no one could be more proud of his 'brave little heterogeneous fleet' than he was. But, struggling to make as effective use as possible of the motley collection of vessels, he was strongly of the opinion that the Grand Fleet's quota of destroyers might have been reduced, and some of the destroyers employed independently to do battle with the U-boats that were wiping out so many merchant ships.

He urgently needed bigger, faster and more heavily armed ships than his trawlers, drifters, ancient torpedo boats, motor launches and armed yachts. He had been encouraged when told that the Admiralty intended assigning sloops to the Queenstown Command. These Flower-Class sloops (all named after a flower), coal-fired, twin-funnelled, 16-knot, 1,200-tonners were twice as fast as the trawlers. Each had a crew of eighty. Because of their shape, the sloops were likely to be, and were, mistaken by U-boat commanders for Cross Channel steamers.

On 1 January 1915 the Admiralty had ordered twelve of them, and followed up that order seven days later with an order for a further twelve. On 4 May another twelve were ordered from the private shipyards. Orders for the final thirty-six were placed in July.

If the sloops had a disadvantage it was that they pitched in a seaway. A fore-and-aft trysail hoisted by a gaff could be set aft. Used only in foul weather, it was a considerable help during Atlantic storms. And as they had single screws, it was easy to keep these vessels hove to in heavy weather, the propeller being deep in the water. The sloops were excellent sea-boats.

The original intended use of these rapidly-built 267-feet-long vessels (they had a 33-foot beam and a draft of just under 11 feet) was minesweeping. However, as each vessel was equipped with two 4-inch guns, a 3-pounder, and depth charges, and the ships were economical with fuel, it was quickly realised that they had a considerable potential for escort and patrol duties. Queenstown Command's first two were scheduled to arrive in July 1915. Others would follow.

Each sloop on patrol, Bayly decided, was required to cover an area of 900 square miles – 30 miles from east to west, and 30 miles from north to south. Eight sloops were on patrol at any given time and, together, they covered an area from 100 miles west of the Fastnet to an area west of the Scilly Isles. The admiral further decided that, as a general rule, each sloop would spend five days at sea, followed by two days in harbour. It took them one day to refuel. On occasions a sloop might have to escort an incoming ship carrying a particularly valuable cargo, and go with her from west of the Fastnet all the way to Liverpool. The sloops performed other duties apart from patrolling and escorting – for instance, towing damaged ships into port, assisting in the beaching of torpedoed ships and saving lives.

Writing in later years about the sloops at Queenstown, Bayly said that they were 'mostly commanded by youngsters who had never commanded anything before, and gales and heavy seas were frequent … and the youngsters who commanded them were splendid. They faced the gales, chanced the fog, and were always ready to face any emergency, no matter how hard the work or how heavy the sea. They never failed me, and always turned up with a smile.'

The sloops were not easy ships to serve in, and there were many occasions when officers' and crews' accommodations alike had half a foot or more of water swilling around in them. On such occasions men rarely lay in dry bunks, and their lives on what Joseph Addison called 'the heavings of this prodigious bulk of waters' were miserable. The conditions wore out anyone whose nerves and determination were not extremely strong.

The admiral invited sloop captains to dine with him and his niece at Admiralty House, to use the quiet restfulness of the gardens to unwind, and, on occasion, to stay overnight in the spacious and comfortable bedroom that he insisted must always be kept in readiness. The flower garden next to the tennis court was itself a small oasis of renewal, and many of the captains found it particularly attractive after a strenuous, dangerous and demanding time at sea. Because trees, high shrubs and a wall surrounded this garden, it was impossible to see the harbour waters from within it. The captains took to planting blooms corresponding to the names of their ships. It soon became known as the sloop garden.

Among the sloops that operated out of Queenstown were: *Bluebell, Camellia, Genista, Jessamine, Laburnum, Myosotis, Poppy, Rosemary, Snowdrop, Sunflower* and *Zinnia.*

Bayly had arrived in Queenstown without a staff, without even a secretary, but that situation couldn't last long. There were so many vessels, so many men, so many ports to be dealt with, so many signals and telegrams, and a U-boat campaign which was causing havoc in the trade route past the south of Ireland, a one-man-and-his-niece operation couldn't possibly handle it all. This was recognised in official circles and, bit-by-bit, he acquired a back-up group.

First to arrive was his secretary, Paymaster H. R. Russell, a man who had served with Bayly in the battle cruisers in 1911. Russell was with the Grand Fleet in 1915 when Bayly contacted him and asked if he would like to come to Queenstown. Russell, one of the ablest secretaries in the navy and something of an organisational genius with a comprehensive knowledge of technical detail, said yes. The setting up of an operations office in Queenstown was an urgent priority, and Bayly and Russell set about it with customary thoroughness.

Three operations officers were appointed – Commanders Stopford Douglas, Grubbe and Herbert. Both Herbert and Stopford Douglas had commanded Q-ships. When Bayly was finally made Commander-in-Chief, Charles Carpendale became his flag captain. Commodore Martin-Leake, captain of the *Pathfinder*, the first British warship to be sunk by submarine, replaced Carpendale later. A specialist in antisubmarine work, Colonel B. F. Trench of the Royal Marines, also joined Bayly's staff.

But the U-boats and the mines weren't the sole causes of concern for Bayly. There were those damned armed merchant raiders which the Germans had sent out onto the high seas. One of them, the *Moewe*, captained by the uniquely-named *Korvettenkapitan* Burgraf

Graf Nikolaus zu Dohna-Schlodien, had put to sea on the day after Christmas 1915 and, after laying a total of 500 mines in two different locations, began in earnest her remarkable career as a commerce raider. She captured merchant ship after merchant ship, took their crews prisoner, and sank the vast majority of the vessels by gunfire, torpedo, bombs, or by scuttling. Bayly himself wanted to hunt down the converted banana ship, but in the circumstances he had to remain shore-based in Queenstown. He wondered if and when the *Moewe* would show up in his bailiwick.

Despite the best efforts to combat the U-boats and sweep up the mines, the bravery of all of those who went to sea, and the best efforts of Admiral Bayly and his staff, casualties mounted in the Western Approaches. The U-boats toll of tonnage rose inexorably. More and more merchant ships were sunk; essential cargoes went to the bottom of the sea, more merchant seamen died. From time to time the Admiralty sent a few British destroyers temporarily to Queenstown to augment the auxiliary patrols, but there were never enough of them, and those that did come never stayed long enough to bring about any major change in the way the sea war was tilting relentlessly in Germany's favour.

For a while the use by the British of decoy ships seemed to promise something like an effective answer.

13

Q-SHIPS AND SAVAGERY

Desperate for some means to supplement the antisubmarine efforts of the Auxiliary Service's trawlers, drifters, motor launches and armed yachts, the British came up with the idea of using decoy ships to lure and, they hoped, sink U-boats. Initially called Special Service vessels, the decoys were variously called Mystery Ships, Q-ships, and (by the Germans), Trap Ships. They became officially known as Q-ships in 1915 after the Admiralty gave 'Q' numbers to all of the ships in the class. One theory was that the designation 'Q' was derived from 'Queenstown' because many of the ships were 'converted' in the dockyard on Haulbowline.

The decoys were armed vessels, disguised as ordinary defenceless merchantmen. The theory was that, sailing alone along the shipping routes and flying the red (merchant navy) ensign, they would, by their innocent-looking appearance, entice a U-boat to the surface. The U-boat would come close, intending to sink the ship either by blowing her up with time-bombs placed on board, or by gunfire, because these methods were far less costly than using an expensive torpedo.

The Q-ship operation required highly disciplined courageous men to carry it out. Each vessel had what was known as a 'panic crew', as well as her regular crew. Each Q-ship also had on board a small group of experienced gunnery experts. The 'panic crew' was composed of Royal Navy personnel disguised as merchant seamen. Uniforms were forbidden on the Q-ships, and the 'panic crew' wore old, worn, scruffy shirts and jerseys bought in hock shops or second-hand clothes stores. When their vessel was fired on by a tricked-to-surface U-boat, the 'panic crew' would abandon ship and row away, behaving as though terrified that they were going to be killed. But they were careful to row to a position which would allow the gun crews concealed on the Q-ship to have clean lines of fire to the U-boat. One of the 'panic crew' was usually detailed to pretend he was the master, and carried a bogus set of ship's papers with him in the lifeboat. U-boat captains were required to provide proof of the sinkings they claimed, and a prisoner or ship's papers were acceptable for that purpose.

Unknown to the Germans on the U-boat, the decoy ship's real captain and his gun crews would remain hidden on board the 'abandoned' vessel, and when the unsuspecting U-boat came into close range, they would open up with the ship's previously concealed guns, and try to sink the U-boat. It was calculated deception, *ruse de guerre*.

Winston Churchill had had a hand in initiating the process. Late in November 1914 he contacted the Commander-in-Chief, Portsmouth, saying it was 'desired to trap the German submarine which sinks vessels by gunfire off Havre', the port in the English Channel on the mouth of the Seine. He suggested that a ship be secretly fitted with two concealed 12-pounder guns. She should carry two disguised, experienced gun-layers. If the ship was stopped by a U-boat, the gunners should make every effort to sink the enemy craft.

The Admiralty, as nearly always when First Lord of the Admiralty Churchill made a suggestion, acceded. In the five months between the outbreak of war and the end of December 1914, two steamships and one fishing vessel entered service as Q-ships. The total number of vessels entering service the following year (1915) jumped to 29, and included a sailing ship.

No single officer was ever appointed to oversee the Q-ship fleet. It was left to the individual admirals in charge of local commands to raise, equip and oversee their own Q-ship operations. This suited

Bayly at Queenstown. It was another opportunity, another outlet for his drive, his inventiveness and his imagination.

The first two Q-ships sent to him by the Admiralty were, he thought, too big. And they had the wrong cargoes – coal. To Bayly's mind a cargo of coal merely guaranteed that the ship would sink extremely quickly after being attacked, thus defeating the purpose for which she was intended, i.e. to engage a U-boat by sustained gunfire at close range and try to sink her. Sustained accurate gunfire from a rapidly sinking ship is a contradictory notion. Bayly got permission to send the two ships to Montreal, there to have their coal cargoes unloaded, and replaced by cargoes of timber. Holds tightly packed with wood should give each ship a buoyancy that would not only slow down sinking but might conceivably keep the ship afloat, perhaps capable of being salvaged.

In acquiring and equipping his own Q-ships, Bayly began by selecting three former colliers, and having them 'converted' in the dockyard on Haulbowline. In considering which ships to acquire for conversion to their new role, the admiral and his dockyard constructor, J. F. Walker, paid close attention to each vessel's suitability for successful disguise. Each ship had to be small enough to induce a U-boat captain to consider her not worthy of an expensive torpedo. In other words she had to be a shellfire candidate, or a time-bomb candidate, a ship that would tempt a U-boat to the surface to sink her by gunfire, or to blow her up.

Walker or his deputy travelled to Wales and England to search for suitable vessels. They decided that ordinary three-island (i.e. with raised forecastle, centre-castle, and poop), 10-knot cargo ships fitted the bill best. Dummy lifeboats, dummy lifebelt lockers, empty cargo crates, false deck fittings, fake deck cabins, hinged bulwarks and gunwales, collapsible screens – all were used by the ingenious Walker in his conversions. The purpose was to conceal the identities and the arms of the Q-ships. A typical Q-ship would have 12-pounders, 6- and 3-pounders, 4-inch guns, machine guns, and depth charges.

The conversions at Haulbowline were carried out by teams of men who had been specially vetted and selected on the basis of trustworthiness. Bayly was pretty sure that there were spies among the dockyard workers and he took steps to guard against information being leaked. For instance, in case a photograph of a new Q-ship was taken by someone sympathetic to the Germans when the Q-ship was ready to put to sea, Bayly devised the idea of altering the ship's appearance one more time once she had cleared the harbour. It was done at night, and might include the taking down of a mast, the alteration of derricks, the changing of the funnel markings, the upper-works being painted a different colour.

The gun crews on the Q-ships had to remain out of sight all the time the ships were at sea. They had to stay still and quiet for hours at a stretch, maybe even when the ship was under attack. The instinct to defend themselves had to be curbed – until such time as the captain gave the order to open fire. Specially installed trapdoors within the ships gave the gun crews access to their weapons without being seen from other vessels, especially U-boats.

The men on the Q-ships lived in overcrowded conditions, and stayed at sea for long periods. Monotony, tediousness and tension took a heavy toll, and some officers and men broke down after only a few months. Bayly won agreement from the Admiralty to give the Q-ship men extra pay which, though not very much, was at least a recognition of the hardships and the extra danger they put up with.

The Q-ship captains often resorted to flying the flags of neutral countries, painting their ships in the colour schemes of well-known shipping companies and changing the ship's name. Wooden funnels, spare ventilators, removable stanchions could be moved about the deck, thus altering the ship's silhouette.

The captains and crews were subject to Standing Orders. These were explicit, saying, for example, that if an enemy submarine was sighted on the surface and began shelling from a distance, every effort was to be made [by the 'panic crew'] to escape, after the engines had been stopped. The ship was to be 'abandoned' – the captain and gun crews of course remaining on board, but out of sight. 'Panic crews' went to great lengths to mimic realistically the fear and distress of a merchant ship's crew rushing to get away from a doomed ship. It was all aimed at fooling the U-boat captain into thinking that the ship had been *completely* abandoned. If all worked according to plan, the U-boat would then move in closer to finish off its quarry.

When he reckoned that the U-boat was close enough, the Q-ship's captain would give the order to fire. The Standing Orders laid down that gunfire from a Q-ship was to be opened on the sound of the ship's whistle or steam siren, and the White Ensign was to be raised. The Q-ship's gunners were not to fire until they were 'pretty sure of making a hit'.

The crews of the Q-ships displayed remarkable bravery in the duels with the U-boats, and the men who captained the Q-ships were a breed apart. Their job called for great coolness under pressure, and exceptional courage in the face of danger. It was the captain who had to wait, and wait, and wait, often lying on his stomach and sneaking looks out through a peephole, or through the gap between the bottom of a canvas dodger and the deck, to see if the U-boat was in range. Through voice pipes, he kept in touch with the gun crews, describing for them developments as they occurred, keeping them calm and informed. In some instances as the captain lay there, and the gun crews crouched in their hiding places, the ship was being shelled, or torpedoed, and was sinking under them. Admiral Bayly said that the strain of captaining a Q-ship was so great that very few officers could stand it for more than about nine months.

In August 1915 the behaviour of an ex-submariner, Lieutenant-Commander Godfrey Herbert, RN, descended into the realms of atrocity when he was in command of the Q-ship *Baralong*. The *Baralong* was one of the vessels that in April had heard the SOS of the doomed *Lusitania* as the liner sank off the Old Head of Kinsale. The Q-ship was nearly 60 miles from the position given by the *Lusitania*'s wireless officer in his SOS messages, and hadn't been able to reach the area in time to be of any help in rescuing survivors.

In Queenstown later that evening, Herbert and his crew saw bodies of children (one child lying in her mother's arms), women, and men, who had died when the liner went down. The sight had shocked and outraged them.

Herbert was described as being deliberate and cool, but he had also won himself a reputation as something of a maverick with a streak of ruthlessness. The *Baralong* was at sea on 19 August 1915 when, around noon, her wireless operator picked up a distress call. It was from a passenger liner, the *Arabic*. She had been attacked by a U-boat. The *Baralong* steamed flat out to the position given in the distress message. There was no sign of the *Arabic* when she arrived, no sign of lifeboats or survivors or bodies or wreckage. The *Baralong*'s crew were once again distressed by what they thought of as their failure to arrive on time to render aid. They didn't know that the *Arabic*'s SOS message had given the wrong co-ordinates.

Then, when they were about 100 miles south of Queenstown, the *Baralong*'s wireless operator picked up another SOS. This time it came from a freighter attempting to shake off a pursuing U-boat. A lookout on the Q-ship soon spotted a merchantman 8 or 9 miles ahead. As the *Baralong* approached the freighter, Herbert ordered the American flag to be run up the flag-staff, and pre-painted boards with the name *Ulysses S. Grant* lettered on them, to be hung over the ship's sides.

He saw U-27 on the surface, shelling the 6,400-ton British freighter *Nicosian*. The *Nicosian* was carrying over 200 mules and munitions from America for use by the British army. On board as passengers was a party of six American muleteers. The U-boat had stopped the ship and, in accordance with prize rules, had sent a boarding party to examine the *Nicosian*'s cargo. The ship's crew and passengers had been ordered to abandon ship, to get away in the lifeboats. All of this had occurred by the time the *Baralong* closed on the *Nicosian*.

With the *Baralong* masquerading as a harmless neutral merchant-man, Herbert made sure to steer his ship so that he kept the *Nicosian* between the *Baralong* and the U-boat. He hoisted the signal VIC-QRA, meaning 'Save life'. Because of the stars and stripes flying on the *Baralong*'s flag-staff, and the American false name on her side, the U-boat captain assumed that she was an American ship, a neutral coming to pick up survivors. He acknowledged the signal.

Herbert edged the *Baralong* closer until he was only 600 yards from the U-boat and in perfect position for accurate firing, whereupon the three concealed 12-pounder guns on the *Baralong* were suddenly revealed, the white ensign was raised, and the 12-pounders roared into action. The *Baralong* fired thirty-four shells at U-27, destroying her conning tower, puncturing her ballast tanks, and causing her to begin to sink extremely rapidly – she was gone within a minute.

Most of her crew went down with her, but her commander, *Kapitanleutnant* Bernhard Wegener, and eleven other men managed to jump into the sea as the submarine sank. Herbert, the *Baralong*'s captain, ordered his twelve Royal Marines marksmen to shoot them. The marksmen took aim and, firing downwards, started to pick off the German sailors thrashing about in the water. One U-boat man, believed to be the submarine's commanding officer, raised both hands in surrender. Two bullets fired at point blank range killed him.

For the marksmen on the *Baralong* it was like being at a fairground shooting gallery, except that this time the targets were human and alive. The marines kept firing at the German seamen below them. The Germans flapped and splashed desperately in the blood-streaked water, trying to get away from the bullets and reach the *Nicosian*. The marksmen killed six of the swimmers. Their training had instilled a cold indifference to killing, and they retained their memories of seeing the *Lusitania* dead on the quay at Queenstown.

Eight survivors of U-27's sinking managed to reach the *Nicosian*, and two of them began to climb the pilot ladder which was hanging down the ship's side. They were picked off by the marines and fell back into the sea. Six others managed to get on board the *Nicosian*. Seeing this, Herbert ordered a party of Royal Marines, led by Sergeant Fred Collins, to board the *Nicosian* and hunt down the German sailors, and shoot them. Two of the German were cut down on the deck of the *Nicosian*. Four kept on running. They found their way, slipping and sliding down the iron ladders into the bowels of the engine room. From there, there was no escape, and in the confined space among the pistons and pipes and the mass of machinery, the marines shot and killed them.

Sergeant Collins (who kept a diary) made a note that when Herbert ordered him to lead the boarding party onto the *Nicosian*, the officer had said, 'Don't forget, Collins, no prisoners aboard this ship. Get rid of them.' Collins said that when one German toppled over the side of the *Nicosian* into the sea, Herbert hurled a revolver at the man and said, 'What about the *Lusitania*, you bastard?'

The *Baralong*'s crew were said to have been excited and satisfied by the killing spree, calling to mind Henry Ward Beecher's Proverb from Plymouth Pulpit: 'It is not merely cruelty that leads men to love war, it is excitement.' Herbert made a report about the affair to the Admiralty. In it he claimed to have been afraid that the survivors from the U-boat would scuttle the *Nicosian* and that that was why he had ordered the marines to shoot the Germans in the water! The Admiralty ordered Herbert's report to be suppressed. But the six American muleteer passengers from the *Nicosian* had witnessed from the lifeboats what they considered to have been the murder of the German U-boat men, and when they went ashore at Liverpool they told the American consul how the Germans had been cold-bloodedly killed by riflemen shooting from a British ship flying the American flag. Three months later, when the muleteers arrived back in the United States, they spoke to American newspapers, and made sworn statements about what they had seen. An American stoker who happened to have been one of the *Baralong*'s complement also made a sworn statement.

It was from the American newspapers that the Germans learned what had happened to the U-boat men who had jumped overboard when their submarine sank. Germany made a formal complaint through the American ambassador, and demanded that Herbert be tried for murder. He never was. The British government dismissed the accusations, saying that the incident had probably happened because the men on the *Baralong* may have been upset by the knowledge that eight British steamers had been sunk that day in the Western Approaches. Herbert eventually requested a return to submarines. He was awarded a DSO, promoted to commander, and served in Queenstown as one of Admiral Bayly's operations officers.

There is no evidence whatsoever that Bayly condoned what Herbert had done when in command of the *Baralong*, but it is highly likely that he would have been shocked, disgusted that in this instance Herbert didn't observe acceptable standards of behaviour. The admiral was aware that in war there is always a percentage of combatants who exult in killing. War frequently brings out the barbarous in mankind, but savagery is savagery, and murder is murder, whatever the circumstances.

Following the publicity that the *Baralong* incident provoked, U-boat commanders became infinitely wary about suspiciously innocent-looking ships, and from then on were rarely taken in by them.

The most famous and distinguished man who commanded Q-ships was Captain Gordon Campbell, RN. A former destroyer captain based in Devonport, he was a competent, but by no means outstanding, thirty-year-old lieutenant when he was given command of the Q-ship *Loderer*, an ex-collier of 3,200 tons whose name was changed to *Farnborough* whilst on her way to Queenstown. She had been equipped with five 12-pounder guns, a couple of 6-pounders and a Maxim, and had had various hinged flaps fitted, as well as a dummy steering house and dummy cabins, all designed to conceal her considerable weaponry. But the Admiralty had been tipped off that information about the *Loderer* and her disguise had been leaked at Devonport – hence the change of name on 5 November during her journey to join Admiral Bayly's command.

Campbell, a short, thick-set, somewhat reticent man who spoke quietly, soon won a reputation for the depth of his concentration, as well as for persistence and patience. Each of the Q-ships he was to command would account for a U-boat, giving him a total of three. No other Q-ship captain equalled that record. And yet, for his first nine months as a Q-ship captain, he never even *saw* a U-boat. However, in March 1916 he sank U-68 with all hands, and was promoted to the rank of commander and awarded the Distinguished Service Order (DSO).

It was another eleven months before his next encounter with a U-boat. At about a quarter to ten on the morning of 17 February 1917, when the ship was off the south-west coast of Ireland, one of the lookouts on the *Farnborough* (Q5) spotted the track of a torpedo heading towards the ship. It looked as if it might miss the *Farnborough*, but Campbell manoeuvred the vessel to ensure that the torpedo *did* strike home. Men like him, and the crews who served with him, deliberately exposed themselves and their ships to destruction in order, it was hoped, to destroy U-boats. The torpedo launched from U-83 struck the *Farnborough* just aft of the engine room. The 'panic crew' rushed about, lowering two lifeboats and a small punt, tumbled into them, and rowed off, 'abandoning' their ship.

The ruse worked. The U-boat came to the surface 300 yards off the port bow of the *Farnborough* and moved in closer to finish off the stricken vessel. At ten minutes past ten Campbell gave the order to open fire. The concealing panels dropped away from the *Farnborough*'s guns, the white ensign was raised, and a hail of withering shellfire from point blank range destroyed the submarine, causing her to go down within minutes, carrying all but one officer and a crewman with her.

The *Farnborough*, however, had developed a dangerous list, seas were breaking over her after-deck, and she was taking water rapidly. She seemed destined to follow the U-boat to the bottom when Campbell sent a wireless message to Admiral Bayly at Admiralty House in Queenstown. It said: 'Q5 slowly sinking respectfully wishes you goodbye.'

Luckily for Campbell and the men on board her, the *Farnborough* didn't sink. Within an hour or so of his sending his wireless message, two patrol vessels arrived on the scene, attached towlines to the badly damaged ship, and began what turned out to be an eighteen hour tow towards the Irish coast where they beached her at Mill Cove near Bearhaven. When they eventually patched up the *Farnborough*, she was taken out of service as a Q-ship and sent back to the merchant navy.

Campbell's next Q-ship was the 2,800-ton collier *Pargust*. On the morning of 7 June 1917 she was struck amidships by a torpedo fired at close range from a submerged U-boat. Twenty minutes later, by which time the 'panic party' had rowed away from the *Pargust* in the ship's boats, the U-boat surfaced less than 100 yards away.

It was a 'can't miss' situation for the *Pargust*'s gun crews. They hammered U-29 with thirty-eight shells, destroying the conning tower, puncturing her fuel tanks, killing her captain. The Germans tried to make their escape. They didn't get far before the *Pargust*'s shells caused an explosion on the U-boat which blew up, slid under the surface stern first, and disappeared for ever. Because his ship was disabled, Campbell sent out a distress signal. A few hours later two sloops from Queenstown, the *Zinnia* and the *Crocus*, arrived, and the *Crocus* towed the *Pargust* into Queenstown where she was patched up and returned to England, to be paid off at Plymouth.

Campbell was promoted to captain, awarded a bar to his DSO and given his final Q-ship, which was also a disguised collier – the

Dunraven. A quarter of an hour before midday on 8 August when she was 130 miles west of Ushant, zig-zagging her way south across the Bay of Biscay, UC-71 began to shell her from over 2¾ miles distance on the starboard side.

At first the U-boat's shooting was inaccurate, but when she closed to around 1,000 yards, her gunners began to drop her four-inch shells right on target. A depth charge exploded on the stern of the *Dunraven,* setting the ship on fire, and creating a real danger of its magazine blowing up. The deck above the ammunition store became red hot and black smoke poured from the after end.

Campbell sent the 'panic party' away in the lifeboats. The gun crews stayed where they were, concealed from the enemy's sight. One of the gunners stripped off his shirt and tore it into pieces which he gave to his companions to protect their mouths from fumes. Then came an explosion which blew out the stern of the ship where depth charges, shells and other ammunition were stored. As well as starting a fire, the explosion hurled the 4-inch gun and its crew into the air, revealing to the U-boat that the *Dunraven* wasn't really a defenceless merchant ship at all, but a disguised and heavily armed trap-ship.

The U-boat crash-dived, and returned to launch a torpedo at the *Dunraven* from under the surface. After a while the U-boat came up again and for twenty minutes poured a hail of shells into the ship. When her ammunition ran out, and having no more torpedoes, the U-boat left the scene and started out on the long voyage home. Two British destroyers and the USS *Noma* arrived to rescue the men of the *Dunraven.* They tried to tow her to Plymouth. They almost made it, but she sank at three o'clock in the morning.

Following the *Dunraven* action, Campbell was awarded the Victoria Cross. The citation said it was in recognition of 'conspicuous gallantry, consummate coolness, and skill in command of one of HM ships in action'. Admiral Bayly told Campbell that he wanted him to give up serving in Q-ships, to be the admiral's flag officer, in command of his cruiser flagship.

The total number of U-boats accounted for between 1914 and 1918 by the entire Q-ship fleet of 193 vessels was just eleven. The cost in Q-ships: thirty-eight were lost. The Q-ships experiment turned out to be no more than a limited success.

14

THE GUNRUNNER

Within a year and a half of the outbreak of war, a 1,400-ton British three-island tramp steamer, the SS *Castro,* underwent two changes of name, and became part of Irish history. The SS *Castro* customarily traded around the Baltic and various North Sea ports. She was in German waters when Britain declared war on Germany, and was arrested by a German destroyer. She was subsequently taken over by the German navy, becoming part of their auxiliary fleet. They renamed her *Libau.*

Her next change of name occurred in 1916, and had its genesis two years earlier when Irish nationalist John Devoy introduced Sir Roger Casement to the German Ambassador to the United States, Count Bernstorff. Casement, himself an ardent nationalist, was a Dubliner, a retired member of the British Foreign Service who had been knighted in 1911 in recognition of his fearless exposure and investigations into Belgian atrocities committed against native workers in the Belgian Congo, and in Peru. His health impaired, he had retired in 1913, and the same year had joined the Irish Volunteers.

Following his meeting with Bernstorff, Casement went to Berlin in October 1914. Helped by Robert Monteith, another member of the Irish Volunteers, he set about trying to raise an Irish brigade from Irishmen in the British army who were prisoners of war in Germany. To Casement's deep disappointment, his efforts failed – only about fifty men came forward. Among them was Sergeant Daniel Bailey. Though failing in his recruitment attempts, Casement nevertheless enlisted help from the Germans for a planned rising in Ireland. He hoped that Count Bernstorff's request that field guns, machine guns, and up to 50,000 rifles be sent to Ireland would be honoured. After all, Irish nationalists and Germans shared a common enemy – England.

The Germans eventually agreed to send 20,000 rifles, less than a dozen machine guns, some explosives, and a million rounds of ammunition – but no backup forces. The *Libau* was chosen to carry the arms and ammunition, and the Germans changed the ship's name again, this time to *Aud*. They were taking a chance with this decision, because there was already a Norwegian three-island tramp steamer of the same name somewhere on the high seas.

The renamed *Libau*, with a crew of twenty-one officers and ratings under the command of a reserve lieutenant named Karl Spindler, loaded her cargo of arms and ammunition at Lubeck in the Baltic Sea. Then, on 9 April 1916, with her cargo camouflaged and concealed beneath timber pit props, baths, window frames, zinc buckets, doors and assorted tin ware, and flying a Norwegian flag, the false *Aud*, gunrunner, put to sea, destination Ireland. She had no wireless equipment.

She went up the North Sea, surprisingly wasn't stopped and boarded by any of the blockade patrol vessels, steamed between Norway and the Shetlands almost as far as the Arctic Circle, and then south between Iceland and the Faroes. She steamed down the west coast of Ireland, passing through patrol areas XVIII and XIX, and into area XX. Patrol vessels for area XX were stationed at Galway, where the senior naval officer was an Irishman, Commander Francis W. Hanan, RN, who had come out of retirement shortly after the start of the war. The *Aud*, because she wasn't equipped with wireless, was completely cut off from any communication with Germany. Spindler had no way of being kept abreast of developments.

Casement, disillusioned and disappointed with the (to his mind) small extent of German help for the nationalist Irish cause, felt that the rising planned for Easter Monday should be postponed. He intended to do his utmost when he reached Ireland to dissuade the leaders from going ahead. He, Monteith and Bailey left Wilhelmshaven on the 12 April on the submarine U-20. The plan was that the *Aud* would rendezvous with the U-boat off Inishtooskert Island north of the Great Blasket Island. It was intended that the *Aud's* cargo be landed in Fenit Harbour in the south-east corner of Tralee Bay, and that Casement would supervise its handover to the Irish nationalists.

Room 40 (Naval Intelligence) at the Admiralty in London had become aware that a cargo of arms from Germany was on the high seas, and suspected that Casement was on his way to Ireland. Admiral Bayly at Queenstown was informed that an attempt to land the munitions was likely to be made on the west or south-west coast of Ireland. He, in turn, routinely instructed his senior naval officers of the west coast patrol areas to keep a sharp lookout.

Room 40's code breakers were by this time gathering an immense amount of information from the intercepts. Many messages between the German ambassador in Washington and his government, about German assistance for the Irish nationalist movement, had been picked up. In one Bernstorff had suggested that 25,000 rifles be sent to Ireland to help with the rebellion.

The Admiralty informed Bayly that it was important that the rebellion, if it couldn't be aborted, must at least be curtailed or limited as far as possible. Any sea link between Germany and Ireland had to be destroyed. Accordingly four destroyers and a cruiser, HMS *Gloucester*, were detached from the Grand Fleet to reinforce Bayly's naval forces at Queenstown.

On Thursday 20 April the signal station at Loop Head at the northern side of the mouth of the Shannon estuary informed Admiralty House in Queenstown that a ship they had under observation was behaving in a suspicious manner. That ship was the *Aud*. Bayly sent an alerting wireless message to two of his sloops, the *Bluebell* and the *Zinnia*, which were in the area.

By noon on the same day the *Aud* was 45 miles from Fenit. Her captain, Spindler, ordered his crew to dump the camouflage cargo overboard so that the arms could be unloaded quickly when the ship tied up at Fenit pier. A quantity of pit props was retained on board to cover the real cargo in the event of an inspection by a patrol vessel. The jettisoning of the camouflage cargo, and the *Aud*'s movements – seemingly unsure of her navigation as she weaved her way towards the Magharees which lie off the north end of a sandy peninsula separating Brandon and Tralee Bays – were probably what drew Loop Head signal station's attention to the ship 'behaving in a suspicious manner'.

An inspection by a patrol vessel materialised when the *Aud* was at anchor. The armed trawler *Setter II,* captained by Skipper John Donaldson, RNR, a former fisherman, went alongside the gunrunner just after dawn to check her out. The boarding party found nothing suspicious. The camouflage cargo fulfilled its intended purpose and the ship's papers seemed in order. Spindler successfully hoodwinked the unfortunate Donaldson, who was later court-martialled, accused of dereliction of duty.

When Spindler reached the agreed rendezvous point, he could see no sign of any U-boat, no sign of any periscope breaking the surface. He'd been ordered to wait for half an hour, so he hove to and waited. Still no sign of a submarine. He took the *Aud* in to within a few hundred yards of Fenit pier. There was no one there. He next spent two hours cruising around the bay. Night came down. Still no sign of any U-boat. Finally he headed back out to sea, leaving the Magharee Islands behind him and steering a course to the south-west, with Brandon Point and Brandon Head well to port.

Another armed trawler, the *Lord Heneage,* saw the fleeing tramp steamer and gave chase, but couldn't catch up with her. However the signal station at Sybil Point, west of Ballyferriter, saw that the *Aud* was ignoring the *Lord Heneage*'s signal flags ordering it to stop. They immediately informed Admiral Bayly at Queenstown. Bayly ordered the sloops HMS *Bluebell* and HMS *Zinnia* to move in on the *Aud* and escort her to Queenstown. If she resisted, they were to fire at her and, if necessary, sink her.

When *Bluebell* caught up with the *Aud*, and communicated with Spindler, the German objected to his ship being taken to Queenstown. The *Bluebell* promptly fired a shot across the *Aud*'s bows, and the objections ceased equally promptly. The *Bluebell*, the *Zinnia*, and the two trawlers escorted the *Aud* towards Queenstown. But as they approached the Daunt Rock lightship near the entrance to the harbour on the calm sunny morning of Saturday 22 April, the *Aud* slowed to a stop, her engines were shut down, her lifeboats were swung out ready for launching, the Norwegian flag was hauled down, and two German naval ensigns were run up instead. She was then about a mile south of the lightship. Spindler and his crew piled into the lifeboats and pulled away from the ship's side.

Suddenly an explosion ripped through the *Aud*, flames and debris shooting into the air. A series of other explosions followed in quick succession, and the ship began to sink, stern first. She was gone inside five minutes, together with her cargo of arms and ammunition, putting an end to the hoped-for wholesale arming of the rebel forces.

The *Bluebell* picked up Spindler and his crew and took them into the harbour. Admiral Bayly sent out his green barge to transfer the *Aud*'s officers to the flagship *Adventure* which eventually took them, and the rest of the crew, to Milford Haven. They spent the rest of the war as POWs.

Spindler admitted later that he thought the *Aud* was already in the navigation channel when he ordered her to be scuttled. He had hoped to block the channel and at least cause some disruption. What Spindler hadn't known was that the U-20, on which Casement was to be taken to Ireland, had developed a serious mechanical fault after only a day and a half at sea, and had had to turn back. Casement, Robert Monteith and Sergeant Daniel Bailey were transferred to U-19 instead. One of the engineers on U-19, Karl Wiedemann, remembered Casement as a pleasant man who soon became their friend and talked to everyone on the boat.

It took them five days to get to Ireland, which they reached on the evening of 20 April 1916. But a pilot boat that was supposed to meet them didn't turn up, nor did they receive the green light signal they'd been told to expect. Off the Kerry coast U-19's captain, Weisbach, tired of waiting and edgy at the danger involved, finally said that he wasn't going to hang around any longer: it was too risky. He told Casement and the other two to get ready for landing. 'Sir Roger,' Wiedemann said, 'walked through the boat and shook hands with every member of the crew.' Casement had shaved off his distinctive beard so that he would not be too easily recognised, and the U-boat captain ran the submarine in close to the shore. The three Irishmen climbed into the small collapsible boat that was lowered into the water for them, and the U-boat captain left them to their fate as he headed off out to sea, unobserved in the dark.

Casement and his two companions landed on Banna Strand in Tralee Bay on Good Friday 21 April 1916. Casement was arrested, Bailey was picked up in Tralee, and Monteith escaped and made his way to Dublin. Casement was sent to London where he was charged with high treason. On 29 June he was sentenced to death. His knighthood was taken from him, and they hanged him at Pentonville Jail at eight o'clock in the morning of 3 August 1916.

Admiral Bayly subsequently sent divers down to the wreck of the *Aud* to gather samples of her cargo. They brought up Russian Mausers, ammunition, and the two German naval ensigns. One of the latter he gave to the captain of the *Bluebell*. Bayly retained the second one, had it framed, and hung it on the wall of his home when he retired.

Years later, in 1936, he returned it to the German navy via *Konteradmiral* (Rear-Admiral) Wassner, the German naval attaché at the embassy in London. Wassner took the ensign to Berlin on the same night. *Großadmiral* (Grand-Admiral) Raeder, Germany's naval chief, sent Bayly a gracious note of thanks.

15

INSURRECTION

The Easter Rising in April 1916 was no surprise to Admiral Bayly. The Admiralty, furnished with intelligence assembled by Room 40 from wireless intercepts, had kept him informed that a rebellion was being planned.

In Ireland, those who wanted emancipation resented British rule, and even though over 250,000 Irishmen had joined the imperial forces, there remained a sizeable hard core of extreme nationalists convinced that the time had arrived to take advantage of Britain's preoccupation with the war in continental Europe. The nationalists believed that force would be the cure for injustice, so they decided to 'strike for liberty'.

Bayly had to deal with the Easter Rebellion from a Royal Navy point of view, as well as continue with the antisubmarine campaign to counter the U-boat depredations in the Western Approaches. He needed reinforcements, both of ships and men. He requested both. Bayly's need of additional manpower was centred on the necessity of providing protection for the dockyard at Haulbowline, and other naval installations. In response, he was sent 2,000 marines, the 14,000-ton battleship HMS *Albemarle*, and the cruiser HMS *Gloucester*. Some of the Royal Marines who arrived at Queenstown were battle-hardened, having fought at the Dardanelles.

The marines arrived in the harbour late at night, set up their bivouacs on Haulbowline, and by the following morning were already in position, their guns threateningly facing Queenstown – in case any insurgents thought of crossing the half-mile of water with a view to destroying the dock gates or burning down the stores. Nobody tried – then, or ever. Nor was there ever any attempt during the war to target Admiral Bayly or Admiralty House.

Some of the marines were assigned guard duty at Admiralty House, replacing soldiers. One foggy night a sentry heard what sounded like footsteps nearby. He challenged the maker of the noise several times to advance and be recognised. Getting no response, he finally fired a shot in the direction the sounds came from. The body of the intruder was found at first light. It was a shaggy old donkey that had strayed onto the property. Bayly paid the animal's owner, an elderly woman, a small amount of money to compensate her for her loss, and rewarded the sentry for his alertness and accurate marksmanship.

The admiral ordered the battleship HMS *Albemarle* to anchor between Ringaskiddy and Passage West, and then put it about that if there were any trouble from insurgents in Cork, the battleship would pound the city with its 12-inch guns and destroy it. Word of the deliberately planted rumour spread like wildfire. A gunnery expert, he admitted later that for the *Albemarle*'s guns to have destroyed Cork, firing from Ringaskiddy Bay, would have been virtually impossible, seeing that Cork was so far away from the ship, and anyway wasn't visible.

He sent motor launches to Waterford to protect the railway bridge, and the cruiser HMS *Gloucester* as well as the sloops HMS *Snowdrop* and HMS *Laburnum* were despatched to Galway. Because the phone lines had been cut, the senior Royal Navy officer at Galway, Commander Francis Hanan, didn't hear during the day on Easter Monday that the Rising had already begun in Dublin. The Admiralty had been unable to contact him. One phone line that hadn't been cut was the one between Galway and Clifden, where Marconi had set up a transatlantic wireless station. Someone at the Admiralty suggested cabling America with the request that news of the Rising be cabled back to Clifden, with Clifden in turn asked to telephone the news to

Hanan in Galway! Foul-ups and delays resulted in Hanan not learning about the Easter Rising until late on Easter Monday night.

HMS *Gloucester* entered Galway Bay and anchored, and local nationalist leaders who had been arrested were put on board ship and subsequently taken to England. On Thursday, 100 marines from Queenstown arrived in Galway by sea (Hanan had asked for 200), and others followed on Sunday. But by 1 May, the insurrection was over, the rebels having surrendered. Those who were to be interned in England were sent across the Irish Sea in two sloops.

Bayly had sent his light cruiser HMS *Adventure* to Kingstown/Dún Laoghaire to ensure that wireless communication between Dublin and the outside world was maintained. The telephone wires between Dublin and Kingstown/Dún Laoghaire had not been cut.

The Rising was confined mainly to Dublin, and little happened in the rest of the country because of the lack of arms and efficient communication. When it was over, the British prime minister, Asquith, desirous of visiting Ireland, included a trip to Queenstown in his itinerary. He wanted to stay overnight at Admiralty House. Foreseeing that crowds would gather at the railway station to catch a glimpse of Britain's prime minister, Admiral Bayly thwarted them by sending his green barge upriver to Cork to collect Asquith. The prime minister was brought down the Lee, past Blackrock, through Lough Mahon, and down past Passage West, Monkstown and Ringaskiddy, to Queenstown where the admiral met him as he stepped ashore.

Asquith visited the operations room at Admiralty House, saw the ships at anchor in the harbour, was shown around the gardens, and dined with Admiral Bayly and his niece that night. The following he day he returned to England, sailing to Milford Haven from Queenstown on the admiral's flagship, HMS *Adventure*.

While Ireland's 1916 Rising occupied the attention of people in Ireland and Britain and elsewhere, the much bigger war at sea went on unabated. And it wasn't just people who became victims. Horses continued to be shipped across the Atlantic from Canada, the first of the thousands having left Canadian ports in 1914. They travelled on horse transports, and these vessels, like any other enemy ships encountered on the oceans and seas of the world, were targeted by Germany's U-boats.

A German writing under the name of Adolf K. G. E. von Spiegel and claiming to have commanded a U-boat, described one of his attacks on just such a vessel in April 1916. He said he saw the captain of the ship walking on the ship's bridge, and the crew cleaning the deck. 'And I saw with surprise, and a slight shudder, long rows of wooden partitions right along all decks, from which gleamed the shining black and brown backs of horses.' His reaction: 'What a pity, those lovely beasts.'

But he didn't allow his admiration of the horses deter him from what he was about to do. 'I went on thinking, "war is war, and every horse fewer on the Western Front is a reduction of England's fighting power",' he said. So he gave the order: 'Fire!' and the torpedo sped through the water towards the horse transport. Von Spiegel saw that the torpedo was spotted from the ship's bridge 'as frightened arms pointed towards the water, and the captain put his hands in front of his eyes and waited resignedly'.

After the explosion and the sudden eruption of water and spray, von Spiegel watched what was happening on board the ship he had just torpedoed. 'From all the hatchways a storming, despairing mass of men were fighting their way on deck – grimy stokers, officers, soldiers, grooms, cooks – they all rushed, ran, screamed for boats, tore and thrust one another from the ladders leading down to them, fought for the lifebelts, and jostled one another on the sloping deck … All amongst them, rearing, slipping horses were wedged.'

Because of the ship's list, the starboard lifeboats couldn't be lowered, as a result of which everyone who could rushed to the port side lifeboats. These were already in the water. Von Spiegel said they had been lowered 'with great stupidity, either half full or overcrowded'. He saw the men who had been left behind on the ship wringing their hands in despair, and running backwards and forwards before finally throwing themselves into the water hoping to swim to the boats.

Then came a second explosion – probably the boilers bursting – and white steam hissed from the hatchways and scuttles. 'The white steam drove the horses mad,' von Spiegel said. 'I saw a beautiful dapple-grey horse take a mighty leap over the berthing rails and land into a fully laden boat … At that point I could not bear the sight any longer, and I lowered the periscope and dived deep.'

By the time the war ended, the British army, according to the official history of the war veterinary service, lost 484,143 horses and mules. The figure included those lost at sea.

On 8 May 1916, Walther Schweiger, the U-boat captain responsible for the sinking of the *Lusitania,* sank another unarmed passenger liner without warning – despite the fact that *Generaladmiral* (Admiral) Scheer, the German Commander-in-Chief of the High Seas Fleet had, on 25 April, recalled by wireless all U-boats to base.

Schweiger claimed never to have received Scheer's signal, and that was why he attacked the 13,300-ton White Star liner *Cymric.* She was steaming westwards on her way to the United States when a torpedo fired from U-20 struck her. She sank the following day, 140 miles west-north-west of the Fastnet. This was a long way further out than the usual limits of the patrol area. Five people lost their lives. The *Cymric* became the thirty-seventh and last passenger liner sunk since the *Lusitania.* Because of Admiral Scheer's temporary suspension of the U-boat campaign, she also became the last ship, until the beginning of August, to be sunk in the Western Approaches or anywhere around the coasts of Ireland and the British Isles. By that time Schweiger, because of his record, had been dubbed 'The Baby Killer' and named on the list of individuals the British Admiralty would want tried as a war criminal. He did not live long enough for anyone to bring a case against him. On 17 September 1917, heading for the French coast, he and his entire crew of the U-88 perished when their boat was destroyed by a mine.

On 31 May 1916, 274 warships and 70,000 sailors clashed in the only major sea battle of the war – the Battle of Jutland, or, as the Germans called it, the Battle of Skagerrak – when Britain's Grand Fleet, under Jellicoe, and Germany's High Seas Fleet, commanded by Admiral Scheer, confronted each other.

The code-breakers of Room 40 at the Admiralty in London had tipped off Jellicoe on 30 May that Scheer and his High Seas Fleet were putting to sea. The British admiral took the Grand Fleet, with its thirty-seven modern battleships, on a sweep down the Danish coast. What he didn't know was that Scheer had decided on a sweep in the opposite direction, up the coast of Denmark. The fleets were thus converging on an unintended collision course. Neither had any definite knowledge of the other.

This was long before radar was developed to detect the presence of ships and the direction in which they were travelling. Sharp-eyed lookouts with binoculars, plus a lot of educated, and some wildly inaccurate, guesswork were the only ways – short of aerial reconnaissance – that warships could find the whereabouts of enemy ships. Aerial reconnaissance was only in its infancy, and anyway the weather conditions of mist and failing light militated against it. So the two great fleets in effect stumbled into each other.

By the end of the battle, the Grand Fleet had lost three battle cruisers, three armoured cruisers and eight destroyers; the German losses were one battleship, one battle cruiser, four light cruisers and five destroyers. Human casualties were: British, 6,097; German, 2,545.

Both sides afterwards claimed victory – the Germans pointing to the number of ships they sank, the British pointing to the fact that the Grand Fleet was ready to put to sea again by 2 June and remained in strategic control of the North Sea. Germany's High Seas Fleet never put to sea again in a major wartime expedition, until its surrender two and a half years later.

Bayly at Queenstown learned about the sea battle off the coast of Denmark. Part of him no doubt longed to be afloat and in the middle of it all with the Grand Fleet, but he had his own fiercely demanding and important part of the sea war to look after from his headquarters on the hill above St Colman's cathedral. And the inescapable truth was that the 'fleet' he had to do it with was farcical when compared with the number and size of the ships under Jellicoe's command.

In the last quarter of the year, the storms of October and the U-boats came back again to the Western Approaches. When the sloop HMS *Genista* was torpedoed whilst on escort duty, Admiral Bayly went out at night in his flagship, the light cruiser HMS *Adventure*, on a rescue mission. Two other sloops had already searched unsuccessfully for survivors. The weather when Bayly steamed out of the harbour was nasty – violent wind gusts, the temperature dropping and the sea rough. It was the worst kind of weather to be wet and cold, shivering and adrift in open boats or exposed on life rafts.

The following morning the cruiser sighted the floating body of a sailor wearing a lifejacket. In the afternoon they came across three Carley Floats (life rafts) with a total of twelve men from the torpedoed sloop on board. When the *Adventure* picked them up, the famished survivors whose bodies had had the heat leached out of them by the cold wind, were given food, rum, warm blankets and a place to rest. Of the sloop's complement, they were the only ones to survive. All of the others, including the officers, perished.

On the slashing passage back to Queenstown, the cruiser had to battle against a gale that increased in strength. She went plunging into the terrible and incessant head winds of the desolate ocean, her bow slamming into the waves, thousands of tons of water dropping onto her decks. The storm continued to rage for the next five days during which an armed trawler disappeared with all hands and two

Royal Navy destroyers on escort duty, after pitching endlessly into deep troughs with stomach-roiling dives, had eventually to run into Bearhaven for shelter.

Bayly said later about the rescue of the twelve men from the *Genista*: 'There is no doubt that some or all of the men on the rafts had been praying hard to be rescued, and that I was sent out to do it.' Though a shore-based Commander-in-Chief, the sea was in his blood, and he loved being at sea. Not that he abused his position by self-indulgence – he was far too disciplined and far too conscientious for that – but he wasn't averse to going out periodically in HMS *Adventure* to visit the patrol areas which the ships under his command steamed every single day and every single night in their duties of escorting convoys or ships sailing independently, rescuing survivors, towing damaged freighters and pursuing U-boats.

On 28 December news came in that the 6,000-ton British tanker *El Zorro* had become the target of a stalking U-boat – Rudolf Schneider's U-24, which had sunk the battleship HMS *Formidable* off Portland in January. The tanker was 10 miles south of the Old Head of Kinsale, had been shelled and torpedoed, and radioed for help. A couple of the old torpedo boats, two tugs and the yacht *Greta* were sent out from Queenstown in response to the distress call, but the foul weather and heavy seas were too much for them. Admiral Bayly, in his bigger, heavier and faster flagship, went out and began a systematic, but fruitless, search for the tanker.

The search was interrupted by another distress call from a different ship in trouble, the liner *Huronian*. She had been torpedoed south-east of the Fastnet. HMS *Adventure* tore off at 22 knots, hunted down and drove off the U-boat while the armed trawler *Bempton* and the sloops *Begonia* and *Camellia* escorted the *Huronian* into Bearhaven. Bayly ordered his flagship to remain at sea, covering for the sloops while they were away from their patrol areas.

The *El Zorro*, fatally damaged, limped towards Queenstown, but the weather conditions beat her and she was driven ashore at Man of

War Cove. The combined force of wind and waves broke her back. The trawler *Freesia* rescued the ship's crew, but the *El Zorro*'s cargo of 8,000 tons of oil poured out of the smashed hull and into the sea, blackening and making slimy the rocks all round.

The Catholic Bishop of Cloyne, Most Reverend Robert Browne, sought help from Bayly one day in 1916. When St Colman's cathedral was nearing completion, the bishop, cultured and imaginative, had the idea of incorporating into it a continental-style set of fixed bells made of bronze, a carillon, the heaviest of all musical instruments. It would be played by a bellmaster, or carillonneur, the bells sounded by hammers or clappers controlled by a keyboard called a baton console and a pedal board, the carillonneur using his fists and his feet. Carillon playing had originated in the Low Countries in the fourteenth century. There were no carillons or carillonneurs in Ireland, so for St Colman's and Queenstown it would be a double first.

Bishop Browne commissioned from bell-founders John Taylor & Son of Loughborough, a set of forty-two bells pitched in chromatic series, each bell tuned to harmonise with the others. The Taylor family had been in the bell-founding business since 1784, and were one of the world's most reputable specialist companies with the largest bell-foundry then in existence.

The first seventeen bells, when completed by Taylors in 1914, had been sent by road from Loughborough to Liverpool, and thence by sea to Queenstown where they were installed in the cathedral. It was 1916 by the time Taylors completed the remaining twenty-five trebles, and these, too, were sent to Liverpool for shipment to Ireland. But by 1916 the Irish Sea was a hunting ground for the marauding U-boats. They tried to attack any and every ship that came within range.

A worried Bishop Browne went to see his new naval friend, Admiral Bayly, and asked if Bayly could help in ensuring the safe transit of the bells from Liverpool to Queenstown. Bayly reportedly said to Bishop Browne, 'Yes ... send them over in the next steamer, and we will obey the Scriptural injunction to watch and pray. I will watch. And you pray.' The bells arrived safely, and were installed, although it took Bishop Browne another eight years before he was able to recruit from Antwerp a brilliant young Belgian named Staf Gebruers to come to Ireland and take up the position of permanent resident carillonneur in the seaside town.

The St Colman's cathedral carillon is the only one in the Republic of Ireland. The only other one in Ireland is in Armagh. St Colman's has the biggest number of bells, forty-nine, of all the fifteen traditional carillons in Britain and Ireland.

In November 1916, U-boats accounted for forty-two ships. By the end of the year Admiral Bayly's Queenstown fleet was made up of fifteen Q-ships, twelve sloops, twenty-three armed steam trawlers, nine drifters, four armed steam yachts, twelve motor launches (MLs), and the four old torpedo boats.

16

THE PRESIDENT'S NAVAL AIDE

William Sowden Sims was born in 1858 on a farm on the shores of Lake Ontario between Toronto and Kingston in Canada. His father, an American, was chief engineer of the East Broad Top Railroad. His mother was Canadian. In later years some people questioned William's right to American citizenship. His biographer, Elting E. Morison, said that Sims himself gave the best answer to that. 'Had I been born in a stable,' William said, 'would I have been a horse?'

At the age of seventeen William sat the entrance examination for the US Naval Academy. He was unsuccessful, failing in geography, spelling and grammar – ironic in view of the fact that he later became one of the US Navy's most prolific producers of reports. But his entrance exam results were so dire that the superintendent of the academy wanted to rule him out permanently. However, six months after he failed at his first attempt at the academy entrance examination, he was allowed to have another shot at it. This time, having put in long hours of study, he managed to pass, albeit barely. In June 1876 he became a cadet midshipman.

Tall, straight-backed, well-built, and meticulous about personal cleanliness, Sims was a strikingly handsome young man. His good looks and impressive appearance remained intact for the whole of his life. He found the rigid discipline of the academy hard to bear. He nevertheless stuck it out for the mandatory four years, and was then assigned to a two-year cruise on the wooden full-rigged ship USS *Tennessee*, the flagship of the US Navy's North Atlantic squadron.

Almost as soon as he joined the ship he began to notice things he felt needed to be changed. He decided to try to get improvements made to the conditions in the steerage accommodation in which he and twenty-four other junior officers had to live. He didn't think, for example, that there was enough space. Much of the furniture was ramshackle and broken, and the ventilation in the sleeping area was totally inadequate. He took his list of complaints to Lieutenant Lyman Arms, the officer in charge of the mess, and spelled out the accommodation's deficiencies, backing up his contentions with drawings and statistics.

Arms was convinced by what Sims brought to his attention, and drafted a letter to the Bureau of Navigation in Washington. He showed the draft to the commander of the *Tennessee*, Captain Harmony, got his approval, and sent the letter. It achieved three satisfying results – the accommodation space was enlarged, a more appropriately sized locker-room was provided for the junior officers' gear, and the ventilation was significantly improved.

One thing the Navy Department refused to do, however, was replace the furniture and fittings. Sims got around that by buying items he knew his colleagues would need, and selling the goods to them at a substantial mark-up. The profits would, he explained, go towards buying the required new furniture. His brother junior officers entered into the spirit of the scheme, the 'business' prospered, and some fine new furniture was eventually purchased. Mission accomplished.

On completion of his two-year cruise, Sims sat his final examinations at Annapolis. Then began a six-year stint at sea, serving on various sailing ships of the US Navy. It was during this time that he began writing reports and submitting them to the Bureau of Navigation. He also started to write newspaper articles about places to which his naval travels took him. His output was prolific.

At the age of thirty he took up the study of French. After a year of struggling with it, and not advancing as quickly as he would have liked, he concluded that the best way of learning the language was to live among the French. The Navy Department granted him a year's leave to go to Paris, and in the capital he applied himself so assiduously to his studies that he became fluent in French.

During the next few years he did stints as a teacher of navigation to boys entering the merchant navy, and as intelligence officer of the ship USS *Charleston*. The latter appointment required him to send reports to the Office of Naval Intelligence in Washington, reports about foreign vessels encountered, harbours visited, and harbour fortifications seen.

The Office of Naval Intelligence came into existence because towards the end of the nineteenth century the US Navy realised that in the navies of other countries there had been a huge surge of technological improvements. It became obvious that the US Navy needed to seek out and report on those advancements.

As the ONI says in its own summary of its history, 'Naval attachés and military affairs officers began a systematic collection of technical information about foreign governments and their naval developments. This formed a library of data for the department of the navy from which vast amounts of information began to flow. Reports of foreign technology advances began to circulate between the various bureaux of the navy ... What began as a small office of borrowed officers from other naval staffs came into its own as the tiny office grew to assume the larger role of war planning for the navy.'

To be able to compile his reports, Sims had to gather information, a task he carried out with a diligence and industry that eventually exhausted him, but which enabled him to compile long, detailed dispatches. Elting E. Morison in *Admiral Sims and the Modern American Navy* wrote: 'The unnecessary length of most of his reports derived largely from the exigencies of a luxuriant prose style developed, perhaps, from an uncritical reading of Herbert Spencer's unpruned sentences.' Spencer was the English revolutionary philosopher who coined the phrase 'survival of the fittest'.

In 1896 Sims was appointed naval attaché at the US embassy in Paris, and US legation at Madrid and St Petersburg. As well as going to Russia, he embarked on a series of wide-ranging visits around Europe to countries that had major naval bases. Reports and letters poured from him, and by the time his three year tour of duty ended he had sent back to America more than 11,000 pages! But Sims wanted to return to sea. He was forty-two years old, and still a lieutenant, so he was delighted when he was posted to the 11,500-ton battleship USS *Kentucky*.

Although familiar with the battleships of other nations, he had never seen an American battleship before. He was unimpressed when he first saw this one. Over time there were elements of the *Kentucky* that alarmed him so much he felt contempt for virtually everything about her. His criticisms almost inevitably became the subjects of lengthy reports that he sent to the Navy Department. He wanted his criticisms either refuted, or accepted.

As early as 1902 he said in a letter to his friend and classmate at Annapolis, Albert Niblack, that he had made up his mind he would give his papers 'such a form that they would be dangerous documents to leave neglected on the files ... I was called a deliberate falsifier of facts and denounced in ordnance, but in respectful and pitying terms of derision ... ' The 'citadel to be attacked' he said, was 'insufferable conceit'.

According to Elting Morison who quoted that letter: 'Informally [Sims] gave release to feelings, never very gracefully restrained, in the observation that the *Kentucky* is not a battleship at all. She is the worst crime in naval construction ever perpetrated by the white race.'

From the *Kentucky* Sims was transferred to the monitor USS *Monterey* at Canton. Monitors were odd-looking shallow-draft ships with exceedingly low freeboards. They were usually equipped with one or two large guns and were mainly used for coastal bombardment. Sims wrote of the *Monterey*, 'She is about the shape of a sweet potato that has burst in the boiling. She draws fourteen feet of mud forward, and sixteen feet and six inches of slime aft, and has three feet of discoloured water over the main deck in fair weather ... The air they built into the ship is there yet, and at the present writing has a gentle odour of mild decay.'

During a short period he spent in Hong Kong before joining the *Monterey*, Sims was introduced to and formed a close professional relationship with Captain Percy Scott, the Royal Navy's greatest and most advanced expert in gunnery. Sims studied Scott's various inventions, carefully examining the way the British officer trained his gun crews and gun layers. Scott's techniques achieved the stunning result: eighty per cent of all shots fired hit the target. Sims urged the US navy to adopt Scott's techniques, and he prepared supporting reports, which he sent to the Navy Department. His recommendations were rejected. Frustrated, he decided to go over the head of the Commander-in-Chief of the China station. He wrote a personal letter to the new president of the United States, Theodore ('Teddy') Roosevelt. For an officer as junior as Sims, a lieutenant, to do such a thing was a risky act of insubordination, and could have resulted in his court martial and dismissal from the service. That it didn't was mainly thanks to Admiral Remey who, although aware of the letter, held back from instituting proceedings against Lieutenant Sims.

Sims' letter drew the president's attention to the reports, many of them couched in strong unofficial language, that he had submitted to the Navy Department. Roosevelt, a former assistant secretary of the navy, was not unaware of the detailed, closely argued paperwork that had in the past flowed from the verbose lieutenant. In his letter to Roosevelt, Sims spoke of 'the extreme danger of the present very inefficient condition of the navy, considered as a fighting force'.

The president replied directly to him, saying that he considered Sims to be unduly pessimistic, but he acknowledged that many of Sims' earlier suggestions had been 'genuinely fruitful'. He thanked the lieutenant for writing to him, and said he would always be pleased to hear from him 'in criticism, or suggestion'. Roosevelt gave instructions that Sims' reports from the China Station were to be condensed, printed, and distributed to every officer in the navy. Between 1900 and 1902 Sims sent thirteen reports to the Navy Department. Some of them were subsequently lost, or mislaid, perhaps deliberately.

For the campaigning Sims, who was devoted to bringing about reforms of the service to which he had committed his life, a door had opened. He had direct access to the most powerful man in America, the president of the United States. Appointment as Inspector of Target Practice in the Navy Department followed in October of 1902. He was promoted to lieutenant-commander. The post was one he held until 1909, and during that period he also acted as naval aide to President Roosevelt.

Because of the methods introduced by Sims, gunnery throughout the US navy improved dramatically. Newspapers summed up his contribution by saying that he taught the navy how to shoot.

Sims' output of reports was prodigious. For example, between 1903 and 1907 he turned out one hundred and thirty-two of them. He couldn't escape ruffling feathers – reformers invariably inspire animosity and ill-feeling. Pockets of resentment seethed among those conservative senior officers who opposed him. They played down his achievements and his influence, tried to deny their existence. Not that Sims was any kind of shrinking violet, or any form of vulnerable whipping cur. Indeed one of his colleagues, urging him to tone down the abrasiveness of his criticisms, to soften his language, went so far as to say that Sims could hardly be more disliked than he already was in certain quarters.

Sims was nevertheless stunned at the lengths to which some of his detractors were prepared to go. Attempts to banish, or at least dramatically to diminish the credit that was his due for the improvements he brought about as Inspector of Target Practice, finally caused him to lay his complaint before the president. He provided adequate proof for President Roosevelt to mull over.

The tawdry anti-Sims campaign disgusted Roosevelt. In a letter to the Secretary of the Navy, the president said, 'Commander Sims has done more than any other man in the United States to improve gunnery, and it is chiefly due to him that we shoot as well as we do.'

Early in 1909, just before Roosevelt went out of office, the president wanted to reward Sims for his loyal and valuable service as naval aide, and for his outstanding success as Inspector of Target Practice. He asked Sims if he would like to take command of a battleship. Sims, delighted, said yes, and named the USS *Minnesota* as the ship he would like to command. The battleship was on her way home from a world cruise at the time. Her commanding officer was Captain John Hubbard. Roosevelt arranged the appointment of Sims, whose rank at the time was commander. By tradition commanders were never given battleships. Only officers holding the rank of captain were given them.

The president's action triggered much rancour in the service. Traditionalists were outraged. Adding fuel to the fire of resentment was the humiliating way Hubbard was relieved of his command at Norfolk in 1909 – before his ship had even completed her cruise. Sims assumed command of the *Minnesota*, and an angry, humiliated Captain Hubbard was appointed naval aide to the Assistant Secretary of the Navy.

Sims' lack of experience in commanding any kind of vessel gave rise to concern both inside and outside the navy. He himself seemed to be not at all worried. He had seventeen years of sea service under his belt and, as he pointed out, he had been both navigator and teacher of navigation. The *Minnesota* was an 18-knot, 16,000 ton ship with a complement of 1,200 men.

Sims, despite the presence of a rear-admiral on board, acquitted himself extremely well in seamanship. He also excelled at the handling of those under his command. Central to this was that he was interested in the officers and men as individuals. He never hesitated to praise, or reward with a promotion, those he felt were deserving. He made a point of trusting his officers and crew, went out of his way to meet the families of the men who served under him, and occasionally dropped into the steerage accommodation, thus encouraging an air of conviviality and relaxation among the junior officers. With his fund of amusing anecdotes and his love of telling a humorous story, he added significantly to the general air of camaraderie on board ship. But he was also keenly aware of the need for discipline, even if he sometimes lessened the severity of the old-fashioned punishments. Through it all he retained an immense natural dignity. Morale was high. The *Minnesota* under Sims was a happy and well-run ship.

As 1910 drew to a close, the fleet was sent to Europe on goodwill visits to England and France. Late in November the four ships of Sims' division steamed into the Thames and anchored at Gravesend on the south bank of the river opposite Tilbury. On 3 December Sims and 800 men attended a special lunch at the Guildhall. Sir Thomas V. Strong, London's lord mayor, hosted it. The band of the Coldstream Guards led the Americans as they marched through the streets from Charing Cross. It was intended that the lunch be a no-speeches affair. Two toasts would be drunk ('The King' and 'The President') and that was all. But things turned out differently.

The lord mayor made a speech and, in replying to it, Sims delivered one which he had been thinking about during the transatlantic voyage. The last words of his talk caused a furore in his own country. The words that triggered the uproar were: 'If the time ever comes when the British Empire is seriously menaced by an external enemy, it is my opinion that you may count upon every man, every dollar, every drop of blood of your kindred across the sea.'

As a serving officer, he should never have voiced this opinion in public. It behoved him not to embarrass his government. Sims' only defence when a torrent of criticism was unleashed at him in America was that he was expressing purely personal opinions. There were calls for disciplinary action to be taken against him, requests that he be relieved of his command, even talk that he should resign.

Because of the ensuing outcry in the United States, Secretary of the Navy George von L. Meyer eventually ordered Sims to tell him exactly what he had said at the Guildhall. Sims informed Meyer that there was no copy of the speech available – it had been extemporaneous. The commander did, however, transmit to the secretary the above quoted words as being, as far as he could remember, how he'd ended his speech.

Uneasy but unafraid, Sims wondered what impact his indiscretion might have on his career. It wasn't until the following January that President Taft decided how to deal with the matter – he delivered Commander Sims a public reprimand, General Order 100.

His cruise on the *Minnesota* over, Sims, promoted to the rank of captain, was sent to the Naval War College at Newport, Rhode Island, to take the first of the new two-year-long courses. Three other officers took the course with him.

He was now fifty-three years old, elegant, loquacious, handsome if somewhat patrician in appearance. And he was, of course, notably non-conforming. He had married Anne Hitchcock in November 1905, and was the father of two girls, Margaret and Adelaide. An affectionate and committed family man, he eventually fathered five children – William, Anne and Ethan were born after Margaret and Adelaide. While he hankered after a post in the Navy Department in Washington, he at least had the considerable consolation of knowing that he would have two years with his family at Newport whilst attending the Naval War College.

The college was the first of its kind in the world. It was founded in 1884 when the then Secretary of the Navy, William E. Chandler, signed General Order 325, the opening words of which were: 'A college is hereby established for an advanced course of professional study for naval officers …'

The building allocated to it was the old Newport Asylum for the Poor on Coaster's Harbour Island at Newport, Rhode Island, and the college's first president was Commodore Stephen B. Luce. Luce said, 'It must strike anyone who thinks about it as extraordinary that we members of the profession of arms should never [before] have undertaken the study of our real business.' He believed that it was only by a philosophical study of military and naval history 'that we can discover those truths upon which we are to generalise and build a science of naval warfare'. In time the Naval War College became 'both a laboratory and a war-planning agency for the Navy Department: tactical, operational, and even technical problems were routinely submitted to the College for solution, and almost every war plan adopted between 1890 and 1917 was prepared by Naval War College officers, alone or in cooperation with the Office of Naval Intelligence'.

During his two years there, Sims was required to attend lectures, readings and seminars on strategy, tactics and operations. Captain Alfred Thayer Mahan, who earned a worldwide reputation for the scope of his strategic thinking and his writings, developed the history course at the college.

The college was an education and research institution, and it was there that Sims learned for the first time about the concept of doctrine. The subject was examined in detail. He learned, for instance, that military doctrine was what was believed about the best way to conduct military affairs; that doctrine was the result of an examination and interpretation of the available evidence; that the interpretation was subject to change if new evidence was introduced, and that the principal source of doctrine was experience. He learned, too, that doctrine was constantly maturing and evolving, and that the real key was the accurate analysis and interpretation of history.

Among those writers apart from Mahan whose works he studied was the British naval historian Julian Corbett. He was familiar with Corbett's 1911 book *Some Principles of Maritime Strategy*, had absorbed what Corbett had to say about a primary objective being to secure your own communications while disrupting those of the enemy; about the physical destruction or capture of enemy ships, and about blockade.

Sims came out of the naval War College having experienced what Dudley W. Knox called 'the mutual understanding necessary for operating large numbers of ships jointly at sea'.

In 1913, when Sims' two-year course was completed, America had thirty-six destroyers in its Atlantic Destroyer Flotilla. They had first come on the scene in the US Navy following the commissioning in 1902 of eleven torpedo boat destroyers. Destroyers were individually capable of inflicting considerable punishment on enemy vessels, but they had never been properly organised and welded into a functioning unit.

As with Lewis Bayly in England, in July 1913 Sims was offered command of the Flotilla. He was in no rush to say yes and, again like Bayly, he wanted a flagship, and a decent sized staff of trained officers. The Navy Department agreed on both counts, giving him a light cruiser, the USS *Birmingham*, for a flagship, and allowing him to select the officers who would form his staff. Most were young men he had met at the War College. Among them was Lieutenant J. V. Babcock, a torpedo specialist, who was to forge a loyal and valued relationship with Sims that would last for many years. Another was Lieutenant-Commander Dudley Knox, who had made a special study of doctrine. Indeed something written by Knox in his article 'The Role of Doctrine in Naval Warfare' was quoted on the flyleaf of *Naval Doctrine Publication 1 – Naval Warfare* published by the Department of the Navy in 1994:

> The only satisfactory method of ensuring unity of effort lies in due preparation of the minds of the various commanders, both chief and subordinate, before the outbreak of hostilities. Such preparation comprehends not only adequate tactical and strategic study and training, but also a common meeting ground of beliefs as to the manner of applying principles to modern war.

Sims applied to the Flotilla everything that he had learned about doctrine at the War College. He received invaluable help and guidance from the impressively informed Knox.

Almost from the beginning of Sims' command of the destroyers, he instituted conferences which were held at frequent regular intervals. Each destroyer's captain was required to attend. Thus was doctrine introduced into the Flotilla. It was agreed, and then made immutable regulation, that the Flotilla would be governed by a doctrine that, as circumstances changed, might have to be revised.

They worked out a doctrine of attack, and repeatedly put it to the test in night manoeuvres at sea, eventually achieving the kind of success that Sims sought. This was long before radar was developed, and being at sea in a destroyer in total darkness and rough seas was an exhausting ordeal. Proper and accurate navigation was frequently impossible, and trying to locate the 'enemy' during exercises made heavy demands on everyone involved. Right through the three years Sims commanded the Flotilla, the encouragement he gave to his officers and men was unceasing. His leadership was outstanding.

In October 1915, by which time war had been raging in Europe for over fourteen months, Sims was assigned command of the new battleship USS *Nevada*, which was then nearing completion. Her 27,500 tonnage was over 11,000 tons more than that of the *Minnesota*. As he had done with the *Minnesota*, Sims installed strong loyalty and pride in his officers and ratings. He was inspirational, and his powerful first-class battleship became another happy and well-run ship.

Following this he was detached from his sea command, after thirty-seven years of service, and appointed the fifteenth president of the Naval War College. He took over on 16 February 1917. In the following month he was summoned to Washington.

17

REASON FOR ALARM

Admiral von Holtzendorff, chief of the German naval staff, said in December 1916 that if the Germans could 'break England's back' the war would at once be decided in Germany's favour. He was convinced that if the U-boat fleet operated in an unrestricted fashion once again, 600,000 tons of British, Allied and neutral shipping could be sunk each month. Germany, he said, would be able to force England to surrender, and there would be peace before 1917's harvest time arrived.

The Kaiser agreed with von Holtzendorff. A decision was taken to inaugurate, 'with the utmost severity', unrestricted submarine warfare from 1 February 1917. Any and every ship – British, Allied and neutral – found in the North Sea, the English Channel, the areas around Britain's and Ireland's coasts, and as far as 400 miles out into the Atlantic west and south-west of Ireland, was to be attacked and sunk without warning.

Bauer, the U-boat chief, wrote explicit orders to his U-boat commanders relating to 'ruthless U-boat warfare'. Every U-boat was to fire all of its torpedoes and all of its gun ammunition on each patrol. The U-boats were to concentrate their attacks on the places where the sea lanes to England converged. They were to aim to be at sea for least half of every month, and only absolutely essential overhauls were to be undertaken when back at base. If they encountered bad weather on a patrol, they were not to move to other locations in search of better conditions, but were to submerge and wait until the bad weather abated. If they encountered armed ships, they were to attack from submerged positions whenever possible. During attacks, each U-boat was to keep moving – a U-boat under way was better able to evade a counter-attack. Whenever possible, the U-boats were to attack by night.

The German decision to commence an unrestricted U-boat campaign caused widespread shock and anger, particularly in the United States where a widely published first-hand account of the sinking of the Cunard liner RMS *Laconia*, written by American journalist Floyd Gibbons, was read from the floor of both houses of congress. The piece, cabled from Queenstown and published in newspapers right across the United States, triggered fury among Americans who had previously been of an isolationist mindset.

The article was graphic in its descriptions of hearing the five quick loud blasts on the ship's horn to signify 'Abandon Ship', of what it was like to be standing on the sloping deck of an 18,000 ton liner at night after she had been hit and began to tilt to starboard, settling deeper in the water as she started to sink. He wrote of what it was like in a lifeboat being lowered into the sea and twice coming close to dangerously upending, nearly tipping everyone out into the dark icy water below; and of seeing the lights dim and go out as the bow of the 600-foot liner rose high into the air and the ship slid down into the depths. The conditions in the lifeboat, where there were blistered hands, tension, panic and loud blasphemy and profanity, Gibbons described as 'bedlam and nightmare'.

He had been on his way to Britain to take up a position as London correspondent of the *Chicago Tribune*. He was one of seventy-five passengers on the *Laconia* along with her crew of 217, under Captain Irvine, when she was torpedoed on Sunday 25 February, 1917, at 10.30 at night. The U-boat that fired two torpedoes at the liner was U-50, captained by thirty-four-year-old *Kapitanleutnant* Gerhard Berger. The ship was 160 miles north-west by west of the Fastnet when the first of the two torpedoes struck her.

Gibbons wrote that the surfaced U-boat approached the lifeboat after the *Laconia* had disappeared. A voice asked in English the name, the tonnage of the ship, if there had been any passengers on board, and if she was carrying cargo. The liner's chief steward answered the enquirer. The people in the lifeboat, Gibbons reported, were told from the U-boat that they would be all right because 'the patrol will pick you up soon'. And then U-50 moved off into the cold night.

The lifeboats tried to stay close to each other, but between violent seasickness, waves sloshing over the gunwales and the water in the boats having to be bailed out continuously, they became dispersed and spent six miserable hours adrift. Eventually, after about six hours in the open boats, they were rescued by the Queenstown sloop HMS *Laburnum* and taken into Cork Harbour.

Among those waiting to meet them when they landed was American Consul Wesley Frost. And for the umpteenth time, Admiral Bayly came down the hill from Admiralty House to meet survivors, to give them hot drinks and snacks and cigarettes – and to listen to their stories.

In England the decision by the Germans to start unrestricted U-boat warfare prompted alarm. The total gross tonnage sunk in February was nearly 540,000. In March the figure climbed to over 600,000. This was a fearsome acceleration in the rate of tonnage being sunk – more than 500 ships destroyed in the first two months of the campaign, the heaviest concentration of them in the South-Western and Western Approaches off the coast of Ireland.

This was what Admiral Bayly was trying to contend with from Queenstown, doing his best with a totally inadequate fleet of ships, and the largely ineffective antisubmarine system that was imposed upon him – the auxiliary patrol system.

The Admiralty considered hunting patrols to be an offensive measure, but some of the U-boat captains thought the patrol ships were all but useless, that their main function, other than steaming along their patrol lines, was to rush to where a call for help came when a U-boat had attacked, rescue any survivors they could find, and endeavour to keep the U-boat submerged. All that the U-boats on station had to do was submerge when a patrol vessel came along, stay out of sight until she had passed, then resurface and wait for the next merchant ships to come by.

On Monday, 26 March 1917, in the United States, Admiral Sims received a telegraphed message from Secretary of the Navy Josephus Daniels summoning him to Washington. There was a cloak-and-dagger, smoke-and-mirrors air of secrecy about it. Sims was to tell no one he'd been called to Washington, was to keep his movements secret and, on arrival in Washington, was *not* to go direct to the Navy Department but, instead, to telephone the chief of the bureau of navigation, Captain Palmer.

The admiral didn't know that the US Ambassador in London, Walter H. Page, had said in his 23 March cable to the Secretary of State that he had informally discussed with Prime Minister Lloyd George, Balfour, Bonar Law, Admiral Jellicoe, and others, the subject of active cooperation between the USA and Britain, and that they would gladly assent to any proposals the USA might make.

'I know personally and informally,' Ambassador Page's cablegram said, 'that they hope for the establishment of full and frank naval interchange of information and cooperation. Knowing their spirit and their methods, I cannot too strongly recommend that our government send here immediately an admiral of our own navy ... The coming of such an officer of high rank would be regarded as a compliment, and he would have all doors opened to him ... Every important ally has an officer of such high rank here.'

Towards the end of the cablegram, Page said, 'Admiral Jellicoe has privately expressed the hope to me that our navy may see its way to patrol [Britain's] coast ... If our Navy Department will send an admiral, it would be advantageous for me to be informed as soon as possible. The confidential information that he would come by would be of immediate help. Such an officer could further definite plans for full cooperation'.

Sims knew nothing about any of this. When he arrived in Washington on Wednesday 28 March and reported to the Navy Department in the afternoon, Captain Palmer, the chief of the Bureau of Navigation, informed him that he was to be 'sent abroad to confer with the Allied admiralties'. But no explicit instructions, no statement of the policy that would govern the US Navy in the event of the United States declaring war against Germany, were given to Sims at that strange meeting. Nor was he told whether or not any naval forces would be sent to Europe, and he was given no hint of who was likely to command them if such forces were sent.

Sims assumed that his mission was to confer with the heads of the Allied navies to learn the actual situation, and to discuss means for naval cooperation in case the United States declared war against the Central Powers. Secretary of the Navy Daniels told him that it had been decided not to issue him with written orders detaching him from his duties at Newport. He was to use the cable freely to advise the Navy Department as to how the Americans could best cooperate with the Allied navies in the event of America being drawn into the war. He was to secure all possible information about what the British were doing, and what plans they had for more effective warfare against the U-boats. (President Wilson believed that the British hadn't taken a vigorous enough offensive to prevent the destruction of shipping.)

Daniels later claimed that in talking with Sims he had mentioned Page's cablegram, and had confidentially informed Sims that the time was near at hand when the United States would enter the war and 'that in that event we must prepare for the fullest cooperation with the British navy'.

Daniels instructed Sims to travel to England under an assumed name, not to take any uniforms with him, and to cross the Atlantic by passenger ship. He was to keep his departure and destination secret, and was to be accompanied by his aide, Commander John Vincent Babcock, who also had to travel under an assumed name. Sims' wife and children were to stay on at the official residence of the president of the War College at Newport, Rhode Island.

Daniels later claimed that he had told Sims, 'You have been selected for this mission not because of your Guildhall speech, but in spite of it.' Sims flatly denied that the Guildhall speech was referred to at that time by anybody in the Navy Department. 'The secretary's recollection on that point is thoroughly mistaken,' Sims said.

The only instructions Sims received were delivered verbally, but Sims maintained that the chief of naval operations, Admiral William S. Benson, said to him, 'Don't let the British pull the wool over your eyes. It is none of our business pulling their chestnuts out of the fire. We would as soon fight the British as the Germans.' Captain Palmer, the Bureau of Navigation chief, revealed that he had heard Benson saying it.

Daniels later stated that he had heard nothing about what Sims claimed was Benson's 'advice', until reading of it in a letter written by Sims in January 1920. Chief of Naval Operations Benson didn't deny having warned Sims to guard against 'British machinations', but, speaking before a congressional investigating committee in 1920, he attempted to negate the notion that he was as anti-British as he was anti-German. 'I never had any idea that we would have to fight any other country,' Benson said. Benson, unlike Sims, was 'a supporter of the principal of civilian supremacy' according to his biographer Mary Klachko. She also said that 'his distrust of Great Britain at times may have passed beyond reasonable limits'.

On 31 March 1917 Sims and Babcock, under the assumed names S. W. Davidson and V. J. Richardson respectively, sailed for Liverpool on the American liner *New York*, a striking-looking Glasgow-built ship with a clipper bow. She had big representations of the American national flag painted on her sides, to proclaim her neutrality.

Sims and Babcock were surprised twice early on the Atlantic crossing. The first time was when a man who had served under Sims on the battleship *Nevada* recognised his former commander. On the liner, the man was a member of the ship's armed guard. Sims took him aside and swore him to secrecy. The second surprise was when a steward noticed the discrepancy between the initials on Sims' and Babcock's pyjamas, and their names on the passenger list. Thinking that the two could well be spies, the steward reported the matter to the ship's master who smiled, reassured the steward, and told him to keep his mouth shut about his discovery.

On 6 April 1917, while Sims and Babcock were on the high seas, President Wilson signed his country's formal declaration of war. The declaration 'authorised and directed' the president 'to employ the entire naval and military forces of the United States, and the resources of the Government, to carry on war against the Imperial German Government ...'

On that same day the British, hoping for help, informed the United States authorities that Britain was in urgent need of financial aid, and that 'all craft from destroyers downwards capable of dealing with submarines would be absolutely invaluable'.

At four o'clock in the afternoon of 9 April 1917, the Isle of Man Steam Packet Company's twin screw steamer SS *Tynwald,* Captain Cojeen commanding, pulled away from her berth at Douglas, the capital of the Isle of Man. She was a smart-looking vessel with two red and black raked funnels, black hull and white upper works. A mini-liner, named after the Isle of Man's ancient parliament, she was the main winter ship on the Douglas/Liverpool service. On that afternoon she was carrying 600 passengers and mail.

The Irish Sea, known by some as U-boat Alley, was strewn with mines, and frequented by U-boats. That day's crossing to Liverpool was initially uneventful, though uncomfortable for the passengers because the *Tynwald* had a pronounced tendency to roll. The lumpy sea, strong wind and occasional snow flurries were not conducive to a smooth passage.

When the *Tynwald* arrived within a few miles of Liverpool Bar, those on board noticed a large ocean liner making her way into the port. Suddenly smoke, and an explosion below the big ship's water line, showed that the liner had either been torpedoed, or had struck a mine. The ocean liner was the 10,500 ton *New York*, and she had struck one of the thousands of mines that U-boats were laying around the coasts of Britain and Ireland, in the approaches to ports.

Captain Cojeen of the *Tynwald* immediately went to the liner's aid, using first-rate seamanship and discipline. All of the *New York*'s sixty-odd passengers, including Rear-Admiral Sims and Commander Babcock, were safely transferred to the *Tynwald* in the liner's own lifeboats. They were put ashore at the Liverpool landing stage.

Tugs towed the *New York* into Liverpool where she was manoeuvred into dry dock. The hole blown in her side by the mine was big enough to drive a horse and cart through. Luckily the bulwark abaft where she was struck remained intact, and though the forward compartments had quickly filled with water, the ship had been able to remain afloat. For Sims and Babcock the incident was a scary reminder that they were in a war zone.

On the quayside to meet them were two officers of the Royal Navy. One was Rear-Admiral Hope, RN, the port admiral. The First Sea Lord of the Admiralty, Admiral Sir John Jellicoe, had sent the other from London. When sending the officer to Liverpool to meet and greet Sims and Babcock, Jellicoe had handed him a letter of welcome and told him to deliver it personally to Sims.

A special train was laid on to take Sims and Babcock to London. In America Sims had followed the progress of the war as best he could by studying newspaper despatches and stories, and certain circulated official reports from US attachés overseas. But having read the contents of Jellicoe's letter, and chatting informally on the train with the officer from Jellicoe's staff, Sims realised how incomplete was the picture of the war's progress that he had pieced together back in the USA. It was clear that his, and virtually every other America-based American's, view of the situation was far from accurate.

Soon after arriving in London on the 10 April, Sims went to the American embassy in Grosvenor Square to meet the ambassador. He and Page had never met before, but the rapport between them was immediate. Sims didn't know then that Ambassador Page had reached a state of intense personal frustration and disappointment, as well as dismay at the behaviour of the White House.

From the embassy, Sims next went to the Admiralty to see the First Sea Lord. Jellicoe and he had first met in China during the Boxer Rebellion, had formed a firm friendship, met frequently afterwards, and had exchanged many letters, swapping views on various subjects relating to naval matters, principally gunnery. Jellicoe knew of the remarkable gunnery results Sims had achieved throughout the US navy during his time as Inspector of Target Practice. He considered Sims to be 'a most distinguished officer', and was attracted by the American's sense of humour, charm, and 'accurate grasp of any problem with which he was confronted'. He admired Sims' habit of speaking his mind 'with absolutely fearless disregard of the consequences' – but was aware that the American also possessed tact, and persuasive eloquence. Jellicoe believed that Sims' overall experience as an officer who had commanded a battleship and the destroyer flotillas, and was president of the War College, plus his close study of naval history, strategy and tactics, 'had peculiarly fitted him for the important post for which he was selected'.

Sims for his part was to point out, 'the First Lord of the Admiralty, the position in England that corresponds to our Secretary of the Navy, has no power to give any order to the fleet – a power which our secretary [Josephus Daniels] possesses'. The American situation, where a civilian, usually a politician, was *de facto* chief of the navy, was anathema to Sims and to many, but not all, other senior US navy officers.

Sims was about to receive a shock when he sat down in Jellicoe's office to confer with the First Sea Lord. British shipping accounted for 43 per cent of the world's total merchant tonnage. At the start of the war the total tonnage of the Allies' merchant shipping was about 21,000,000. That left them a margin of roughly 6,000,000 tons over and above what was absolutely essential in order to ferry into England the country's basic needs (food and raw materials), and arms and munitions for the forces fighting the land war in Europe. Two-thirds of all Britain's food was imported. But the Germans' relentless and successful U-boat campaign was ripping the merchant fleet asunder, and the rate of shipbuilding to replace the lost vessels was seriously inadequate.

A few days before Christmas 1916, Germany's Chief of Naval Staff, Admiral von Holzendorff, had sent a lengthy document to the Kaiser and supreme command laying out the statistical reasons for believing that if the U-boats could attain and maintain a sinkings rate of 600,000 tons per month, Britain would cave in. Her oil reserves were already perilously low, down to barely two month's supply. Von Holzendorff had predicted a German victory before harvest time.

Jellicoe told Sims that the U-boats had, in two months, destroyed one-third of the precious six million ton margin. The First Sea Lord opened a drawer in his desk, withdrew a sheet of paper, and pushed it across to the American. On it were written the actual figures for February and March.

What he read astounded Sims: 540,000 tons of shipping had been sunk in February – an increase of roughly 170,000 tons over January. The figure for March sinkings read, 603,000 tons. The projected figure for April, the month in which they were speaking, was 900,000 tons – and Britain had only a few weeks supply of grain left. The statistics were nearly four times bigger than the public had been led to assume. Shaken, Sims said he had never imagined the situation to be so terrible.

'It is impossible for us to go on with the war if losses like this continue,' said Jellicoe quietly.

'It looks as if the Germans are winning the war,' Sims said.

'They *will* win,' Jellicoe replied, 'unless we can stop these losses, and stop them soon.'

The First Sea Lord estimated that if things continued the way they were going, Britain would be defeated before the end of November. More and more new U-boats were joining Germany's submarine fleet, and even if the rate of sinkings levelled off at around one million tons a month, Britain's endurance was likely to end, according to some calculations, by 1 November 1917.

It struck Sims that American leaders in general, and the Navy Department in particular, had only the vaguest notion of the naval situation in Europe. No extensive efforts, as far as he knew, had been made to analyse the situation. There was no realistic conception in Washington of the extent and seriousness of the U-boat campaign. Jellicoe admitted that he could understand how difficult it was for those in Washington to fully appreciate the conditions in European waters. They were, after all, separated by 3,000 miles of sea from the theatres of war. The information they relied upon was incomplete and inaccurate, and European censorship had ensured that crucial information was held back.

When Sims later told Ambassador Page about the conversation he'd had with Jellicoe, gave him the statistics and passed on the opinions not only of Jellicoe, but also of other senior officers, Page said baldly, 'What we are facing is the defeat of Great Britain.'

On each of two successive days in the third week of April, 27,000 tons of British shipping went to the bottom of the sea. Sinkings had reached a horrendous peak. The Western Approaches, and in particular the sea area off the south-west coast of Ireland, were becoming, in Churchill's words, 'a veritable cemetery of British shipping'.

Sims moved into the Carlton Hotel where he remained for the whole of his time in the capital. He dismissed the idea of acquiring a house, because it would be wasting his government's money when all he needed was a place to sleep.

Four days after he arrived in London he sent his first cablegram to Washington. By then Ambassador Page had introduced him to Britain's prime minister, David Lloyd George. The four days were spent gathering as much information as possible. He ran up against resistance in some quarters because of British reluctance to share detailed information with anyone, but particularly Americans. It took considerable effort on Sims' part to persuade officials to allow him to pass to Washington such figures and facts as were reluctantly given to him.

The British didn't trust Americans. They were afraid that confidential information passed to Washington would not be kept secret. There had been too many cases in the past of secret intelligence transmitted across the Atlantic, finding its way into the newspapers, fuelling anger and suspicion in London. The British authorities were dead set against the Germans learning from *any* source just how crushingly successful the U-boat campaign was, so Sims had to use all his considerable charm and persuasive powers to overcome their resistance.

His first cablegram to the Secretary of the Navy in Washington was sent on 14 April 1917. On the previous day, unbeknownst to Sims, Wilson had approved the sending of six US destroyers to Europe. Sims wrote his message based on his conviction that destroyers and other fast, light vessels were the best means of defence against submarines, primarily because they could force U-boats to remain submerged and so curb their effectiveness.

He used the British naval code for his cablegram, necessitating its translation at the British embassy in Washington. The cablegram didn't contain all he had to say – he would write at length a few days later, giving more details, background, and explanation. Nevertheless, his first message filled four long pages. This is the essence of what he said:

- The submarine issue is very much more serious than the people realise in America ... The reports of our press are greatly in error.

- Supplies and communications of forces on all fronts, including the Russians, are threatened, and control of the sea actually imperilled.
- German submarines are constantly extending their operations into the Atlantic, increasing areas and the difficulties of patrolling.
- The Allies were notified that hospital ships will continue to be sunk, this in order to draw destroyers away from operations against submarines [in order] to convoy hospital ships.
- To accelerate and ensure defeat of the submarine campaign, immediate active cooperation absolutely necessary.
- The issue is and must inevitably be decided at the focus of all lines of communications in the Eastern Atlantic, therefore I very urgently recommend the following naval cooperation: *Maximum number of destroyers to be sent, accompanied by small antisubmarine craft; the former to patrol designated high seas area westward of Ireland, based on Queenstown*, with an advance base at Bantry Bay, latter to be an inshore patrol for destroyers … Also repair ships and staffs for base … [Italics added]
- The chief other and urgent practical cooperation is merchant tonnage and a continuous augmentation of antisubmarine craft to reinforce our advanced forces.
- The cooperation outlined above should be expedited with the utmost dispatch in order to break the enemy submarine morale.
- Maximum augmentation merchant tonnage and antisubmarine work where most effective constitute the paramount immediate necessity.

In 1922 when Secretary of the Navy Daniels wrote his book *Our Navy at War,* he quoted from that cablegram and then added: 'What were the British doing to meet this perilous situation? What plans did they have to defeat the U-boats? That was what we particularly wanted to know, and were surprised when it was not stated in that dispatch.' But the sparse verbal orders given to Sims in Washington had been no more than 'to get immediately in communication with the British Admiralty, and send to Washington detailed reports on prevailing conditions'. Which is precisely what he did.

On 19 April 1917 Sims wrote a long letter to the Secretary of the Navy. Its subject was: 'Confirmation and elaboration of recent cablegram concerning War situation and recommendations for US Naval cooperation.' In it he gave detailed information about what the British were doing to protect merchant shipping. It contained facts he had gleaned from such people as Jellicoe, with whom he had daily conferences; Lloyd George; the First Lord of the Admiralty, Sir Edward Carson; the chief of naval staff; the directors of intelligence, antisubmarine operations, torpedoes and mines; and the ministers of shipping, trade, munitions and mines. He also conferred with several cabinet officials.

Sims revealed that considerable criticism had been and was still being concentrated on the Admiralty 'for not taking more effective steps, and for failing to produce more substantial and visible results. One of the principal demands is for convoys of merchant shipping, and more definite and real protection within the war zone.' And he added, 'The answer, which manifestly is not publicly known, is simply that the necessary vessels are not available, and further, that those which are available are suffering from the effects of three years of arduous service.' He also said that until very recently the Admiralty had been unable to convince some members of the cabinet 'that the submarine issue is the deciding factor in the war. The civilian mind, here as at home, is loath to believe in unseen dangers …'

Whether or not Daniels read into that last sentence an implied criticism of himself as a civilian is not known, but certainly long after the war was over, Daniels would do a complete about-face on a lot of his previously expressed congratulatory views about Sims. In public hearings he did his utmost to discredit the admiral.

On 21 April 1917 a communication from Sims was received by Secretary of State Robert Lansing, in which he reported that 408,000 tons of shipping had already been lost in that month alone. 'Of utmost urgency that we give maximum assistance immediately; every other consideration should be subordinated. I urge the immediate sailing of all available destroyers followed at earliest possible moment by reinforcement of destroyers and all light draft craft available.' Lansing took the message immediately to Secretary of the Navy Daniels. Three days later, the first six destroyers were on their way across the Atlantic.

In London at the end of April 1917, the British Admiralty significantly relaxed its resistance to sharing information with Sims. What triggered the change of heart was the late acknowledgement that Britain needed every possible assistance it could get from the United States in connection with submarine warfare and other important war operations. An order was therefore issued that 'all information that may be of use to the United States Navy' should be communicated by the departments concerned with operational matters to Admiral Sims. The First Sea Lord was to be consulted if any doubt arose as to the expediency of communicating any particular item of secret information.

Knowing that Sims and Babcock would need somewhere in which to work, Ambassador Page allocated them two rooms directly above his own at the embassy. He told Sims, 'You can have everything we've got. If necessary to give you room, we'll turn the whole embassy force out into the street.' Although America was now participating in the most gigantic war there had ever been, and Sims was the representative in London of one of the world's greatest naval powers, for four months the two rooms at the embassy constituted the only office accommodation the admiral had. Nor did he have any back-up staff other than Babcock. He repeatedly asked Daniels for staff, but Daniels ignored the requests, as seemingly he ignored most of what Sims sent in the way of information and recommendations.

Sims finally became so frustrated that on 27 April he said to the ambassador that either the Navy Department in Washington didn't believe what he had been saying, or they didn't believe what the British were saying, as Washington presumed that the British were exaggerating the peril. 'They think I am hopelessly pro-British and that I am being used,' said Sims.

Page knew from bitter personal experience what it felt like to have such accusations made. Sims asked if Page would take the matter up directly with the president, saying, 'then they may be convinced'. Each was convinced that the realities of this war were still not realised in Washington

Page took pen and paper, and rewrote a communication to the Secretary of State that Sims and Babcock together had drafted. He signed it, headed it, *Very Confidential for Secretary and President*, and promptly despatched it. His opening sentence was: 'There is reason for the greatest alarm about the issue of the war caused by the increasing success of the German submarines.' Having given the numbers and tonnage of Allied and neutral ships sunk during the week ending 22 April, and emphasising that almost a million tons were being lost every month, he said that most of the ships were sunk 'to the westward and southward of Ireland'.

He went on to say, 'The British have in that area every available antisubmarine craft, but their force is so insufficient that they hardly discourage the submarines.'

The strongly worded dispatch included such passages as, 'Whatever help the United States may render at any time in the future, or in any theatre of the war, our help is now more seriously needed in this submarine area for the sake of all the Allies than it can ever be needed again, or anywhere else'; and, 'I cannot refrain from most strongly recommending the immediate sending over of every destroyer and all other craft that can be of antisubmarine use … I cannot exaggerate the pressing and increasing danger of this situation … There is no time to be lost.'

Throughout the following two months, Page and Sims kept up a constant flow of requests, information and pleas to Washington. On

28 April 1917, Sims was notified that he was to assume command of all American destroyers operating from British bases, and on 26 May he was promoted to vice-admiral. Shortly after that he was given the title, Commander, United States Naval Forces Operating in European Waters.

Jellicoe and the other senior officers at the Admiralty became increasingly irritated by some of the criticism and proposals emanating from the US Navy's Chief of Naval Operations, Admiral Benson. But Benson wasn't the only one in Washington in criticising mode. President Wilson was repeatedly saying to Josephus Daniels, his Secretary of the Navy, that the British Admiralty 'had done absolutely nothing constructive in the use of their navy'. The president was equally forthright to Sims, writing to him in London: 'From the beginning of the war I have been greatly surprised at the failure of the British Admiralty to use Great Britain's great naval superiority in an effective way. In the presence of the present submarine emergency, they are helpless to the point of panic.' He spoke of 'the absolute necessity of finding and ending the hornet's nest and destroying the poison or removing the cork ... We cannot win this war by merely hunting submarines when they have gotten in to the great ocean.'

Benson advocated the Royal Navy taking the offensive against the U-boats in their bases. This proposal was considered by Jellicoe to be unsound, and prompted him to comment in a letter to Admiral Browning, RN, 'The real truth is that Admiral Benson has an idea in his head that the gun and a sharp pair of eyes are the answer to a submerged submarine. One would hardly believe that such ideas could be held by any naval officer – but there it is.'

Sims and Jellicoe on the other hand saw eye-to-eye on virtually everything. Jellicoe said, 'as he is absolutely independent and does not care a hang what they say to him from the other side, he strengthens my hand considerably'.

Sims continued to bombard Washington with communications – throughout May, June and July 1917, he called thirty-two times for ships, including ocean-going tugs. Their response was to send a further twelve destroyers and the tender *Dixie* in May, ten more destroyers and another tender in June, and a further nine destroyers in July.

18

TWO OF A KIND, BUT DIFFERENT

In London in April 1917 Admiral Bayly met Admiral Sims for the first time. Bayly had been summoned from Queenstown for a meeting with Jellicoe, First Sea Lord, and Sir Edward Carson, the First Lord. Jellicoe's departure from the Grand Fleet, incidentally, had caused many officers and other ranks to weep openly, as he had been a popular leader.

Bayly was in an impatient mood when he arrived in London, resentful at being called away from Queenstown. Didn't they realise how much he had on his plate? There was the U-boat campaign, the torrents of telegrams and signals that had to be dealt with, the survivors from torpedoed ships who had to be looked after. The survivors were men and women who had been fished out of freezing seas, or who had been adrift without food or water, exposed to wind and slashing rain in open boats, or clinging to rafts, and who could not be ignored when brought ashore.

People like James M'Cartney from Belfast, first officer of the *Bray Head*, which was torpedoed hundreds of miles off the Irish coast on the bitterly cold 14 March. The crew of thirty-eight took to the two lifeboats in the teeth of a gale which got stronger by the minute. The ship's master, John Hay, took command of one of the boats, and the first officer took command of the other. He said that both boats were shipping water. During the night, the master's boat occasionally shone a lantern across the darkness. The weather deteriorated, became so bad that at 3 a.m. on the Friday morning in the driving wind M'Cartney ordered the sail taken down and a sea anchor put out.

They had had to bale unceasingly to keep the boat afloat, and the men became exhausted. M'Cartney rationed their small quantity of drinking water and spoke constantly to the men, encouraging them to hold on, not to give in. One crew member died from cold and exposure. They had no option but to throw him overboard. A second man died the following night. The master's boat foundered and everyone on board perished. At eight a.m. on Sunday 18 March, M'Cartney's lifeboat with its half-dead occupants was sighted by a patrol vessel, and the survivors were brought ashore.

Their story was typical of thousands poured into the sympathetic ears of Admiral Bayly and his niece in the Customs Hall in Queenstown, as they fed and comforted the haunted-looking survivors. In the three and a half years following the sinking of the *Lusitania*, an estimated 7,000 survivors were brought ashore at Queenstown. The admiral never once failed to meet those who were rescued from the sea when their ships were destroyed by enemy action.

He made a habit of inviting up to Admiralty House the captains of torpedoed ships so that they could tell him the details of the deadly attacks. He believed that there was always something to learn from such men. Smoking his short black pipe, he listened patiently to gruesome stories of sudden death in the night, of seas 'brilliant with burning oil, and men screaming in agony, dying in the flaming water under dark implacable skies'.

But as well as the demands on his patience and compassion, Bayly also had hundreds of vessels around the coast to deal with, all of them under his command. Added to all that were the naval installations, the dockyard at Haulbowline, and the volatile political situation in Ireland. He was seething with chagrin at the Admiralty for not leaving him alone to get on with his job. Didn't they realise that he couldn't afford to be away from Queenstown, wasting valuable time travelling from County Cork across to London and back? And for what? Talk. And more talk. Why couldn't whatever they wanted to discuss be dealt with through the customary means of communication?

Never naturally affable, and with a reputation for being cantankerous, Bayly was feeling particularly tetchy when he arrived at the Admiralty. Jellicoe and Carson broke the news to him that America was on the verge of officially entering the war, and that US destroyers would soon be arriving at Queenstown. What had been a matter of conjecture was now a matter of fact. The destroyers would be under his operational command, would sail under orders from him.

Jellicoe and Sims had already discussed in detail the intricacies of this arrangement. Since the American destroyers would be operating from the base and within the district under Bayly's command, and their activities would have to be co-ordinated with British naval units, the most efficient arrangement would be to allow Bayly to direct the American ships. It would call for tact, consideration, professional ability and businesslike methods from Bayly. The Americans would themselves deal with their own disciplinary and maintenance matters.

Jellicoe told Bayly that he hoped he would be nice to the Americans. The First Sea Lord then introduced him to the tall, elegant man wearing the unmistakeable high-collared uniform of the US Navy, who had been sitting quietly in the background, listening. He was Admiral William S. Sims, USN, Commander of the US Naval Forces Operating in European Waters. Sims, whose career in the US Navy had taken a parallel course to Bayly's in the Royal Navy, said later, 'On that occasion he was as rude to me as one man can well be to another.'

Jellicoe had had misgivings about the likelihood of the men and ships of the two separate navies working cooperatively together under one admiral (and a British one at that), and had seen fit to warn Sims that Bayly could be 'very difficult'. Even so, the American was taken aback by Bayly's chilly taciturnity and rudeness. Jellicoe was so embarrassed by the episode that he later suggested to Sims that perhaps Bayly should be removed from command at Queenstown. But Sims said no, he wanted to see if he could sort things out.

On his way back to Queenstown, Bayly kept wondering just how to be 'nice' to the Americans who'd soon be arriving at the port. He decided he'd treat them in exactly the same way as he treated the British. A short while after their uncomfortable London meeting, Sims received a letter from Bayly. It was an invitation to come to Queenstown and stay at Admiralty House. Sims, surprised, accepted and went.

Though cool at first, Bayly gradually thawed and within a few days the two admirals established a friendship characterised by tact, instinct and intuition, underpinned by a mutual respect that deepened as the weeks and months passed. They had much in common, a fact which cemented a friendship that would last to the end of their lives.

Sims became, as Bayly put it, 'practically an honorary member of Admiralty House, Queenstown'. Bayly sent a letter to Sims at the end of May containing an unprecedented proposal. Bayly had slogged away unceasingly for almost two years with enormous responsibility and pressure, and had had no time off. He wrote to Sims saying that if he went on leave from 18 June to 23 June, 'would you like to run the show from here in my absence? I should like it (and you are the only man of whom I could truthfully say that), your fellows would like it, and it would have a good effect all round.'

Sims replied immediately that the proposal was the surprise of his life, and that he would hesitate to accept were it not that he would simply be carrying out Admiral Bayly's plans, by Bayly's methods, and with the assistance of a staff trained by Bayly. He would be more than glad, he said, to act as Admiral Bayly's representative.

Sims travelled over from London, Admiral Bayly's flag was hauled down at Admiralty House and, at the British officer's insistence, Admiral Sims' flag was raised in its place. Sims was hesitant about complying with this, because US Navy regulations stipulated that an admiral's flag could be flown only from the mast of a ship afloat. Among the wilder rumours that started circulating was that the two admirals had quarrelled and Sims had banished Bayly from the country, and that the Americans were about to take over the governance of Ireland!

Sims' flag flew from the Admiralty House flagmast for five days while Bayly and his niece took a short motoring holiday in the west of Ireland. It was the first time in history that an American admiral commanded part of Britain's Royal Navy in a time of war. It had been a truly historic moment when Bayly's flag, with its red cross, was hauled down from in front of Admiralty House and Admiral Sims' flag, with its white star, was raised in its place.

From then until the end of the war Admiralty House in Queenstown was like a second home to Sims. Although his headquarters were in London, and he had ships based in many ports, he took to spending three or four days in Queenstown every few weeks. The base became closer to his heart than any other, and he found that the people of Queenstown and Cork 'received our men with genuine Irish cordiality'.

His admiration for Bayly continued to grow, and he saw a side of the British admiral he couldn't even have guessed at in the beginning. He discovered that Bayly kept a stock of kettles, tea, coffee, sugar, cigarettes and tobacco in a hall behind the Customs House and that when ship survivors were brought ashore, no matter what time of the night or day, Bayly and his niece went down from Admiralty House to meet them. Many of the survivors were in a state of shock – wet, bedraggled, frightened. Neither Bayly nor Violet Voysey was indifferent to their pain, despair and anguish. The admiral and his niece handed out hot drinks, snacks and cigarettes to the survivors. They listened sympathetically to all they had to say about their feelings, their fears, their experiences on rafts and in lifeboats where they didn't have room to stretch their legs, and how they shivered with the cold as they were drenched by waves. The survivors spoke of how some people couldn't take any more and simply gave up, dying where they sat or huddled on the flooded floor boards.

Sims saw Bayly with his sleeves rolled up, washing dishes in a big pan of hot water, looking just like any grizzled elderly man putting away the plates and mugs, so that they were ready for the next group that came in from torpedoed ships.

The American was full of admiration and gratitude for the way Bayly 'watched over our ships and their men with the jealous eye of a father', and how Bayly called them 'my Americans'. He became angry when he learned that an American officer in Queenstown had unfavourably criticised Bayly, referring to him as 'Old Frozen Face'. Sims wrote personally to the officer, telling him that such behaviour was a dangerous business, even when no harm was intended. The chastened officer never again publicly referred to Bayly as 'Old Frozen Face'. He and his colleagues daren't risk the wrath of Sims by bad mouthing someone Sims called 'this very lovable man'.

19

'LONG AND DISTANT SERVICE'

The Kaiser's secret message of 9 January 1917 to all the ships in the German navy said, 'I order that unrestricted submarine warfare be launched with the greatest vigour on February 1. You will immediately take the necessary steps.'

In America, President Wilson didn't hear about this development until the German Ambassador to the United States, Count Johann-Heinrich von Bernstorff, told Secretary of State Robert Lansing, about it.

On 3 February 1917 Wilson announced to congress that diplomatic relations with Germany had been severed. The die was cast as far as America's formal entry into the war was concerned, because the aim of Germany's U-boats was to sink on sight, and without warning, *all* ships, neutral and otherwise, in the war zone around Ireland and the British Isles, France and Italy, and the eastern Mediterranean. Wilson said that he couldn't believe that the Germans 'meant to do in fact what they have warned us they feel at liberty to do'. Incensed, he issued a warning that if American ships were sunk and American lives lost, he would take steps.

Very early in the conflict Britain had cut Germany off from direct communication with the Americas by severing its transcontinental cables. As a result, Germany had to rely mainly on wireless transmissions. But Britain, unknown to them, was intercepting the German despatches – as many as 200 a day. What became known as the Zimmermann Telegram was one of them.

On 23 February 1917 Britain's Director of Naval Intelligence, William Reginald 'Blinker' Hall, gave the Foreign Minister, Arthur Balfour, a copy of a deciphered wireless intercept which had first come into the hands of British naval intelligence on 17 January. When the unusually long intercept had first arrived in Room 40 (the intelligence service of the Admiralty) it was passed on to the political section, because it was written in non-naval code. The two civilian cryptographers on duty in the political section examined the rows of numbers on the paper arranged in groups. An irregular jumble of figures confronted the two men.

Working from German codebook No. 13040 (the diplomatic code, which Room 40 had acquired), the cryptographers tackled what they assumed was the signature at the bottom of the intercept, trying to transform the numbers into a name. Eventually they succeeded. The name turned out to be Alfred Zimmermann. Zimmermann was Germany's foreign secretary. The cryptographers then turned to the groups of numbers at the start of the intercept and found that the first words were: 'most secret'. The unusual length of the message was because it contained not one, but two separate telegrams.

The first was to the German Ambassador in Washington, Count von Bernstorff. The second, shorter, telegram was for the Imperial German minister in Mexico. For the British, this was one of the great intelligence coups of the war. Ironically, it had been the American Colonel Edward M. House who arranged for Germany to route its messages to its ambassador in Washington via the American embassy in Berlin. He did so in order, as he thought, to facilitate hoped-for peace negotiations.

Director of British Naval Intelligence Reginald Hall had warned the two cryptographers to say nothing to anyone about the explosive document. He held on to the deciphered message because he didn't want the Germans to know that it had been intercepted and decoded. Eventually a Western Union official in Mexico was bribed to provide a copy of the telegram. Bernstorff, the German ambassador in Washington, had sent it via Western Union to the German ambassador in Mexico. The ploy worked. It hoodwinked the Germans into believing that the *Americans* had intercepted the telegram. Indeed some accounts declared that it was 'captured' by America's secret service on the Texas border.

Thus it was that on 23 February Arthur Balfour formally handed a copy of the deciphered message to the American Ambassador in London, Walter Hines Page. Page forwarded it immediately to President Wilson in Washington. Frank L. Polk, America's Deputy Secretary of State (Secretary Lansing was on vacation) showed the telegram to President Wilson on 25 February. Wilson became furiously angry. On the following day he requested approval from congress to arm American merchant ships. He got that approval from the House of Representatives by a 403 to 14 votes.

The part of the Zimmermann Telegram that most enraged Wilson was:

> We intend to begin unrestricted submarine warfare on February 1. We shall endeavour to keep the United States neutral. In the event of this not succeeding, we make Mexico a proposal of alliance on the following basis: make war together, make peace together, general financial support, and an understanding on our part that Mexico is to reconquer the lost territory in Texas, New Mexico, and Arizona.

The whole concept was fundamentally flawed. Mexico was militarily powerless, poverty-stricken, close to anarchy. And those in power in Mexico surely knew that no ships, men or munitions from Germany could possibly reach Mexico. The proposition contained in the telegram was so absurd that initially many people didn't believe that it was genuine, though Woodrow Wilson never for a moment doubted its authenticity. At the end of the following month Zimmermann himself confirmed having sent it.

On 28 February the still angry Wilson released the text of the

Zimmermann Telegram to the Associated Press. Within hours the story was headlined in virtually every major newspaper in the United States, and in many across the world. Within the United States the telegram had the psychological effect of hardening the public's attitude towards Germany.

Meanwhile Germany's unrestricted U-boat warfare was proving terrifyingly successful – 781,500 tons of shipping sunk by the end of February 1917. What finally propelled the United States into becoming a belligerent in the war was the loss of American lives in the sinking of three American merchant ships, the *Illinois*, the *Vigilancia* and the *City of Memphis* on 18 March.

On the night of 2 April 1917 a special joint session of the congress of the United States was held in a packed House of Representatives. The gallery was filled to overflowing. The Supreme Court justices were there, as were cabinet colleagues, and many distinguished visitors. The president began by saying that he had called the congress into extraordinary session because there were very serious choices of policy to be made immediately. It was neither right nor constitutionally permissible, he said, that he should assume the responsibility of making those choices. In his speech he used all of his formidable intellectual capacities, and his considerable talent for clear expression. Commentators, analysts, and fellow politicians considered this – his War Message – one of the most powerful speeches of his entire career.

He reminded the assembly that on 3 February 'I officially laid before you the extraordinary announcement of the Imperial German government that, on and after the first day of February, it was its purpose to put aside all restraints of law or of humanity, and use its submarines to sink every vessel that sought to approach either the ports of Great Britain and Ireland, or the western coasts of Europe, or any of the ports controlled by the enemies of Germany within the Mediterranean.' He referred to the submarine campaign as 'the cruel and unmanly business', and said, 'Vessels of every kind, whatever their flag, their character, their cargo, their destination, their errand have been ruthlessly sent to the bottom without warning and without thought of help or mercy for those on board, the vessels of friendly neutrals along with those of belligerents.' He spoke of ships sunk with 'reckless lack of compassion or of principle'. International law, he said, had its origin in the attempt to set up some law that would be respected and observed 'upon the seas, where no nation had right of dominion and where laid the free highways of the world'.

He accused the German government of 'throwing to the winds all scruples of humanity or of respect for the understandings that were supposed to underlie the intercourse of the world', and said that he was thinking of 'the wanton and wholesale destruction of the lives of non-combatants, men, women and children, engaged in pursuits which have always, even in the darkest periods of modern history, been deemed innocent and legitimate'.

Property could be paid for, he said, but 'the lives of innocent and peaceful people cannot be. The present German submarine warfare against commerce is a warfare against mankind. It is a war against all nations. American ships have been sunk, American lives taken in ways it has stirred us very deeply to learn of, but the ships and people of other neutral and friendly nations have been sunk and overwhelmed in the waters in the same way ... The challenge is to all mankind.'

He said that because submarines were in effect outlaws 'when used as the German submarines have been used against merchant shipping', it was impossible to defend ships against their attacks as the law of nations had assumed that merchantmen would defend themselves against privateers or cruisers, 'visible craft giving chase upon the open sea'. There was one choice the Americans could not make, were incapable of making: 'We will not choose the path of submission, and suffer the most sacred rights of our nation and our people to be ignored or violated. The wrongs against which we now array ourselves are no common wrongs; they cut to the very roots of human life.'

Edward Douglass White, the chief justice and a veteran of the Civil War, was so moved at this point that he wept openly.

Wilson advised that the congress 'declare the recent course of the Imperial German government to be in fact nothing less than war against the government and people of the United States'; that it 'formally accept the status of belligerent' which had been thrust upon it, and that it take immediate steps to exert all its power and employ all its resources 'to bring the government of the German Empire to terms, and end the war'.

Regarding the requirements as far as the US Navy was concerned, he said, 'It will involve the immediate full equipment of the navy in all respects, but particularly in supplying it with the best means of dealing with the enemy's submarines ... Neutrality is no longer feasible or desirable, where the peace of the world is involved and the freedom of its peoples ...' The object was 'to vindicate the principles of peace and justice in the life of the world as against selfish and autocratic power ...' he stated. 'We have no quarrel with the German people. We have no feeling towards them but one of sympathy and friendship. It was not upon their impulse that their Government acted in entering this war. It was not with their previous knowledge or approval. It was a war determined upon, as wars used to be determined upon in the old, unhappy days when people were nowhere consulted by their rulers, and wars were provoked and waged in the interest of dynasties, or of little groups of ambitious men who were accustomed to use their fellow men as pawns and tools.'

He said that 'a steadfast concert for peace' could never be maintained except by a partnership of 'democratic nations', and later in his address he said Americans were 'now about to accept gage of battle with this natural foe to liberty' and would, if necessary, 'spend the whole force of the nation to check and nullify its pretensions and its power ... We are glad, now that we see the facts with no veil of false pretence about them, to fight thus for the ultimate peace of the world and for the liberation of its peoples, the German peoples included: for the rights of nations great and small, and the privilege of men everywhere to choose their way of life and of obedience. The world must be made safe for democracy.'

He ended by saying that it was a distressing and oppressive duty that he had performed in thus addressing them. It was 'a fearful thing to lead this great peaceful people into war, into the most terrible and disastrous of all wars, civilisation itself seeming to be in the balance. But the right is more precious than peace and we shall fight for the things which we have always carried nearest our hearts – for democracy, for the right of those who submit to authority to have a voice in their own governments, for the rights and liberties of small nations, for a universal dominion of right by such a concert of free peoples as shall bring peace and safety to all nations, and make the world itself at last free.' He asked congress for a joint resolution declaring war against Germany.

When he finished, he received a roaring, shouting, clapping, stamping, standing ovation. Commenting on that later to his private secretary, Joseph Tumulty, he said, 'Think of what it was they were applauding – my message today was a message of death for our young men. How strange it seems to applaud that.' The Senate subsequently voted 82 to 6 in favour of supporting the president; the House voted 373 to 50. What it added up to was that of a total of 531 congressmen and senators, only 56 objected, and Woodrow Wilson mobilised the nation for total war. It was the first time in his country's history that it had gone to war as one body. But the president didn't sign any alliance with Britain or France – America intended operating as an independent force.

America's Secretary of the Navy, Josephus Daniels, recalled that five minutes after President Wilson signed the war resolution that congress passed on 6 April 1917, the following message was radioed to every ship in the US Navy, and to every US naval station:

> Sixteen Alnav. The President has signed act of Congress which de-
> clares a state of war exists between the United States and Germany.
> Acknowledge. 131106.
> SECNAV

'Alnav' signified 'all navy', and 'SECNAV' indicated that the message
was from the Secretary of the Navy.

Dresden-born Commander Joseph K. Taussig (38), who had already
spent over twenty years in the United States Navy, was on board the
destroyer USS *Wadsworth* (Destroyer No. 60) at Base 2, the protected
deep water harbour inside the York river in Virginia, when the signal
came through. The United States Fleet had left Hampton Roads for
Base 2 on 3 April, the day after President Wilson had delivered his war
message to congress. The ships had steamed up the Chesapeake to the
mouth of the York river, the Fleet's movement and rendezvous having
been kept secret.

Daniels sent the following mobilisation signal to the navy's five
flagships, the USS *Vestal*, the USS *Columbia*, the USS *Minnesota*, the
USS *Seattle* and the USS *Pennsylvania*, at about 1.30 p.m. of the day
he'd sent the signal about the president's declaration of war:

> Mobilise for war in accordance department's confidential mobilisa-
> tion plan of March 21. Particular attention invited paragraphs six and
> eight.

Paragraph six of the mobilisation plan was about the assigned rendezvous
of the various forces; paragraph eight contained instructions relating to
vessels fitting out at navy yards. The flagships passed the signal to the
ships under their command.

The *Pennsylvania* was the flagship of the Commander-in-Chief of
the Atlantic Fleet, Admiral Henry T. Mayo. As soon as he received the
telegram, he hoisted the signal 'War has commenced'.

The Tucker Class destroyer *Wadsworth* (commissioned in July 1915) flew Taussig's pennant because he had taken command of Eighth Division, Destroyer Force, Atlantic Fleet, in July of the previous year. *Wadsworth* was just over 1,000 tons displacement, was a twin-screw ship with a top speed of 29.5 knots at full revolutions, and had a crew of 99. The other five ships of Taussig's division were the USS *Conyngham*, the USS *Jacob Jones*, the USS *Porter*, the USS *Tucker* and the USS *Wainright*. All of their captains were lieutenant-commanders. Taussig had been promoted to commander on 29 August 1916, but he hadn't yet received the paperwork. The six ships of Eighth Division varied in size from just over 1,000 tons to 1,250 tons. Each was 315 feet long with a 30-foot beam and a draft of 10 feet. Each was equipped with eight torpedo tubes and four 4-inch guns.

On the night of 14 April Taussig was just about to get into a car with his wife to go to a dance when the phone rang. He answered it. The caller was his gunnery officer on the *Wadsworth*, Lieutenant (Junior Grade) J. H. Falge. Orders had just been received, Falge said, 'to leave at daylight for New York, to fit out for long and distant service'. Any way you looked at that 'long and distant service' phrase, you were left with the conclusion that in all likelihood they were being sent abroad. The big question was: Where to? Taussig explained to his wife that he couldn't now go to the dance – he had to return immediately to his ship.

When he went on board the *Wadsworth* he was handed and read the confidential movement orders. The *Wadsworth* was to go to the New York navy yard; the other destroyers of Eighth Division would join her at Cape Henry. On reaching New York they were to dock 'and expedite all necessary preparations for special service'. Other than those few facts, all that Taussig had to go on was the mystifying phrase, 'long and distant service'. He was irritated at being kept in the dark.

The *Wadsworth* got under way at half-past five in the morning, leaving fifteen of her crew behind – liberty men who weren't due back from shore leave until 8 a.m. Through an administrative mix-up, three of Eighth Division's destroyers, including the *Wadsworth*, were diverted from New York to Boston because, as Taussig recorded, 'it never was intended that they go to New York'.

Taussig was by no means a fan of the Navy Department which, he felt, was 'absolutely unorganised so far as its duty in connection with carrying on a war is concerned'. He cited lack of communication, and wrote damningly in his diary: 'Our doctrine in the flotilla teaches us that, in order to carry out instructions intelligently, the commanding officer should know the reason for the issuing of such instructions. But doctrine has no weight with the department, which appears to go along with its eyes only half open.'

When he eventually managed to speak on the phone with the Chief of Naval Operations, Admiral William S. Benson (who assumed office three days after the *Lusitania* was torpedoed), the conversation, from Taussig's point of view, was 'very unsatisfactory'. Benson wouldn't give him a sailing date, and yet insisted that the Eighth Division destroyers 'must sail immediately on receipt of orders' and 'be ready for any contingency'.

On 23 April Taussig received a 'Strictly Secret and Confidential' telegram from the commandant in operations which stated baldly that Taussig's division had to be 'ready to sail immediately urgent'; he was to 'report as soon as ready'. It also gave the first inkling of where they were going: 'destination English Channel'.

Taussig had been across the Atlantic with the Fleet in 1910, the year that Sims made his contentious speech at London's Guildhall. But Taussig's frustration and anger at the way he and his division were being treated in 1917 spilled over into his diary: 'All ships refuelled and took on fresh provisions so as to be ready to sail in case the department should order us out before we were really ready,' he wrote. 'I would not be surprised if this were done, as it would seem that the whole result of this war, which has been going on for nearly three years, depends on whether or not six little destroyers sail from Boston for the English Channel on a certain indefinite date known to no one – not even those who are issuing the orders. Can you beat it!'

He was glad he hadn't been on board the *Wadsworth* when Commander Frank Schofield telephoned from operations and spoke to Lieutenant Falge – glad, Taussig said, because 'perhaps I would have said things I might be sorry for'. Schofield had commented to Falge that 'No excuses would be accepted' if Eighth Division did not sail when orders were received. That, Taussig said, 'implied that the department considers that we are stalling. I consider the remark nothing else than insulting.'

Two officers from operations eventually came to see him. One handed him confidential signal books for use with the British and French navies. The other officer had sealed orders for Taussig as Commander of Eighth Division. When the division was 'in all respects ready for sea', he was informed, the six destroyers were to proceed to a position 50 miles due east from Cape Cod, and only then was Taussig to break the seal and carry out the orders.

Eighth Division sailed on 24 April 1917. It now consisted of the destroyers *Wadsworth, Conyngham, Porter, McDougal, Davis* and *Wainright*. They left port at around five o'clock in the afternoon of a pleasant day, and headed east at 14 knots. Taussig's mood didn't match the benign weather. 'Instead of nagging us and not giving us any information,' he wrote in his diary, 'I feel sure that the proper procedure in this case would have been for me to be ordered to Washington and get the situation explained to me confidentially. I feel that the department kicked us out rather discourteously.'

Just after midnight, when the destroyers were 50 miles out in the Atlantic, Commander Taussig opened his sealed orders. The Secretary of the Navy, Josephus Daniels had signed them. The 'Secret and Confidential' document had as its subject: 'Protection of Commerce near the coasts of Great Britain and Ireland'. It said:

1. The British Admiralty have requested the cooperation of a division of American destroyers in the protection of commerce near the coasts of Great Britain and France.

2. Your mission is to assist naval operations of Entente Powers in every way possible.

3. Proceed to Queenstown, Ireland. Report to Senior British Naval Officer present, and thereafter cooperate fully with the British navy. Should it be decided that your force act in cooperation with French Naval Forces, your mission and method of cooperating under French Admiralty authority remain unchanged.

Route to Queenstown:
Boston to latitude 50 N., Long. 20 W., to arrive at daybreak, then to latitude 50 N., Long. 12 W., thence to Queenstown.

When within radio communication of the British naval forces off Ireland, call GCK and inform the Vice Admiral at Queenstown in British general code of your position, course, and speed. You will be met outside of Queenstown.

4. Base facilities will be provided by the British Admiralty.

5. Communicate your orders and operations to Rear Admiral Sims at London and be guided by such instructions as he may give you. Make no reports of arrival to Navy Department direct.

Taussig and the other destroyer commanders knew nothing of this Queenstown place. To them it was just a name on the map of Ireland, about midway along the south coast of that small country on the western edge of Europe. And who was the senior British naval officer they were to report to at Queenstown? What was his name? What rank did he hold? And what exactly did 'cooperate fully with the British navy' entail? Who'd be in charge? Who'd issue orders? How much was Josephus Daniels, that civilian who was *de facto* chief of their navy, holding back from them?

Questions, questions, to which there were no immediate answers out on the Atlantic with ominous signs of nasty weather looming up. Josephus Daniels' background had nothing to do with the sea, boats or ships, and yet he wanted to have full power to direct naval policy. A journalist by profession, he was the publisher of a North Carolina newspaper, the *Democratic News and Observer*. A man of strong pacifist tendencies, he was said by some to possess both graciousness and charm.

Having supported Woodrow Wilson for president in 1912, Daniels was rewarded by being appointed Secretary of the Navy. The assistant secretary was an energetic and ambitious thirty-five-year-old politician named Franklin Delano Roosevelt who became responsible for, among other things, overseeing the Office of Naval Intelligence and, in 1916, organising the Naval reserve force.

Daniels viewed naval officers as would-be aristocrats. It coloured his dealings with them. In 1913, in his first 'Annual Report of the Secretary of the Navy', he had revealed a hope that the US Navy might become a great university where men could obtain an academic education. Opposed to the system of aides, which existed when he took over, he started to sideline and then ignore the advice of his aide for operations, Rear-Admiral Bradley Alan Fiske, a thirty-year veteran.

Fiske found Daniels' ignorance of, and lack of respect for, naval traditions and customs, alongside his lack of technical knowledge, hard to put up with. In Fiske's estimation, Daniels was devoid of the ability, knowledge and foresight required of the individual holding the powerful position of secretary. Daniels had stymied the admiral's plans to have the various bureaux prepare for war, and he frequently ignored Fiske's counsel in favour of the advice of some of Fiske's subordinates. To Fiske, it all became 'excessively disagreeable'. He asked to be relieved of his duties. The management of the navy, he was convinced, was in unworthy hands. Daniels accepted his resignation, and Rear-Admiral

Fiske became president of the Naval War College at Newport, Rhode Island.

In 1921, in a short foreword to the book *Naval Lessons of the Great War* by Tracy Barrett Kittredge, Admiral Fiske all but branded the Secretary of the Navy a liar. After stating unequivocally that Kittredge's book showed that the principal naval lesson of the war was 'the menace to the national honour and safety that was involved in committing the management of its navy to unworthy hands', and that the Secretary of the Navy should be 'a man of the highest order of ability, knowledge and foresight', he went on to say that the book showed 'that Secretary Daniels was so far below this standard that the navy would have been caught wholly unprepared when we entered the war, and would have been ineffective during the war if certain navy officers had not sacrificed or endangered their positions by putting through important measures without [Daniels'] knowledge'. He ended by accusing Daniels of 'making many statements about important naval matters within his cognizance, that were absolutely false'.

In his 'Official Report on the US Navy during Wartime' Daniels said that it was at a secret conference on 10 April 1917 – only three days before Eighth Division received the order to 'fit out for long and distant service' – and later at a meeting with Assistant Secretary of the Navy Franklin D. Roosevelt, that the decision had been made to send destroyers to Europe. That secret conference was held at Fortress Monroe in Hampton Rhodes, and was attended by admirals from Britain and France as well as from the USA. The officers and men who served in destroyers, Daniels would say, were 'engaged in this most rigorous service', which he characterised as 'the hardest and most exacting service in the navy'.

The good weather and calm sea that the destroyers of the Eighth Division enjoyed at the start of their voyage from Boston to Queenstown didn't last long. The weather worsened, and for six days they steamed eastwards with half a gale blowing from the south-south-east. A rough sea on their starboard beam forced them to reduce speed to 12 knots. Now they knew with a vengeance that they were in the stormy Atlantic.

In the high winds and rough seas, the long, narrow, shallow-draft vessels rolled and pitched violently. It was impossible to set up the mess tables, and plates of food had to be held in the lap. The wind howled above the roar of waves crashing onto the forecastles as the ships took green water over the bows. When sheets of heavy spray smashed against a destroyer's bridge, it was impossible for anyone on bridge watch to stand without holding on tightly to something, to prevent himself from being hurled about and badly injured. Anything that wasn't secured or tied down careened all over the place when the destroyers buried their bows, or heeled right over at crazy, terrifying angles.

The Americans were getting a brutal foretaste of what they could expect on North Atlantic patrols. It was very different from what they were accustomed to; the US fleet usually spent the winter in the West Indies. On the Atlantic during the most violent part of their crossing, the tranquillity of tropic seas was a long way behind them.

Out on the ocean when the steep waves were running and vessels shipped huge quantities of water, destroyers were notoriously difficult to steer. There were swinging surges as they slewed to port and starboard, often by as much as 20 degrees. Trying to keep exactly on a preferred course was impossible. The helmsmen had to try to average out the swings, while the ships shuddered, slammed, pitched and rolled. There was nowhere to run for shelter. It was a nerve-racking ordeal.

Repairs to the *Conyngham*'s circulating pump, and later to the *Wainright*'s main condenser, forced the group to stop for several hours on three different occasions. Everybody was on edge about the possibility of being attacked by U-boats. They felt instinctively safer when they were under way, even though for some it meant sleepless vigilance and courage of the first order.

Before leaving Boston, Taussig had sent an order to all his destroyers setting out the actions to be taken should a U-boat be sighted, or should any of the destroyers be torpedoed or damaged by a mine. Lookouts were sent aloft with powerful binoculars. The American's knowledge about U-boat attacks was extremely sketchy. They didn't know where waiting submarines might be – astern, ahead, on bow, beam or quarter. Would, or could, U-boats attack in a heavy sea? In a long Atlantic swell? What was a U-boat's most favourable firing range? From how far off could a watching U-boat see their masts? More questions they didn't know the answers to. There was much they were going to have to learn, and learn quickly.

On 2 May 1917 Eighth Division made radio contact with the British destroyer HMS *Parthian*, but although Taussig transmitted details of position, course and speed to her, by the time it got dark the *Parthian* still hadn't managed to locate them. The *Parthian*'s captain then decided to steam on the same course and at the same speed as the Americans, intending to search for them again at daybreak. But mist and poor visibility again intervened. The *Parthian* couldn't find them.

On Friday 4 May another British destroyer, the 'M' class HMS *Mary Rose*, hove into view. The sea by now was calm and it was a beautiful day. When the *Mary Rose* closed with the *Wadsworth*, the British ship hoisted the signal: 'Welcome to the American colours'. The *Wadsworth*'s response was: 'Thank you, I am glad of your company'.

A tug carrying an official photographer who had been specially sent from London was waiting for the American destroyers near the Daunt Rock lightship. The cameraman had been instructed to film the arrival of the American destroyers, and to follow Taussig and his fellow captains wherever they went for the rest of that day. As they approached the entrance to Cork Harbour, the men on the destroyers had a clear view of Roche's Point lighthouse standing 50 feet above sea level. The light itself was a further 50 feet higher up, atop a squat tower. It was a sight the Americans were to become very familiar with, to depend on, and to be very grateful for.

The entrance to the harbour looked narrow, although it was three-quarters of a mile wide between Roche's Point on the east side of The Sound, and Weaver's Point on the west side. It could be entered without difficulty by day or night, and had east and west approach channels, divided by Harbour Rock. The Americans knew nothing about the navigation aids in and around Cork Harbour. There were lighted and unlighted can buoys, and lighted and unlighted conical buoys along with the seamarks inside the harbour, beacons and posts. The most important landmark was the spire of the ruin of Templebreedy church when they were outside the harbour. They would have to learn about the white leading lights and the red leading lights, and where they were placed. It was all new to them.

Just outside Roche's Point the destroyers slowed to a stop as a motor launch, HMML *181*, approached. She was one of nearly 600 similar craft ordered and built for the British Admiralty. They were seaworthy boats, but it was said of them that 'they'd roll the heart out of a rocking horse'. However, they performed their tasks with courage and distinction.

HMML *181* went alongside the *Wadsworth*, and two Royal Navy officers, two US Navy officers, and a civilian boarded the destroyer. They'd been only a few minutes on board when two enormous explosions a few hundred yards to the south of Eighth Division burst the silence. The sea erupted. The Germans had laid at least twelve mines at the harbour approaches on the previous night. A couple of minesweeping trawlers from Queenstown had just dealt with the last of them. The explosions brought home to the Americans that they had arrived in a dangerous place. But over the course of the entire war no US ship was damaged or sunk when arriving at Queenstown.

The two US officers who had been delivered to the *Wadsworth* by the motor launch were Lieutenant-Commander Babcock (Admiral Sims' aide), and Paymaster E. C. Tobey. Taussig knew both of them. They had been friends for years. The civilian was Mr Sherman from the American consulate at Queenstown.

One of the British officers was Lieutenant-Commander Thomas H. Robinson. He and five other Royal Navy officers had been detailed by Admiral Bayly to pilot the American vessels into the harbour and through the navigation channel to their moorings. The other British officer was Commander Edward R.G.R. Evans, who in June 1910 had been navigator and second-in-command to Captain Scott on the *Terra Nova*, the ship from which Scott made his epic and tragic trek to the South Pole.

On the night of 20 April 1917 Evans, a commander on active duty with the Dover Patrol, had engaged in a violent naval action in the English Channel. Captaining the destroyer HMS *Broke*, Evans and the flotilla leader HMS *Swift* (captained by Commander Peck), encountered a group of six modern two-funnelled German torpedo boats about 7 miles east of Dover. The *Swift* raced into the attack, closely followed by the *Broke*. The *Broke* fired a torpedo that struck the German ship *G.85* full amidships, causing a huge explosion and clouds of smoke and spray. The torpedo boat was put out of action, crippled.

Evans immediately brought his destroyer about and onto a collision course with the torpedo boat *G.42*. He had decided to ram, and he drove the *Broke* straight at the German ship at full speed. The torpedo boat tried desperately to get out of the way, but failed. The bow of the *Broke* smashed into the port side of the German vessel opposite her after-funnel. There was a tremendous shrieking, crashing sound of rending metal as the German ship was forced over on her beam ends, the *Broke*'s guns firing shells into her at point blank range.

Evans recalled 'pouring a deadly fire into her terrorised crew'. He said that many Germans clambered off the wrecked torpedo boat and onto the forecastle of the *Broke* 'only to meet with instant death from our well-armed [with rifles, bayonets and cutlasses] seamen and stokers'. The officers on the *Broke*'s bridge were said to have used their revolvers and pistols.

The *Broke*, with the *G.42* impaled on her bow, was now an easy target, and in danger of being sunk by the 10.5 centimetre shells that one of the German ships was firing at her. Four-inch cordite cartridges on board the *Broke* caught fire, and an explosion in the boiler room damaged the main steam pipe. The destroyer began losing feed-water to the boilers. By the time the battle was over, twenty-one of the *Broke*'s crew were dead, thirty-six injured, and there was blood all over the upper decks. Evans' ship tore herself clear of the wrecked German vessel, and then his crew concentrated on picking up German survivors from the water. They rescued 140 of them. Both Evans and Commander Peck were awarded the DSO, and Evans became known as 'Evans of the *Broke*'.

While his ship was in dry-dock undergoing repairs, Evans was assigned to Queenstown for a couple of weeks to act as temporary liaison officer with the Americans. A promotion from commander to captain came through while he was there. When he boarded the *Wadsworth* he handed Taussig an envelope containing a personal letter from Britain's First Sea Lord, Admiral Sir John Jellicoe.

Taussig had met Jellicoe in 1900 when both of them had served in the Seymour column in China during the Boxer Rebellion. Jellicoe was then a forty-year-old captain, Taussig a twenty-one-year-old junior officer. Each had been wounded on the same day – Jellicoe was shot in the chest, the bullet remaining in his lung for the rest of his life; Taussig was wounded in one of his legs by a dumdum bullet. The two men lay in adjoining beds for a time whilst receiving medical attention, and had become friendly with each other. But that was seventeen years ago. By the time Taussig arrived at Queenstown, he had no reason to think that Jellicoe would remember him after such a long interval, let alone have delivered to him a personal handwritten letter. The American was amazed. The letter, dated 1-5-17 and written on Admiralty paper, said:

My dear Taussig

I still retain very pleasant and vivid recollection of our association in China and I am indeed delighted that you should have been selected for the command of the first force which is coming to fight for freedom, humanity and civilisation. We shall all have our work cut out to subdue piracy. My experience in China makes me feel perfectly convinced that the two nations will work in the closest cooperation and I won't flatter you by saying too much about the value of your help.

I must say this however, there is no navy in the world that can possibly give us more assistance, and there is no personnel in any navy that will fight better than yours.

If only my dear friend McCalla [a US navy captain who commanded the American landing force in the Boxer Rebellion] could have seen this day, how glad I would have been.

I must offer you and all your officers and men the warmest welcome possible in the name of the British Nation and British Admiralty, and add to it every possible good wish from myself. May every good fortune attend you and speedy victory be with us.

Yours very sincerely,

J. A. R. Jellicoe

Rear-Admiral Sims, who had been called to Paris and was therefore unable to be at Queenstown for the destroyers' arrival, also wrote Taussig a letter of welcome. And there was a note from Vice-Admiral Sir Lewis Bayly, written from Admiralty House. It was short and to the point.

Dear Lieut. Comdr. Taussig

I hope that you and the other fine officers in command of the US destroyers in your flotilla will come and dine here tonight, Friday, at 7:45 and that you and three others will remain to sleep here so as to get a good rest after your long journey. Allow me to welcome you and to thank you for coming.

Yours sincerely

Lewis Bayly

Dine in undress: no speeches.

The destroyers of the Eighth Division, long and lean with four funnels, very high masts, and unusual bridge structures, entered the harbour in a single line, the ships a thousand yards apart, HMS *Mary Rose* leading them in. Taussig's ship, with the big figures '61' showing prominently on her bows, was immediately behind the *Mary Rose*. To people watching from the cluster of houses at Roche's Point, and looking out from White Bay, the difference in appearance between the American destroyers and the British one was immediately noticeable. The line of ships steamed in between Forts Camden and Carlisle, which were just a half mile apart and a mile inside the lighthouse. Taussig said later he heard welcoming cheers coming from the forts.

Having passed the forts, the ships then had a two-mile run to the Spit Bank lighthouse. They left Corkbeg, Whitegate and Aghada to starboard, the Curlane Bank, Spike Island, Rocky Island and Haulbowline Island to port. The (to them) strange-looking Spit Bank lighthouse on its octagonal pile structure stood on the north-east point of the mud bank which extends from there all the way to Haulbowline. The Americans would get used to and value the sound of the Spit's fog bell – it rang twice every thirty seconds when the harbour was shrouded in impenetrable mist, and visibility was down to mere feet.

The destroyers turned through 90 degrees left when they rounded the Spit and ran west past the Batteries, the Holy Ground, the Baths (formerly Inman) Quay, and the town's oldest quay, Lynches, built in the eighteenth century and used by sailing ships during America's War of Independence.

The men on the destroyers had a perfect view of the steeply terraced multi-hued town and the massive, granite St Colman's cathedral, 'clinging miraculously to the side of the hill'. To the right of the cathedral was the row of priests' houses and, higher up the hill, an imposing building with balconies, and a high mast in its grounds. It was the Americans' first glimpse of Admiralty House – whose name was almost always pronounced locally as Admiralty House. As the vessels manoeuvred towards their moorings, stars-and-stripes flags could be seen fluttering from the windows of houses, shops and offices all over the town. It was obvious that the ships had been expected, the security and secrecy surrounding their departure from Boston notwithstanding.

The *Wadsworth* and the *Conyngham* went alongside the oiling jetty, the other four destroyers moored at buoys in midstream. Taussig sent a signal of thanks to the British destroyer *Mary Rose* which had led them into the harbour. The *Wadsworth* received an answering signal, 'Captain, officers and ship's company of HMS *Mary Rose* are very gratified to have the honour of being the first to meet you and your squadron.' Within a few months the *Mary Rose* became another victim of the war – sunk in October in the North Sea. Not one member of her company survived.

To facilitate the film cameraman sent from London, Taussig had to 'walk over the gangway alone so that the moving picture man could take my photograph as the commanding officer of the first American squadron to cooperate with the Allies'. Stepping ashore, he was greeted by American Consul Wesley Frost, who was formally dressed, complete with top hat, in recognition of the historic occasion. The Lord Mayor of Cork, Councillor Butterfield, and some of his officials, had driven down to Queenstown to greet the Americans. They waited at the consulate along with, in Taussig's words, 'the leading citizens of Queenstown'. They included the resident magistrate, Walter Allan and the chairman of Queenstown Urban Council, Timothy Campbell.

After the speeches of welcome, Taussig replied briefly on behalf of the Americans. Then the motorcars that Consul Frost had laid on took them up the hill to Admiralty House to report to Admiral Bayly. The Americans weren't sure what to expect. They'd heard on the way in that Bayly had a reputation for being gruff and brusque, and was a tough disciplinarian. Unsmiling, and dressed in a worn-out-looking uniform, Bayly greeted them, deliberately keeping his back to the official cameraman. His self-effacement when it came to publicity was consistent and incomplete. He looked the embodiment of a flint-featured old sea-dog. He shook hands with Taussig, spoke a few terse words of welcome, then asked, 'At what time will your ships be ready for sea operations?'

Various versions of Taussig's answer became part of American navy folklore. Even Secretary of the Navy Josephus Daniels quoted a version of it.

Taussig is reported to have said, 'We are ready now, sir.'

What he actually said was, 'Ready when fuelled, sir.'

'Require any repairs?'

'No, sir.'

'Stores?'

'No, sir. Each vessel has enough stores on board to last for seventy days.'

A small pause, then Admiral Bayly said, 'You will take four days rest.'

The six destroyer captains of Eighth Division assembled at 7.30 that evening in the Royal Cork Yacht Club. From there they made their way up the hill to Admiralty House for their 7.45 p.m. dinner date with Admiral Bayly. Before going in they caught a glimpse of the large, well kept gardens, and the tall flagpole, the signal station which they had noticed as they steamed to their moorings. They had a magnificent view of the harbour, looking down over the roof of the cathedral to Haulbowline with its dockyard, the Martello tower and the green flat topped Spike Island to its east.

At the dining table Taussig was placed next to the admiral's niece, Violet Voysey, who acted as her uncle's hostess. She was the only female at the dinner, as she was for so many dinners at Admiralty House. Taussig's impressions of her were that she was charming and friendly. He guessed her to be about thirty years of age, ten years younger than Taussig. The other dinner guests that evening were the officer who was in charge of the coast guard at Queenstown, Rear-Admiral H. V. Elliott, RN (Retired); Captain Carpendale, RN; Commander Evans,

RN; Lieutenant-Commander Babcock, USN; Paymaster Tobey, USN, and Wesley Frost, the American consul.

As Admiralty House was 'dry', no wine was served with dinner, nor aperitifs afterwards. It was, nevertheless, a convivial occasion that lasted until shortly after nine o'clock. On this mild evening, with some daylight still left and a bright moon climbing the sky, the admiral and his niece led the dinner guests on a tour of the grounds where Taussig described 'the air [as] very sweet with flowers in bloom and birds singing'. He said it was hard to realise that they had completed an uncomfortable ten-day trip across the ocean, and 'were suddenly transported to this peaceful place. It seemed like a dream.' Bayly repeated his invitation for four of them to stay the night. They decided among themselves that the four would be Taussig, Zogbaum of the USS *Davis*, Johnson of the USS *Conyngham* and Fairfield of the USS *McDougal*.

The four left after breakfast on the Saturday morning and were back on board their destroyers by ten o'clock. In the afternoon they went up the River Lee to Cork's City Hall in the admiral's green barge, to return the previous day's call made on them by Cork's Lord Mayor.

On Sunday morning all the US destroyer captains climbed the steep narrow streets to Admiralty House to be addressed by Admiral Bayly at 10 a.m. Fighting the U-boat menace was a different kind of fighting from anything they had been trained for, and they were keen to learn from him as much as they could and as quickly as they could. Having already experienced the kind of extreme weather they could expect to have to deal with off the coast of Ireland, they knew that patrolling the seas of the Western Approaches was not going to be easy. Before the year was out an American destroyer, the *Ammen*, would have one of her four funnels ripped off by a gale and hurled into the waves. Crewmen were lost overboard from several ships, and an instance was recorded of a destroyer heeling an astonishing 56 degrees to port under the force of wind and wave. Deck plates were known to buckle, rivets to pop.

But on this Sunday morning in May in the calm atmosphere of Admiralty House the American officers sat down to listen to Admiral Bayly. English and officerly his accent may have been, but his speech was without undue pedantry or affectation. He began by telling them that the Admiralty in London had been afraid that he would be rude to the Americans. 'I *won't* be,' he assured them, 'if you do your work … I *shall* be if you don't.' That set the tone.

He told them that the areas they would be patrolling were to the south and south-west of Ireland, from 100 miles west of the Fastnet to a position west of the Scilly Isles. On the days they were going out on patrol, the destroyers were to leave harbour at 8.30 a.m. Destroyers returning from patrol were to enter the harbour at the same time. They must not on any account underrate the ability of the German U-boat commanders who, he said, had repeatedly shown remarkable cleverness, 'never acting according to any fixed routine'. From the time they left harbour to the time they returned, they should assume that a U-boat was watching them. Constant twenty-four hour alertness was an absolute necessity. Taussig was struck by the bluntness of Bayly's saying that as soon as they passed beyond the defence of the harbour, they faced death until they returned.

They would, the admiral told them, have three main duties:

1. to destroy U-boats
2. to protect and escort merchantmen
3. to save the crews and passengers of torpedoed ships

If there was a chance of destroying a U-boat, they must take it – even if they saw men and women in lifeboats, or struggling in the water. 'To let a submarine escape in order to save life only means the loss of more lives later,' he asserted. If there was a danger of their own ship being torpedoed, they must not stop to rescue people. Survivors picked up at sea were to be kept on board the destroyers. They were not to be brought into harbour until the patrol was completed – unless there was a very special reason.

If they sighted a periscope, they were not to try to ram it, but instead to use their guns to shell it, because there was always a possibility that it was actually a decoy attached to a mine. And he told them of a ruse the U-boats sometimes employed of rigging sails when on the surface to look like sailing boats from a distance.

'When approaching a surfaced U-boat,' he said, 'approach her with the sun at your back.' Thirteen knots was the minimum speed at which they were to steam, and they must steer zig-zag courses. Full-speed runs in pursuit of U-boats could leave a ship short of fuel, and therefore unable to remain at sea for its allotted time. He proposed that their allotted time be six days. If a fuel shortage arose among any of the destroyers, they were to return to base when two-thirds of their fuel stocks had been used up.

At night, no lights were to be shown, no matches struck on deck, no searchlights used. If they had to send signals, they were to make them short, and they were to avoid as far as possible repeating the names of ships. He said that officers and crews of both nations would be treated exactly alike. And he stipulated that when more than one ship happened to be at sea together, the senior officer, whether American or British, was to take charge.

Before the Americans left Admiralty House to return to their destroyers, Admiral Bayly handed out explicit written orders, and the pairings in which he proposed the destroyers should work. As far as possible the USS *Wadsworth* was to be paired with the USS *McDougal*, the USS *Conyngham* with the USS *Davis*, and the USS *Porter* with the USS *Wainright*. As well as the six American destroyers, there were eight British destroyers on a short stay at Queenstown. These were the M class ships HMS *Magic*, HMS *Narwhal*, HMS *Peyton*, HMS *Parthian*, HMS *Marne* and HMS *Mary Rose*; and two R class destroyers, HMS *Sapedon* and HMS *Rigorous*.

Bayly's plain, direct speaking impressed the Americans. Taussig's reaction was, 'I think all of us will be able to get along with him without any difficulty or friction.' Lieutenant-Commander Zogbaum who, like

Taussig, later became an admiral, told the writer Keble Chatterton that he thought Admiral Bayly's frankness in his opening remarks 'laid the foundation stone of the fine spirit which was ever present in the Queenstown Command throughout the war'.

Blunt and often impatient Bayly certainly was, and small talk was not his forte. He was more interested in action than in words. He was now in command of an international force, and though in some quarters he was thought of as being notoriously difficult, cantankerous and of not getting on with people he disliked, he had qualities that inspired the imagination and the loyalty of those who served with him.

'As grim and strict as a Prussian,' one American destroyer officer said of him later. 'But very just, and runs things in a way that secures all our imagination.' Bayly could be tactful, and was generously endowed with common sense. These two attributes, added to his intelligence and his tactical knowledge, and because he truly *wanted* the two navies to pull together, resulted in the likelihood of friction being nullified.

On the Sunday afternoon, Taussig and three other destroyer captains were invited to Consul Wesley Frost's house for tea. Frost arranged for jaunting cars to meet them at the pier. On the way to the Frosts' home they picked up Evans and his wife. Taussig found the jaunting car uncomfortable, but at the Frosts' home he was much taken by their two-year-old daughter who showed off her toy doll.

Within days, depth charge racks were installed in the American destroyers at Haulbowline dockyard, and the ships' tall topmasts were removed to lower their silhouettes and decrease their distance of visibility from searching eyes on U-boats. The ships also unloaded most of their surplus stores to lessen their draft and make them slightly less vulnerable to mines.

In due course they were given the 'dazzle painting' treatment that had been invented by the marine painter and designer Lieutenant Norman Wilkinson, RN. He had come up with the idea of distorting the periscope view of a ship by painting its hull with high contrast unrelated shapes, thus breaking up her form and confusing U-boat officers as to the course she was steering.

Admiral Sims wrote to Admiral Bayly on 8 May saying:

You will, I am sure, find our officers more than willing to carry out your orders and instructions, and to cooperate with your forces as completely as their present inexperience in this peculiar warfare will allow.

My aide, Lieut.-Commander Babcock, reports them enthusiastically grateful over the reception you have given them, and anxious to be of the maximum service to the common cause.

Bayly, impressed by Sims' graciousness, wrote to the American admiral saying that he did not consider that he was in charge of two different kinds of destroyers, or that there was any reason to make a difference. 'We are all one here,' he said, 'and an order is sent out to such destroyer as is in any particular place, whether she is American or English.'

Though under the overall command of Admiral Sims, the American destroyers at Queenstown were under the operational control of Admiral Bayly whose command extended over 25,000 square miles, covering the Western Approaches as far as 20 degrees west, the entire Irish coast, the Irish Sea, and the south-western entry to the English Channel. Bayly was constantly aware that the sea lines of communication with countries all over the world converged in the narrow approaches to Ireland and Britain, and were crowded with merchant ships – the prime targets of German U-boats.

Sims' first operation order issued on 29 April, six days before the destroyers arrived, gave instructions that the US destroyer force commander (Sims) was to be 'informed periodically of military services performed'. He sent copies of it to: the Secretary of the Navy; Admiral Bayly; the First Sea Lord of the Admiralty; the US naval attachés in London and Paris, and to all the ships under his command. All official routine correspondence was to be eliminated, and particular heed given to the physical condition of the personnel. In the absence of US supply vessels, the destroyers would receive necessary supplies and repairs 'by direct request on British Headquarters, Queenstown'. Two destroyer tenders, mother-ships, arrived from America in due course.

Bayly, knowing there was much that the Americans were unfamiliar with in what he called 'this different kind of fighting', planned that the US destroyers work a schedule of each ship spending six consecutive days at sea, followed by two days in port. The captains coming in off patrol were to report to him at Admiralty House at 10 o'clock on the morning following their arrival back. He wanted to know from them what they had seen and done, what their views and problems were; and he wanted to learn from them. He also wanted to give them the chance to relax, perhaps stay the night in Admiralty House, sleeping in a comfortable bed that wasn't heaving and rocking to the violent rhythms of the sea. He arranged for the American radio operators and signals officers to be given instructions in the coding and decoding practices in the Royal Navy. And he took the opportunity of getting 'Evans of the *Broke*' to talk to them of his experiences in British destroyers.

20

FIRST PATROL

At 2 o'clock on the afternoon of Tuesday 8 May, 1917, the *Wadsworth* set out on her first patrol. Evans and a Royal Navy radio expert, Lieutenant Alston, were on board. Alston was seasick for the entire four days he was at sea, recovering only when they went into Bantry Bay. They went in past Dursey Island and Black Ball Head, Bear Island and Whiddy Island, and landed him in the town shortly after eight o'clock on Saturday morning 12 May. Evans, who had an appointment back at Queenstown, also disembarked at Bantry.

He later described Taussig as 'full of brains and go', and said he was very much impressed by the American. He was struck, too, by the Queenstown Command operation, and before he left he said to Vice-Admiral Bayly, 'I had quite made up my mind that the Dover Patrol did more sea time and running than in any other command. However, I take my hat off to your ships … I hope some day that I may have the honour to serve under you, sir.' He got that chance when Admiral Bayly's flagship HMS *Adventure* was replaced by the cruiser HMS *Active* with Evans as captain. Evans became a rear-admiral in 1928, and was raised to the peerage in 1945 as 1st Baron Mountevans.

On the way into Bantry Bay, the *Wadsworth* passed four ships that had been torpedoed, towed into Bearhaven and grounded. They were being patched up so that they could be towed to Queenstown for permanent repairs in the dockyard.

The USS *McDougal*, the destroyer with which the *Wadsworth* had been paired for this first patrol, was already at anchor in Bearhaven ahead of them when the *Wadsworth* came out from Bantry having landed Alston and Evans. Taussig steered his destroyer in through the east entrance, easing between Lonehort Point, and the Roancarrigmore lighthouse. The *Wadsworth* left Bearhaven again at 8.30 on Monday morning of 14 May, and went back to her patrol station. They passed four other destroyers from their squadron, the *Porter*, *Wainright*, *Davis* and *Conyngham*, all coming in after six consecutive days at sea.

Taussig thought that six days was too long a period to keep up the strain of a vigilant lookout such as was required by all hands. It was particularly taxing when for days on end they lived in a world of fog and mist and rain and wind and waves and spray and salt-stung eyes, and perhaps snow and sleet as well. And, of course, danger. The executive officer of one of the American destroyers would tell his wife that they 'fussed a bit when, expecting two or three comfortable days in port, we got chased out [by Admiral Bayly] on short notice into a raging gale outside'.

The Americans' first patrol was fatiguing, a harsh introduction to new sea duties for the *Wadsworth*'s captain and crew. There were false alarms, such as when a lookout spotted a 'periscope' which, on investigation, turned out to be nothing more threatening than a floating boat hook. Spars in the water were occasionally mistaken for something much more ominous. Nevertheless the crew went to general quarters at least half a dozen times on sighting suspicious objects.

Taussig, his officers and crew were on a steep learning curve. They grasped such facts that a periscope could protrude anything from 3 feet to just 6 inches above the surface – when its object glass would be almost awash – and for as short a duration as ten or fifteen seconds; they learned that they might encounter a dummy periscope with a mine attached to it, primed to explode if rammed; they were taught that they might encounter a booby-trapped lifeboat. They were instructed about the tactic of circling at speed around a sinking ship before going in to pick up survivors, and that zig-zagging should be done irregularly, so as not to be predictable.

Steaming in varying directions over the patrol area instead of doing geometrically regular sweeps from one end to another and thereby allowing the U-boat to calculate where the patrol ship would be at any given time was of the utmost importance, as was knowing that at night, if the background was dark, a U-boat could approach within 500 yards without being seen. 'A submarine's conning tower seen in the dark might look like a small boat,' one of the British officers at Admiralty House told them. 'And the hour of morning twilight is reckoned to be the most dangerous hour of all.'

And then there were the depth charges. They had to remember that a depth charge's sinking rate was 6½ feet a second, and the radius of destruction 70 feet. Contact with the enemy depended largely upon chance.

The *Wadsworth* came across several plodding cargo ships being escorted by sloops, drifting empty lifeboats, and much floating wreckage. And on 11 May they escorted, until it got dark, a lone merchantman bound for Liverpool.

Almost as soon as the *Wadsworth* put to sea from Bearhaven after refuelling, Admiral Bayly sent Taussig a wireless message ordering him to escort the 14,000-ton former Cunard liner *Tuscania*, which was doing duty as a troopship. The *Tuscania* hammered along at a brisk 15 knots while Taussig drove the *Wadsworth* ahead of her, zig-zagging at 20 knots. The destroyer had to plough through flotsam, thread a way through a fleet of fishing trawlers in fading daylight, and evade an empty lifeboat. They finally handed over the *Tuscania* to the British destroyer HMS *Peyton* at a quarter past eleven that night.

The following morning, 15 May, they escorted a Liverpool-bound ship loaded with ammunition. 'Not a pleasant occupation,' was Taussig's reaction. He knew as well as anyone that an ammunition ship would almost certainly explode if she struck a mine, or was hit by a shell or torpedo.

Increasingly strong winds and rising seas made things very un-comfortable on the *Wadsworth*. On following day, while escorting the *Orduna,* seas crashed over the forecastle, and spray came over the bridge and funnels as the *Wadsworth* forged ahead at over 15 knots. The conditions made it impossible to zig-zag. It may have entered Taussig's mind, and the minds of others, that a ship's back could break if driven too hard in turbulent seas. The forces exerted on the metal hulls were tremendous. With squalls raging at maximum intensity, hail, sleet, biting cold whining winds swept down from the Arctic. Everything below decks swimming in water, deck seams parting, water streaming in through hatchway cracks – these became the norms when the weather was dirty, which was very often.

The *Orduna* had fifty American Red Cross nurses on board. They were going to Europe to help deal with the carnage on the battlefields. The girls waved small American flags to the men on the destroyer whenever the *Wadsworth* drew near.

The *Cork Examiner*'s first mention of the American destroyer flotilla's arrival in Ireland wasn't until Thursday 17 May, 1917. The first mention in the *Irish Independent* was on the same day – it appeared near the bottom of page 3 in the second column under the heading WAR AT SEA. A Press Association War Specials report said: 'The Admiralty states "A flotilla of US destroyers has recently arrived in this country to cooperate with our naval forces."' In mentioning Rear-Admiral Sims, the Admiralty release said he was 'in daily touch with the Chief of the Naval Staff. The services which the US vessels are rendering to the Allied cause are of the greatest value and are deeply appreciated.' On 18 May the *Cork Examiner* again noted the destroyers' arrival, describing the ships as 'business-like, grim-looking torpedo-boat destroyers'.

By the time the *Wadsworth* returned to Queenstown on 19 May from her first patrol, six additional American destroyers had already arrived from the United States. They had put into Queenstown on 17 May led by Commander Charles Courtney in the USS *Renown*, and anchored in Monkstown Bay. The other five destroyers in Courtney's division were: *Jacob Jones, Ericsson, Tucker, Winslow* and *Cassin*. They, too, had had a rough passage on the Atlantic, but, as they acknowledged, at least the sea was behind them all the way.

They'd soon experience what it was like to leave a snug berth tied to a buoy in harbour, and head out on patrol through a gale and lashing rain. They, like Taussig and all the personnel in Eighth Division, and all those destined to come after them, would become familiar with the rugged south and south-west coast of Ireland, and would come to know the names and location of such places as Mizen Head, Crookhaven, Roaringwater Bay, the Fastnet Rock, Cape Clear, Sheep's Head, Galley Cove, Toe Head Bay, Galley Head, the Old Head of Kinsale, Man of War Cove, Daunt's Rock, Ram Head, Mine Head, Helvick Head, Hook Head, the Saltee Islands, Carnsore Point, the Tuskar Rock, and so many others.

On 19 May Admiral Sims arrived in Queenstown from London. He was warmly greeted by Bayly on the platform of the local railway station as he stepped down out of the train. The American met all his destroyer captains, and to them he emphasised the need for efficiency, and for preserving the best of relations with the British authorities at the Queenstown base. There was an absolute need, he said, for total cooperation with their British counterparts, and the best joint result could and would come through Admiral Bayly directing the employment of the American destroyers. Sims impressed upon his officers that they and their men were pioneers, and that he was delighted with and proud of them. He stayed at Admiralty House for the whole of his short visit.

21

A DECENT MAN BANISHED

Four days after the second American destroyer flotilla arrived at Queenstown, the bottom dropped out of American Consul Wesley Frost's world. He received a devastating letter from the American embassy in London informing him that he was being removed from his job. He immediately sent a copy of that letter to the Secretary of State in Washington, accompanied by 'the most earnest and emphatic protest of which I am capable'.

He was distraught, deeply conscious of how serious was 'this impeachment of my capacity to exercise my profession'. He was angered as well as dismayed. In his letter to the Secretary of State, he said, 'It seems incredible that I should have been accused without specification, tried without opportunity to know of the charge, and severely chastised without consultation with my superiors in the consular service … I did not suppose there to be a civilised government in the world under which a commissioned official in active service could be convicted by secret fiat without any open confrontation with his accusers, or the possibility of a syllable in self defence.'

Frost went immediately to London to see Ambassador Page. His meeting with Page on 23 May convinced him that the ambassador had 'acted with the utmost sincerity … and with a kindly feeling towards myself'. Page told him that his removal from office was 'due to the suggestion of officers of the British Admiralty at Queenstown'. The consul was 'too much astounded to ask for the manner and particulars of the charge against my discretion'.

Frost had worked himself to physical and mental exhaustion by his humane efforts at the time of the *Lusitania* sinking, and during the time he was in Queenstown, he diligently and painstakingly gathered information for the State Department about the U-boat campaign. Not knowing specifically what was now alleged against him, he had to resort to conjecture – 'since the facts are withheld, I cannot allege'.

His guess was that information copies of two of his despatches to the State Department in Washington – communication numbers 371 and 375 – were shown to Admiral Sims, and that Sims resented the publicity that had been given to the arrival of the Eighth Division destroyers at Queenstown. Frost also thought that Sims had taken exception to 'my setting down in writing, even to the department, the facts as to the movements of these vessels'.

He speculated that 'filled with the ideals of inexperience, Admiral Sims proceeded to Queenstown, and mentioned what he regarded as my dereliction to some of the British naval staff, probably eliciting some informal expression to the effect that the consul had indeed been rather prying as to naval matters.' He conjectured that Sims 'apparently urged upon the ambassador that my immediate removal was desired by the Admiralty, and actually induced the ambassador to act drastically without any investigation – thus heaping humiliation and hardship, both physical and financial, upon me at a time when I might least have been expected to be able to support them'.

He went on to say that there seemed to have arisen an absurd belief on the part of the embassy and Admiral Sims that because Frost had chronicled the reception that the Eighth Division destroyers received in Queenstown, and had participated in it in his official capacity, he was in some way responsible for it. Nothing, he pointed out, could be further from the truth.

On the Sunday prior to the destroyers' arrival, Admiralty House had told him about their impending appearance. Frost had contacted Admiral Bayly's secretary, saying that he hoped at some stage to meet, informally, the officers of the flotilla. Two or three days later Admiral

Bayly had asked the consul to come to Admiralty House as he wished to talk with him about the ships' imminent arrival. Frost and Vice-Consul Sherman met the admiral, and Frost repeated to Bayly that his wish was to meet the American officers on an informal basis. Sherman heard him saying it.

'A little later in the day,' Frost told the Secretary of State, 'the admiral appeared to get the impression, from the advent of the chief British official photographer and his kinema man, that some authority at London wished some little display to be made; and accordingly he asked me, in a very kind note, if I would waive my rank and meet the officers at the pier, to which I of course assented.' Frost did exactly what Admiral Bayly asked him to do – photographs taken at the time prove it.

The Admiralty arranged for three motor cars to be at the pier when the American officers stepped ashore. Wesley Frost had procured the loan of an additional two cars from an American living in the area. While Frost was at lunch on the day of the destroyers' arrival, a telephone message was received at the office saying that the Lord Mayor of Cork was motoring down to meet and officially welcome to Ireland the American ships' officers. As soon as he'd received the message, Frost had phoned the mayor's office, hoping to put the Lord Mayor off. But he was too late – the mayor was already on his way. The consul had then phoned Admiralty House and told Admiral Bayly's secretary of these developments. It was suggested that the civic authorities should meet the officers at the consulate. As Frost's letter to the Secretary of State said, 'Throughout all the day's proceedings, and the calls at Cork on the following day, I was entirely an inert factor, never making a single proposal, and being merely moved about, *at the Admiral's convenience*, as a useful lay figure [Italics added].'

How Admiral Sims might have received the impression that ceremonial features were of Frost's contriving was wholly inexplicable to Frost. He took up the matter of the view expressed to him by

Admiral Sims that Frost had been injudicious in writing his despatch No. 375. The admiral had said that the consul's mail to the department might be tampered with, 'or that my subordinates might be corrupt'.

In his Protest against Removal (which is how he captioned his letter), Frost maintained that no comment was called for from him on the justifiability of his reporting to his superiors all the information in his possession 'both on general principles, and in responses to the various instructions on the matter'. And about the employees of the consulate, he said that they were selected and retained 'in no small measure expressly for their loyalty and discretion'.

He allowed that some naval officers might have spontaneously said they found the acquisition and use by him of naval information to be 'unpleasant', because, as he put it, it was 'highly natural for British naval men to have the feeling referred to'. It will be remembered that Sims had already encountered his own problems with the Royal Navy's reluctance to share information and it was only Admiral Jellicoe's intervention that had brought about the release of the information he needed (see chapter 19). Frost pointed out to the Secretary of State that, to the British mind, many perfectly insignificant matters which no one in America would dream of keeping confidential, were regarded as sacrosanct.

About his ongoing investigation of what he called 'submarine cases', he said that he had had to intrude necessarily into matters 'either actually or fanciedly confidential, and the intrusion *has been usually automatically resented, in fine disregard of the purpose it has been designed to serve* [Italics added]'. Not all the Royal Navy officers with whom he had contact in Queenstown behaved in an obstructive way, and he admitted that in many cases officers had shown a helpfulness and patience which, considering their bias, had evoked his admiration and gratitude. But there were 'atrocious cases of insult', which he accepted as part of the day's work, because he conceived it to be his duty as an official, and as an American, to give the department 'the uncoloured facts as to the submarine warfare'.

Regarding Admiral Sims' view of statements made in despatch No. 375 to the State Department as 'betraying facts otherwise locked in the breast of the Admiralty', Frost pointed out that naval news was almost universally accessible in Queenstown and Cork; that 'scores of men who detest England conscientiously' were in regular possession of all such facts as those in his despatch No. 375. He instanced the arrival of the first American destroyer flotilla, Taussig's Eighth Division, which was known about in Queenstown for at least a fortnight beforehand. (This suggested a leak from the USA.) An eighteen-year-old girl had given him his first news of the flotilla at a private afternoon tea party and all the other persons in the room already knew of it.

In the case of important submarine disasters, the streets of Queens-town and Cork usually hummed with the facts 'long before the Admiralty lets me know them'. And as for ship movements, businessmen and fishermen at all parts of the coast were well informed at all times. For British naval men to complain at lack of discretion on his part, he wrote, 'is calling attention to a mote in my eye, while a beam is in their own. And for Admiral Sims to undertake to punish me so unmercifully for reporting facts in my dispatches to the Secretary of State, is merely an evidence of rudimentary ignorance of local conditions.'

Towards the end of his letter, Frost wrote about being physically and financially destitute. He pointed out that with a plethora of able consuls unassigned at that particular time, it was an especially unfavourable time to detach a consul from his post. The manner of his removal, he said, was such as to humiliate him fatally among the officers and gentlemen who were his friends in Queenstown. The cause of his removal, he thought, 'like all other Admiralty information, is probably already club talk here, and I am quitting as furtively as possible the post where I have spent three of the best years of any man's life.'

He asked that the department carry out an immediate and thorough investigation, 'to culminate in my reinstatement at Queenstown, or some such measure which will notify all parties concerned, in a manner as striking as has been my summary ejection from my post, that a consul is not a marionette to be cavalierly moved at the caprice of the first naval man who happens to step ashore in his district'. Wesley Frost was never reinstated at Queenstown.

Whether or not it was solely Admiral Sims who was the main catalyst in the withdrawal from Queenstown of an able, compassionate and cool consul, a man whose moral courage enabled him to stake career, happiness, his whole future on his judgement of what he thought was right and worthwhile, what is undeniable is that his removal was shabby in the extreme. It reflected no credit on anyone who contributed to dishonouring an honourable man. Wesley Frost was gone from Queenstown before June 1917 ended.

Frank Lyon Polk, Counsellor for the Department of State, subsequently wrote about 'the extent and importance of the submarine atrocities which the American consul at Queenstown was called upon to report to our government', and said that a cablegram of commendation was sent to the consul by the Secretary of State, 'an unusual expression of merit in the consular service'. In an Introduction to the book, *German Submarine Warfare*, which Frost published in 1918, Polk said that Frost's health had suffered severely under the strain, and that the consul 'was brought back to America upon furlough, and was assigned to duty in the Department of State'. Almost as soon as he arrived back in the United States, the committee on public information recruited Frost. He was sent out on tours throughout the west, south-west and mid-west as a speaker in the government's information campaign. 'The success of his tours,' Polk reported, 'was immediate and striking.'

Life during the remaining days of the war still had one additional cruel blow to deliver to Wesley Frost. It centred on a former German cargo ship whose name was changed from *Kamilla Rickmers* to USS *Ticonderoga* when the United States government seized her in 1917 and handed her over to the US Navy. On the night of 29/30 September 1918, when 1,700 miles out from America's Atlantic coast, the *Ticonderoga* was attacked by U-152. Gunfire from the U-boat set the ship ablaze, killed several men, and wrecked the ship's forward gun as well as her wireless equipment. U-152 then torpedoed the ship and shelled her even as she sank.

Only one lifeboat survived the shellfire. All the others were either demolished, swamped, or sank upon launching. The one lifeboat to get away drifted in the Atlantic for four days before the British vessel *Moorish Prince* rescued the twenty-four men who were still alive. There were 237 people on board the *Ticonderoga*: 112 sailors and 101 soldiers died. It was the greatest combat loss of life on any US Navy ship during the First World War. Among those who died was Wesley Frost's only brother, Lieutenant Cleveland T. Frost.

The consul who, up to halfway through 1917, had done so much in caring for survivors of torpedoed ships and who, as instructed, had gathered so much evidence about submarine warfare, lost his brother in the same merciless conflict with which he himself had been so intimately associated.

He remained in the consular service, and was at Marseilles from 1921 to 1924, followed by another four years as consul general in the same city. From 1928 to 1935 he was consul general at Montreal. From 1941 to 1942 he was US minister to Paraguay, and was appointed ambassador for the period 1942–1944. Wesley Frost died on 9 January 1968. He was eighty-four.

22

POINSETT PRINGLE

The day after Wesley Frost received the letter telling him of his removal from Queenstown, the USS *Melville*, Destroyer Tender No. 2, arrived in the harbour. She was a 417-foot-long vessel of 7,150 tons displacement. Her captain on commissioning was Commander Henry B. Price. He had been promoted to captain by the time he brought the ship into Queenstown.

The *Dixie*, another tender, at 6,144 tons and 391 feet long, was not only smaller than the *Melville* but was also older. Leaving Philadelphia on 31 May 1917, she arrived off Cork Harbour on 12 June under the command of forty-four-year-old Captain Joel Roberts Poinsett Pringle.

The Germans had mined the approaches to the harbour on the nights preceding the arrivals of both ships. Clearly they had been provided with important secret information relating to ship movements. Bayly was unsure whether the leak was from Queenstown, or from cables sent from the USA to Germany. He thought it likely that it was a combination of the two.

In the *Melville*'s case, the minesweepers did a successful sweeping job late on the night prior to her arrival, and in due course she passed the Daunt Rock lightship and headed safely in past Roche's Point.

At six o'clock on the morning of 12 June, the vessels on mine-sweeping duty, although they had swept the approaches the night before, discovered that a U-boat must have come back again before dawn and laid more mines. The *Dixie* was due in from the Atlantic at 8 a.m. When Admiral Bayly heard this he sent a signal to the *Dixie* telling her that she should remain outside the harbour until the mines had been swept. Shortly afterwards, looking out his bedroom window, he saw the *Dixie* about to enter the stretch of water where the mines were! He was powerless to do anything to stop her. All he could do was wait for the explosion. He kept peering out at the American ship. What words had her captain not understood? The signal had been explicit – remain *outside*. The *Dixie* kept on coming. And then, after what seemed like an age, she was *in* and heading towards the Spit. No explosion.

When Captain Pringle met Admiral Bayly later, the American officer explained that the signal hadn't reached him until he had already entered the mined area. He then had two options – turn his ship around and go back out, or continue. Because it was high water, he took a chance and pressed ahead. It was the kind of decision Bayly himself would have made.

By 5 July 1915 there were thirty-four American destroyers at Queenstown, as well as the two destroyer tenders, the *Melville* and the *Dixie*. The *Melville* was the principal destroyer mother ship. Pringle was senior to the *Melville*'s commanding officer, Captain Price, so at Queenstown, because the *Melville* was the larger of the destroyer tenders, they swapped commands. Additionally, the *Melville* was named Admiral Sims' flagship, though the admiral was based in London.

As Sims' biographer Elting E. Morison pointed out, Queenstown, of all the bases, was closest to Sims' heart. 'Indeed for all the men who worked out of this port during the war,' Morison wrote, 'the duty was one of the great experiences of their lives … Queenstown was the one place where [Sims] could intimately see and hear and touch the realities of the war that at times seemed so remote in London.'

Sims appointed Pringle his chief-of-staff at Queenstown, which was the centre of convoying activity for all the trade from the Americas and as such was vital to Allied success. Sims himself had to spend the greater part of his time at his headquarters, or attending the Allied

Naval Council in Paris, and therefore felt it necessary that he should be represented at Queenstown 'by a man of marked ability'. This was why he chose Pringle. The state of readiness and efficiency in which supplies, maintenance and administration were constantly maintained was, Sims said, the strongest possible evidence of Captain Pringle's ability.

Admiral Bayly appointed Pringle his United States chief-of-staff, entering him on the navy list. Never before had a foreign naval officer appeared in the navy list of a Royal Navy admiral's staff. For one man to hold these dual appointments was an irregular arrangement, but Pringle succeeded in making it work. Sims later paid him the compliment of saying that the fact that the Americans cooperated so harmoniously and so successfully with the British was chiefly due to Pringle.

Pringle was both disciplinarian and diplomat, and was seen as being both fair and frank. He had a cool brain and a well-balanced, powerful mind. Bayly thought him the best man to handle the American destroyer captains 'to get the most work out of them, and to keep them smiling'. He said Pringle would have been an outstanding officer in any navy, and described the American as his *beau ideal* of what a naval officer should be.

Pringle, sophisticated and consummately skilled, had an intuitive wisdom that was called into play in serving his two masters: the individualistic Bayly and the equally individualistic Sims. He fully understood and accepted that when the American destroyers went to sea, they were under the orders of the senior officer of the group while on duty, whether that officer was British or American, but before the American destroyer captains reported to Admiral Bayly when they came in from patrol, they had first to report to Pringle aboard the *Melville*, a procedure with which Bayly was fully in agreement.

The British admiral dealt with the American officers directly regarding their orders and duties, but Pringle, as the senior American naval officer at Queenstown, took care of all disciplinary matters. To emphasise and encourage the best possible cooperation between the two navies, Admiral Bayly arranged to have a piece of timber (it was a signal board from a sunken German U-boat) fitted with prominent brass lettering that said PULL TOGETHER. With the agreement of Captain Pringle, it was mounted on the topside bulkhead of the *Melville,* inboard of the starboard gangway main deck platform.

With so many ships now stationed in the harbour, there were thousands of American sailors whose recreational and entertainment requirements had to be catered for. The sailors wanted a library. They wanted to watch films. They wanted to see plays and musicals, comedies and variety shows, vaudeville. Queenstown had no variety theatre, no opera house, no large clubs to which the men could go to relax, drink, eat, play pool and be entertained.

Cork was the nearest city, and the train service was handy, cheap and frequent. At first the American sailors used the rail link with great frequency when they came in from the sea. British author Keble Chatterton said the Americans went to Cork 'rather than remain among the dismal unattractiveness of Queenstown'.

American uniforms and American accents became commonplace in the Cork streets, shops, restaurants, entertainment places and public houses. Cork businesspeople did very well out of the Yanks – for a while. The sailors had money to spend, and willingly spent it. They were attracted to the Irish girls who in turn were attracted to the Americans' easy-going charm and willingness to spend their dollars. Cork businesses benefited to the tune of an estimated £4,000 a week.

It was inevitable that jealousies would arise among some Irish males. Taunts led to arguments, the arguments led to brawls, and within a short while serious fights between American sailors and Irishmen broke out in the streets of Cork city. The level of violence was so serious that it was believed there were political undertones and motivations behind fights in which groups of Irishmen attacked American sailors.

When Admiral Sims wrote his prize-winning *The Victory at Sea* in 1920, he said that during the nearly two years which the American naval forces spent in Europe, only one element in the population showed them any hostility or even unfriendliness. He decided to inform Americans 'just what kind of treatment their brave sailors met with at the hands of the [*sic*] Sinn Féin in Ireland'. While the people of Queenstown, he said, 'received our men with genuine Irish cordiality', hostility in certain quarters became evident.

He characterised the members of Sinn Féin as being not only disloyal, but openly pro-German, and said that the fact that the American sailors did not openly manifest a hatred of Great Britain and a love of Germany infuriated the Sinn Féin faction. Sims said that when the Sinn Féin element saw their sweethearts deserting them for the American boys, 'their hitherto suppressed anger took the form of overt acts'. According to him, occasionally an American sailor would be brought from Cork to Queenstown in a condition that demanded pressing medical attention, having 'suddenly been set upon … and beaten into a state of insensibility'. He told of American sailors severely injured, stoned, at the receiving end of hostile demonstrations in cinemas and theatres, with some bloody battles taking place.

He downplayed the incident of a priest in St Colman's cathedral in Queenstown denouncing the American sailors as vandals and betrayers of Irish womanhood, and said that Bishop Browne had subsequently called upon Admiral Bayly and apologised for the insult.

Sims revealed that it had been discovered that blacksmiths on board the *Melville* were surreptitiously making weapons for sailors who were intent on doing battle with Sinn Féiners. 'So for the whole period of our stay in Queenstown our sailors were compelled to keep away from the dangerous city.'

Admiral Bayly was his usual decisive self when it came to dealing with the Cork brawls. Upon hearing that knuckle-dusters were being manufactured on board the *Melville*, he imposed a ban on any British or American officers or ratings going within 3 miles of Cork city. The Lord Mayor of Cork and a number of the city's prominent businessmen asked for and were granted a meeting with Admiral Bayly. The Lord

Mayor read a prepared apology, and then asked the admiral if he would rescind his order prohibiting visits to the city, so that American and British sailors might once again be allowed to go there.

Bayly asked if the people who had fomented the fights were still at large, and was told that they were. He then asked the Lord Mayor if he could guarantee that the sailors of both countries would not in future be insulted and attacked. The lord mayor said he couldn't give such a guarantee. And when his answer to the question as to whether Sinn Féin volunteers had assembled in Cork the previous Sunday, contrary to the law, was 'Yes', Bayly told him bluntly that the order would not be rescinded. End of meeting.

When Secretary of the Navy Josephus Daniels wrote a book about the American navy in the First World War, he referred to 'the one regrettable incident at Cork where an unruly element attacked some of our sailors', and said it was recognised as an exception. He highlighted the people's 'feeling of friendship for our sailors and our country', and described 'the great Irish people who received us with open arms, and showed hospitality and cordiality towards our forces domiciled in that country'.

By August 1917 Admiral Bayly at Queenstown was receiving daily situation reports from London about U-boats. They emanated from Room 40 at the Admiralty, and were based on intercepted wireless traffic between U-boats at sea and their land-based headquarters.

It had been discovered in 1904 that by a technique of cross-intersection by listening receiver stations (DF, or direction finding), the position of a transmitter could be located. Although the wireless traffic was enciphered, the British had broken the German codes before the end of November 1914. When U-boats used radio to announce their departures, and followed up by daily giving their position (for obvious reasons they transmitted on the surface at night), as well as outlining the progress of their patrols (number of ships attacked, etc.), the intercepts were deciphered in Room 40, and the results sent to the appropriate sources. Hence Admiral Bayly was receiving valuable information on the numbers of U-boats at sea, and where they were heading.

The mining by German U-boats of approaches to busy ports was of continuous concern. The approaches to Cork Harbour were repeatedly mined, and the minesweepers could never afford to relax in the hazardous work of trying to ensure that the approaches were clear. The U-boat minelayers worked on the principle that minefields laid in the entrance and exit channels of heavy-traffic ports stood a good chance of sinking some of that traffic. Even if that wasn't achieved, the likely existence of a minefield would at the very least give rise to anxiety, might even cause the withdrawal of some vessels from patrol duties in order to carry out minesweeping duties.

The German E-mines carried 330-pound charges, and had the Hertz horn method of detonation. They accounted for many hundreds of ships over the course of the war.

The auxiliary patrol was always on the lookout for new minefields, and when any were discovered and swept, the information was broadcast, using a special code. When Room 40 in the Old Buildings of the Admiralty discovered that the German wireless intelligence service had broken the code used by the British when broadcasting information about minefields that had been discovered and swept, a plot was hatched which, if it worked, might yield valuable information.

Room 40 had realised that when the Germans decoded the intercepts of British information about minefields, they acted on it by sending U-boat minelayers back to the swept minefields to lay more mines. On 15 June 1917, minesweepers from Admiral Bayly's Queenstown Command discovered a minefield between Hook Point and Swine head – the 3½ mile wide entrance to Waterford Harbour. Bayly instructed them not to sweep up the mines in this particular instance. He then issued instructions to close the port of Waterford to all shipping for a fortnight. Next he broadcast a fake signal saying that a minefield had been discovered off the entrance to Waterford

Harbour, that it had been swept, and that the area was now clear of all German mines.

The Germans fell for it. They intercepted Bayly's signal, not knowing it was a hoax. On 31 July they sent UC-44 from Heligoland to lay more mines between Hook Point and Swine Head. Whenever moored mines were laid, the minelaying vessel was required to record the exact co-ordinates for each, so that any future craft belonging to the navy laying the mines would know where not to venture. *Kapitanleutnant* Kurt Tebbenjohanns of the UC-44 was therefore given the co-ordinates recorded by the earlier minelayer. It enabled him, he thought, to go back and lay new mines in roughly, not exactly, the same places.

Just after midnight on 4 August, after lying on the seabed until the tide turned, Tebbenjohanns was in the conning tower as the UC-44 began laying the mines in the approaches to Waterford Harbour. The first four had been dropped, and the U-boat was proceeding to her next position when suddenly a shattering explosion ripped through the submarine, slamming the captain against the periscope and stunning him. The two men with him in the conning tower were hurled about by the force of the explosion. Water gushed through the massive hole in the submarine's pressure hull when the mine blew up. She began to sink, went down rapidly and hit the seabed hard, 90 feet below the surface.

Tebbenjohanns, using the speaking tube, tried to contact the rest of the crew. He received no reply. The water rose very quickly in the conning tower. The situation of the three men in the confined space was desperate. Tebbenjohanns told the other two that there was just one slim chance to escape, and that was through the conning tower hatch. If they could get it open, and get out, they just might make it to the surface. He struggled with the wheel of the locking mechanism and then, after a tense struggle, and with the water rising towards their shins, he managed to turn the wheel slowly. When the mechanism disengaged, with a great *whoosh* the cover flew open. The three men were shot out of the conning tower by the pressure, and upwards towards the surface.

It was a pitch-black night, and when they broke the surface, at first they could see nothing. After a while they saw a light in the distance but couldn't make any headway when they tried to swim towards it. The current was too strong, so they decided to swim towards the opposite shore, which was shrouded in darkness. The three became separated, but kept shouting to each other. Then they lost contact, their yelled cries for help sounding weaker the further apart they were carried by the tide. Tebbenjohanns eventually couldn't hear them anymore. He never saw them again. Two Irishmen in a rowing boat found Tebbenjohanns about an hour-and-a-half later. They had heard the explosion, and had pulled out from the shore to search.

Interrogated in Waterford later in the morning, Tebbenjohanns was made a prisoner of war. He didn't learn until well after the war was ended that he had been the victim of a deliberate ruse set up by Bayly and Room 40. Between them they had managed to lure a U-boat into an area where the water was shallow enough for the Royal Navy to recover and examine her papers and equipment. UC-44 had hit one of nine mines laid on 14 June by UC-42.

The Royal Navy raised UC-44 in September. On board they found a valuable set of secret documents and detailed charts laying out the precise courses that U-boats should steer to pass safely through the 'impregnable' Dover Strait. Not only did the charts show the courses, they also indicated the depths at which the submarines should travel, together with dates, times and tides. Bayly sent the charts and documents to the Admiralty in London. The bodies of the German crew of the U-boat were buried, and the U-boat itself was destroyed.

On 10 September, a mine – one of her own – sank another U-boat just off the Irish coast. This time it was UC-42. She went down close to the Daunt Rock lightship outside Roche's Point. Divers were sent down to her, too, and additional valuable books and documents were recovered.

At Queenstown, the American sailors still urgently needed recreational facilities. A building was eventually identified and earmarked as a suitable place to rent and refurbish. Then a site was found on which additional huts could be erected – *if* the requisite money was forthcoming. A group of American businessmen in London contributed about £4,000 and work began straight away.

On 25 August 1917 the US Naval Men's Club was opened in Queenstown. The long wooden huts on the Baths Quay below Harbour Row had all the things the men needed: a library, restaurant, a facility for showing films, a performance stage, dormitory, billiards and pool tables and showers. A slipway was built at Whitepoint to facilitate traffic between there and Haulbowline, a skating rink up on Sunny Heights, and another next to the Water's Edge or Five-Foot Way. The Americans were thus well catered for.

The British sailors, in contrast, hadn't even a hut where they could go to relax. Their desire and need of a meeting place ashore were underlined by the opening of the new American facilities. The problem again was money. There was none available. And then the YMCA came to the rescue. They erected a hut for use by the Royal Navy sailors.

23

CONVOYS

The Admiralty continually refused to adopt a tactic that, if introduced, would have protected Britain's merchant fleet against U-boats far more effectively than the antisubmarine patrol system. Historian Sir Basil Liddell Hart in his *A History of the World War, 1914-1918* said, 'The blindest blunder of the British Admiralty was in opposing the introduction of the convoy system in face of the futility of other methods to avert the close-looming disaster.' The Admiralty had condemned the convoy system as unworkable.

Towards the end of April 1917, however, the tonnage figures for shipping lost to German submarines were so catastrophic that on the 26 April Rear-Admiral Sir Alexander Duff, assistant chief of the naval staff and head of the Admiralty's antisubmarine division, sent a memo to the First Sea Lord, Admiral Jellicoe, saying, 'It seems to me evident that the time has arrived when we must be ready to introduce a comprehensive scheme of convoy at any moment.'

Convoy literally meant groups of ships sailing in company under naval protection, and the system had been used successfully since medieval times. But in January 1917 the operations division of the Admiralty war staff had written: 'Wherever possible, vessels should sail singly ... convoy *is not recommended in any area where submarine attack is a possibility*. It is evident that the larger the number of ships forming the convoy, the greater is the chance of a submarine being able to attack successfully, and the greater the difficulty of the escort in preventing such an attack. [Italics added]'

Jellicoe was sceptical about Duff's 26 April recommendation on the necessity of being ready to adopt convoy 'at any moment', but he nevertheless supported it.

Von Holtzendorff's December 1916 prediction that an average rate of sinking of 600,000 tons of shipping per month would bring peace before harvest time, was coming dangerously close to being proved right. The average for February, March and April reached 602,000 tons per month – at a cost of only ten U-boats. Two of those had blown up on their own mines, and another had run aground and been arrested by the Dutch. Only seven U-boats were accounted for by British antisubmarine action.

Neutral countries began to avoid trading with Britain, and in many cases neutral merchant ships refused to go to sea from British ports. For Britain the picture could hardly have been bleaker; if things didn't dramatically change for the better, disaster was about to descend. Between 120 and 145 ocean-going ships were traversing the U-boat danger zone each week – rich pickings.

Bayly's opinion was that it was difficult to see why the introduction of convoys was so long delayed. 'We used [the convoy] over and over again in past wars,' he said, 'and found it especially useful when … the enemy gave up using their battle fleets and went for the destruction of commerce … Considering, therefore, the benefits we derived from the convoy system in the past, no objection to it should have been allowed to be sustained in the Great War.'

Of course conditions had changed enormously since the time of those 'past wars'. Convoy as a protection of sailing ships against attack by other sailing ships was an entirely different matter from convoy as a protection of steamships from torpedo attack by an invisible underwater enemy. Bayly pointed out that a U-boat found it very difficult to position itself favourably to attack a convoy, because of the constant threat and danger posed by the escorts.

There had been an outstandingly successful use of the system of convoy in the coal trade to France which most urgently needed one and a half million tons of coal each month from Britain to keep her armament factories in full production. After the U-boats took a heavy toll of the cross-channel colliers during the last quarter of 1916, a convoy system was instituted, though it was not officially designated 'convoy', but 'controlled sailings'. But convoy was what it was.

Eight hundred colliers (some of them sailing ships) crossed the English Channel each month. A few armed trawlers escorted convoys of about forty-five colliers at a time; occasionally destroyers of the Dover Patrol took part. The loss rate once the 'controlled sailings' were introduced was only 0.19 per cent. Between March and August 1917, nearly 9,000 vessels crossed the Channel under convoy. Only fourteen ships were lost. The figures were remarkable by any standard. Jellicoe's view of what he called 'the extraordinary immunity of the French coal trade convoy' was that it was probably due to the short passage, which enabled most of the distance to be traversed at night, and to the ships being of light draft.

But although the question of introducing ocean convoys had been discussed and considered several times, and a younger group of officers led by Commander Richard Henderson, who had been in charge of the French coal convoys since the beginning, favoured it, the senior men at the Admiralty had continued to advance what they believed to be compelling reasons for rejecting the move. These were the reasons they gave:

- There were not enough suitable ships available for escort duty through the U-boat danger zone.
- Ships in convoy would present a more desirable target than ships steaming alone. (In February, when President Wilson had asked Secretary of the Navy Josephus Daniels why the British had not adopted the convoy system, Daniels told him that the Admiralty thought dispersing ships over wide tracts of ocean a sounder principle).
- Convoys having to travel at the speed of the slowest ship in the

group would make all of the ships in that group more vulnerable to attack by submarines, and would cause delays in the delivering of essential cargos.

- Large groups of ships arriving at ports at the same time would cause congestion, and jam the unloading facilities.
- Merchant ship masters would be incapable of maintaining station in groups of ships – in convoys, the keeping of close and accurate station would be absolutely essential.
- Convoys entering minefields would in all probability result in a number of ships being sunk whereas, in the case of ships sailing alone, the first ship to hit a mine would reveal the existence of the minefield, and thus act as a warning to other vessels to skirt it.
- Convoy wouldn't work as protection against an *invisible* enemy.

Added to all of the above, senior Admiralty officers held that the Royal Navy's role should always be based on taking the offensive. They looked upon trade protection as a purely *defensive* role. So, in the circumstances and context, Jellicoe's scepticism was understandable.

Regarding the perceived difficulty that merchant ship masters would have in station-keeping in a convoy, a surprising degree of support for that perception came from merchant ship masters themselves. In February 1917, ten masters of ships in the port of London attended a meeting with officers from the Admiralty's naval staff. The masters were asked if they thought their ships could keep station in a twelve-to-twenty-ship convoy. They said 'No'. They believed that the biggest number of merchant ships that would be able to manoeuvre together safely was three. Uppermost in their minds were problems that they felt sure would arise when sailing in darkened ships, in close formation, in fog and mist, zig-zagging by day and by night, and course alterations. They cited the inexperience of many of their deck officers as most of the experienced ones had joined the Royal Naval Reserve; the shortage of seasoned engineers; the difficulties in making speed adjustments, and the poor quality of bunker coal, which made keeping to a consistent speed almost impossible. Other ship masters, when consulted later, confirmed the views expressed by those who had conferred with the naval staff.

Admiral Sims was strongly in favour of the use of convoy. Moreover he insisted that convoy was a genuinely *offensive* measure because, as he explained, it forced the U-boats to fight at a disadvantage. For weeks after his arrival in London he urged the Admiralty to adopt the convoy system. He knew that under the patrol system, each patrolling vessel was assigned a square area of sea measuring 30 miles by 30 miles, and had to steam back and forth endlessly within that box, looking for U-boats.

But the overall U-boat danger zone was so enormous, and the number of destroyers and sloops available for patrol duties was so small, that the total zone was incapable of being covered effectively. The patrol ships only rarely came across submarines, for the simple reason that on the approach of a patrolling destroyer or sloop, a U-boat had merely to submerge out of sight and remain under the surface until the patrol craft passed. Then the U-boat could surface again and resume its hunt for ships to sink. There was an abundance of ships coming through the sea lanes.

Sims, and others who thought like him, believed that it was necessary to 'make the submarines come to the antisubmarine vessels and fight, in order to get merchantmen'. Convoy, he maintained, was the way to accomplish that. He argued that it was the patrol system that was the defensive measure. The power of his persuasion helped to accelerate the Admiralty's decision to think again. That, plus sheer necessity, finally forced them on 1 May reluctantly to try an experimental convoy, as had been suggested by Duff and Henderson.

It was to sail from Gibraltar to Britain, and the convoy commodore was Captain H. C. Lockyer. Naval officers made the preparatory arrangements, briefed the masters of the seventeen ships about the role of the commodore, the signals that would be used which the masters had to obey, the convoy formation, the number of columns, the position of each ship, and the speed the convoy would have to keep to. On the evening of 10 May, the convoy of 8-knot merchant ships left Gibraltar with an escort force comprising a couple of Q-ships and three armed yachts. They all arrived safely in the UK on 20 May. Success!

No submarine had been sighted, not a single ship was lost, and the merchant shipmasters had proved to themselves, as well as to other doubters, that they could well handle the practicalities of station-keeping. They kept station excellently, contending with fog and heavy weather; they understood the signals and complied with them.

It was, Sims believed, one of the great decisive moments of the war. On 21 May the Admiralty voted to adopt the ocean convoy system for merchant shipping on the North Atlantic. Sims naturally supported the decision wholeheartedly, contending that any other choice by the Admiralty would almost certainly lead to a German victory. A convoy room was set up at the Admiralty with Vice-Admiral Duff in charge. From August on, co-ordinating the movements of American convoys with the numerous other Allied convoys was Captain Byron A. Long, USN, who had been sent to London by the US Navy Department.

The schedule, rendezvous and escorts for troop ships would be decided upon in London, and the convoys run with the precision of a railway timetable. One entire wall of the convoy room was covered by a huge map on which were plotted daily the movements of convoys, and the positions of U-boats as supplied by Room 40. Because the U-boats at sea were constantly communicating with each other, the assiduously listening operators at the British wireless intercept stations were intercepting valuable information. Radio-direction finders were also sources of invaluable intelligence. If a convoy was seen to be sailing towards the known position of a U-boat, it could, by wireless communication, be routed away from the lurking submarine.

When lone merchantmen steamed unescorted into the Western Approaches along the shipping lanes on their way to Britain with vital supplies, they were easy targets. A U-boat captain had only to station his boat astride one of the lanes, and ship after ship would turn up, easy targets to attack. The picture changed utterly when a group of ships (an escorted convoy) arrived, zig-zagging quickly past the U-boat's position, giving the submarine only a fleeting opportunity to launch a torpedo, before the ships were out of range. Another convoy might not come by for days, leaving the U-boat in the interim without a ship to sink. Convoy eliminated the steady supply of individual targets.

The Admiralty's decision to adopt convoy was generally well received in the United States, though the chief of naval operations, Admiral Benson, at first expressed reservations. When the effectiveness of convoy was eventually conclusively proved, and both the Americans and the Allies embraced its adoption, differences in emphasis arose almost immediately. The Admiralty in London, backed unreservedly by Sims, decreed that the priority had to be the protection of the merchant shipping bringing desperately needed supplies to Britain. The outcome of the German U-boat offensive against merchant shipping would definitely influence who the winner of the war would be.

The Americans had a different priority from that of the British – their prime concern was the protection of transports carrying American forces to Europe. Sims was informed accordingly. Secretary of the Navy Daniels fired off a missive to him. 'Be certain,' Daniels told Sims, 'to detail an adequate convoy of destroyers, and in making the detail, bear in mind that everything is secondary to having a sufficient number to insure protection of American troops.'

Initially the convoy system applied only to inward bound ships, and vessels capable of 16 knots or more continued to sail independently. Because there was a perceived danger that German surface raiders might attack convoys in mid ocean, it was decided that the ocean convoys coming in from the Atlantic should be escorted by pre-dreadnought battleships or cruisers, as far east as the U-boat danger zone. At the outward limits of the danger zone, about 300 miles out to sea, convoy escorts based on Queenstown would take over. But it wasn't just ocean-going merchant ships in the Western Approaches that attracted the attention of the U-boats. An *Irish Independent* story on 28 May 1917 was headlined: **Fishing Fleets Sunk**. Its sub-head said: **7 Baltimore Boats Down – Threats by the Germans**. The story also carried a 'Passed by the Censor' note beneath its headlines.

The report stated that German submarines were 'destroying Irish fishing fleets from Kenmare to Howth, says our Skibbereen correspondent, writing on May 4, and many boats are at the bottom of the sea'. It went on to say that the Baltimore fleet of eighty boats had set out at around seven o'clock on the evening of 3 May, and four hours later seven of them were sunk about 20 miles off Baltimore. The fishermen were allegedly given minutes to launch their punts, and were not allowed to take the boats' oars with them. One of the fishermen was reported to have said to the U-boat commander, 'I thought the Germans would do nothing to the Irish – that ye liked us.' The reply he was reported to have received was, 'You don't know the Germans yet.'

The report concluded with this paragraph: 'The Germans said they had sunk the Kinsale fleet, and, off Dunmore, the Waterford boats, boasting that they would have every Irish fishing boat sunk in a month, while one of the crew is stated to have said that they intended shelling villages shortly.' It was said in the course of the story that the boats that escaped 'brought back abundance of mackerel, but did not venture out again, so that the whole fleet is "put out of action", meaning a loss of thousands to the fisherfolk'.

How much of the story is fabrication or innocent exaggeration is impossible to say but it probably contains at least grains of truth. A reported appearance of a British patrol boat (most likely a sloop out of Queenstown), causing the U-boat to submerge, rings true.

The following day the *Independent* picked up a story from London's *Daily Mail*. In the Irish newspaper the story was headlined: **U Boats**

& Irish Fishermen. Its sub-head, complete with quotation marks, was: 'You Are Feeding Our Enemies'.

It was about a reported attack by a U-boat on a motor fishing boat off the south-west coast of Ireland, and told how the motor boat was on her way to her home port laden with fish when 'a rifle shot rang out, the arm of the man on the tiller immediately spurting blood'. A voice from the U-boat reportedly said, 'I'll teach you to stop when you are told.' According to the *Daily Mail*, the motor boat's owner answered, 'We heard no order to stop. We are Irish – we are doing nothing to you.'

'I don't care what you are,' the U-boat commander's response was said to have been. 'The next time you are ordered to stop, do so. Further, you are feeding our enemies, the English.'

As the *Irish Independent* related it, 'The Germans then took what fish they wanted, throwing the rest overboard with some valuable lines and a sail, and smashed the sparking plug and other parts of the engine, but the commander said he would not destroy the boat then, as he had other use for it.' The 'other use' was to transfer to it a number of Irish fishermen who had been captured and kept on board the submarine. The *Independent*'s account concluded with these words, 'the owner was ordered to use a pair of sweeps to row them ashore. The *Daily Mail* added that an intense hatred of the pirates had replaced any other feeling the people of the district may have ever had.

The first eastbound Atlantic convoy of twelve ships sailed from Hampton Roads, Virginia, on 24 June 1917. Its ocean escort was the cruiser *Roxburgh*. On arrival in the U-boat danger zone, eight destroyers from Queenstown met the convoy. The absence of the destroyers from Queenstown temporarily reduced the port's force to ten destroyers and ten sloops. The absence was prolonged because the destroyers were retained at St Nazaire until the empty transports were ready to put to sea again, whereupon the Queenstown based destroyers had to escort them back out into the Atlantic to the edge of the U-boat danger zone.

Convoys from North America thereafter left from New York, Hampton Roads, Sidney (Cape Breton) and Halifax. They sailed on regular schedules according to a strict timetable. For example, convoys sailed from Hampton Roads every eight days, from New York every eight days, and so on. Convoy soon established itself as by far the most effective way to foil the U-boats, to thwart them in their objective of sinking Allied shipping. No one was more conscious of this than the resourceful and imaginative Commodore Bauer, Germany's U-boat chief.

Karl Dönitz, a young U-boat commander in the First World War and who, in the Second World War, brilliantly directed Germany's U-boat fleet and became the German navy's Commander-in-Chief, wrote that the introduction of the convoy system in 1917 'robbed the U-boat of its opportunity to become a decisive factor. The oceans at once became bare and empty; for long periods at a time the U-boats, operating individually, would see nothing at all; and then suddenly up would loom a huge concourse of ships ... surrounded by a strong escort of warships of all types ... The lone U-boat might well sink one or two of the ships, or even several, but that was a poor percentage of the whole. The convoy would steam on.'

Dwelling on the fact that quite obviously U-boats operating singly had little chance of numerical success against escorted convoys, Bauer, in 1917, tried to figure out if there might be an alternative and more effective way to use these submersible torpedo boats. He began to formulate a plan for using *concentrations* of U-boats against the concentrations of surface vessels crossing the ocean under escort. His idea was to appoint a flotilla commander who would operate from a specially adapted cruiser U-boat. This officer would tactically direct and co-ordinate the attacks of the other U-boats in the group, communicating with them by wireless. Bauer's was a brilliant innovative idea. It was one that led to the formation of the enormously successful

Wolf Packs in the Second World War – for which Karl Dönitz would be given most of the credit. But in 1917 Bauer's idea was rejected, as indeed was Bauer himself. In June the German navy appointed a new U-boat chief, Andreas Michelsen, to replace him.

A typical eastbound convoy crossing could take between fifteen and twenty days, the ships steaming roughly a thousand yards apart, and covering an overall sea area of approximately 10 square miles. From the second week of August 1917 onwards, convoys were introduced for the westbound voyages of ships that in most cases were empty, in ballast – a condition that often rendered them almost unmanageable in heavy weather. The assembly ports for the outward-bound convoys were: Queenstown, Buncrana, Milford, Devonport and Falmouth.

In the case of Queenstown, the freighters assembled inside the harbour. Convoys sailing from Queenstown were given identifying letters and numbers, such as: OQ 11 – the 'O' standing for 'Outward', the 'Q' standing for 'Queenstown', and the '11' meaning that it was the eleventh such convoy.

Destroyers or sloops escorted these convoys to beyond the far western edge of the U-boat danger zone, and there the merchantmen would disperse. Those same destroyers or sloops would then meet an incoming convoy at a pre-arranged rendezvous and time, and escort it through the danger zone. It was essential that merchant ships adhere strictly to the convoy instructions they were issued with.

The adoption of convoy brought about a significant change in the war at sea. Between the time of its adoption and the end of September, 1,288 out of 1,306 ships arrived safely in Britain, coming in through the Western Approaches in eighty-three separate convoys. And of the 789 ships that sailed outwards in fifty-five convoys, just two ships were sunk.

Convoy proved itself the great tactic against the U-boat. By the end of the war, it was calculated that Admiral Bayly in Queenstown supplied 91 per cent of the escort for 360 convoys. The success of convoy in countering the attacks of U-boats that had been operating far out to sea, forced a decision to withdraw them from the deep Atlantic and to operate closer to the coasts. They were sent to the areas where incoming convoys dispersed, or outward-bound convoys assembled.

24

COLLISION

Commander Taussig made many visits to Admiralty House, invariably on foot, trudging up the demanding slopes from the pier. Apart from the occasions when he was obliged to report there before going out on patrol, or at 10 o'clock on the mornings after returning from patrol, there were many times he went to the house at the invitation of Admiral Bayly. Sometimes he was invited for tea, sometimes for dinner, sometimes to play tip-and-run or tennis, sometimes just to take it easy, to sit in the quietness and colour of the Sloop Garden and relax or, if he wished, to pick gooseberries, known in local slang as goozahs. The visits to Admiralty House were always memorable and habitually enjoyable. Although he and Bayly came from totally different backgrounds with different histories, cultures and habits, and from different navies, Queenstown in those days of war brought the two men close and mutually respectful of each other.

One afternoon Taussig went to the low redbrick railway station by the Deepwater Quay and took the train to Cork. It was his first visit to the city since the fleeting stop-off at the City Hall the day after the Eighth Division arrived from Boston. The scenery he saw from his carriage windows once they came to Rushbrooke and onwards past Carrigaloe and Fota Island he described as 'pleasing', and the carriage itself was 'comfortable'. He and a fellow officer went by jaunting car to the cricket ground on the Mardyke where a crowd of about 3,000 had turned out to watch a baseball game between teams from the USS

Melville and the USS *Trippe*. The gate receipts that day were handed over to the Red Cross.

The peaceful scene and the atmosphere in the picturesque little ground were such that Taussig found it 'hard to realise that a war was going on anywhere. It seemed like a dream that only a few days ago I was out at sea with my ship shooting at a hostile submarine.' He and his colleague took in a variety show at the Palace Theatre later, and then caught the last train back to Queenstown at 11.20 p.m. The following day it would be back to sea again, out to where such messages as 'Torpedoed, am sinking fast' came all too frequently.

One officer said that when that happened you looked at the chart and decided whether to go to the rescue at full speed, or to stay on your patrol line and let some ship that was closer to the incident deal with it. If the alarm was sounded on your own ship, you grabbed mechanically for your life-jacket, binoculars, pistol, wool coat, and jumped to your station, whether what the lookout had seen was really a periscope or a stick floating out of the water.

On the night of 20 August the sloop HMS *Zinnia* and the American destroyer USS *Benham* were about 14 miles off the south coast in squally weather, when a serious accident occurred. The *Benham* was altering course having come out of a rain squall. Suddenly there, right in front of her, was the sloop. The two ships were unable to avoid each other, and collided. The *Zinnia*'s bow was badly twisted by the impact, but it was the *Benham* that was the more seriously damaged. Her after fire-room, engine room, auxiliary engine room and after magazine all flooded, and she looked as if she might sink. The *Zinnia* went alongside and took off most of the destroyer's crew, then began to tow the crippled destroyer towards Queenstown. When they finally arrived into the harbour, the *Benham* had to be taken into the dry dock at Haulbowline for extensive major repairs.

The incident called for a court of enquiry. It was held on Admiral Bayly's flagship HMS *Adventure* on 23 August. President of the court was Captain Hyde, RN, of the *Adventure*. The two other members were American – Commander Taussig and Lieutenant-Commander Platt. After all the witnesses and their evidence were examined, blame was assigned to no one.

The hard slog of escort duty went unceasingly on, and the punishing weather when it came made life on the escort ships unavoidably miserable. On 29 August Taussig wrote in his diary:

At midnight the barometer suddenly began to fall by leaps and bounds. The wind gradually increased and the seas kept getting bigger. By one o'clock Monday afternoon the barometer had fallen to 28.78, and a half hour later the storm broke with its full strength.

The rain came down in torrents and the spray from the top of the waves was blinding.

There was no danger from submarine attacks in this kind of weather and the vessels of the convoy could not possibly keep together. So I ordered the destroyers by wireless to part company with the convoy and to make the best of their way to the rendezvous at noon the next day where we were to meet the morning convoy.

I gave orders for them to heave to if necessary and not risk damaging their ships.

I headed on a course that brought the sea on our starboard quarter and kept the engines running over for 8 knots. Although the waves were tremendous, we rode them easily, but with much discomfort owing to the motion of the ship. I think I never saw it blow harder.

Bayly as Commander-in-Chief was aware of the strain under which the destroyer crews worked. He recorded that except under good weather conditions it was almost impossible for the personnel of the destroyers to get any rest at sea, even when off duty. He said he was amazed at the way all the small craft kept going in spite of all the discomforts and continuous work. He was very proud of what they accomplished, the many acts of bravery they performed and the good seamanship they displayed.

On 11 September 1917 a communication went out from Admiral Bayly's office addressed to:

The Commanding Officers
US Ships and *DIXIE*;
H.M.S *Adventure*
And all US Destroyers and H.M. Sloops Based on Queenstown

Its text was as follows:

MEMORANDUM

(1)   The Commander-in-Chief wishes to congratulate Commanding Officers on the ability, quickness of decision and willingness that they have shown in their duties of attacking submarines and protecting trade. These duties have been new to all and have had to be learned from the beginning and the greatest credit is due for the results.

(2)   The winter is approaching with storms and thick weather; the enemy shows an intention to strike harder and more often; but I feel perfect confidence in those who are working with me that we shall wear him down and utterly defeat him in the face of all difficulties. It has been an asset of the greatest value that the two Navies have worked together with such perfect confidence in each other and with that friendship which mutual respect alone can produce.

Lewis Bayly
Vice-Admiral
Commander-in-Chief

On 7 November Commander Taussig heard from Admiral Sims that he was being detached from command of the USS *Wadsworth* from 15 November and would be returning to the United States where he was to report to the Navy Department, Bureau of Navigation, and await further orders. In the months between the time he had led his Eighth Division destroyers across the Atlantic to Queenstown, Taussig had steamed over 37,000 miles on patrol and escort duties. He had spent 143 days at sea between April and the end of the first week in November.

On the morning of Saturday 17 November he went up the hill to Admiralty House for the last time, to say goodbye to Admiral Bayly, Miss Voysey and the staff officers. He told the admiral that he had never operated under pleasanter or more satisfactory conditions. Bayly said the Americans had done splendidly, and when Taussig thanked him, the admiral replied that he would not have said the Americans had done well if he had not really thought so.

As Taussig was leaving him, Bayly said, 'Tell your father that I say you have done splendidly.' As the American left Admiralty House, Miss Voysey handed him a small photograph of Bayly, saying that her uncle (who hated publicity and who had very few photographs taken), had said that Taussig and one brother officer were the only ones to whom photographs were to be given.

Writing about Bayly later in his diary, Taussig said he thought the only two times the admiral had shaken hands with him were when they had first met, and when they were saying goodbye. 'Although [Bayly] undoubtedly feels deeply, he does not show it, and his manner belies the cordiality which I really believe he feels,' Taussig wrote. He referred to the 'honour and pleasure' of serving under Bayly, 'a most efficient officer … It has been a pleasure to serve under him directly, and in the numerous times when we have had to use our own initiative in deciding knotty questions, he has backed us to the limit and made commendatory remarks on our reports.'

He also said that Admiral Bayly had always treated him 'with the utmost courtesy and consideration'. Bayly he saw as 'a man with the highest sense of duty – of a naturally retiring disposition but of quick perception and action … He is very religious, and I have often been impressed when talking with him that he is a Christian in heart and action.'

Late in the afternoon when the USS *Bridge*, the ship on which Taussig was returning to America, steamed down the harbour, it was accompanied as far as the boom by the admiral's green barge. The admiral, Miss Voysey, and Captain Pringle waved goodbye as the *Bridge* went out through the boom gate towards Roche's Point, and the start of the long voyage home.

On the same afternoon, with a westbound convoy about to leave the harbour, the destroyer escorts were manoeuvring into position when the lookout, Coxswain David D. Loomis, on the USS *Fanning* caught a momentary sight of a periscope poking up through the sea's surface about 400 yards away and three points on the port bow. It appeared to be moving towards the convoy.

The *Fanning*, commanded by Lieutenant A. S. Carpender, immediately turned and raced for the spot where the periscope had showed. When she got there, depth charges were dropped. They went off close enough to the U-boat to damage her and she surfaced. She had sustained jammed diving rudders, broken oil pipes and a wrecked motor. Another destroyer of the escort group, the USS *Nicholson*, under Commander Berrien, immediately pounced upon her. With the U-58 trying to escape, the *Nicholson* fired at her with her stern gun. The *Fanning* turned and came back at the submarine, firing at the enemy with her forward gun.

The captain and crew of U-58 realised that they were defeated and they poured out onto the U-boat's deck at 4.30 p.m., hands raised in surrender. It was only eighteen minutes after Loomis had first seen the periscope. But the Germans had no intention of allowing the Americans to capture the U-boat. Two of the crew were sent below and opened the seacocks and scuttled U-58. As she began to sink, *Kapitanleutnant* Gustav Amberger and his crew jumped into the sea and started to swim towards the *Fanning*. Ropes and life-belts were thrown to them from the destroyer. All but one of the U-boat men were hauled out of the sea. The one who couldn't make it began to sink, and two of the *Fanning*'s crew jumped into the water to help him. They managed to get him onto the deck of the destroyer, but Fritz Glinder never regained consciousness.

The *Fanning*'s crew gave the others coffee and cigarettes and a change of clothing. The destroyer took them into Queenstown and put them on board the *Melville*. As the Germans left the *Fanning*, they cheered their captor/rescuers. They were subsequently transferred to one of the Royal Navy sloops and taken to Milford Haven and handed over to the military. They spent the rest of the war in a prisoner of war camp. Admiral Bayly went on board the *Fanning* to congratulate Lieutenant Carpender and his crew on their achievement. Carpender was subsequently awarded the DSO. The *Fanning* was the only American destroyer to sink a U-boat.

25

JELLICOE JETTISONED

A week before Christmas 1917 the American troop transport *Leviathan*, carrying around 8,000 American troops and bound for Liverpool, was due to be met by Queenstown-based escorts. The *Leviathan*'s captain was given three separate rendezvous points; one was south-west of Ireland, the second was south of Ireland, and the third was off Tuskar Rock, which is 7 miles off the south-east tip of Ireland. He was specifically instructed to pass his ship through each rendezvous.

Admiral Bayly assigned eight American destroyers to meet the enormous transport and to escort her. He sent them first to the rendezvous furthest out in the Atlantic, about 300 miles offshore. Having waited there for two hours, the patrol leader sent a wireless message back to Admiralty House at Queenstown saying that because the *Leviathan* hadn't turned up, the destroyers were now going to proceed to the next rendezvous. But the no-show was repeated. Bayly considered the situation serious enough to warrant going out in his flagship to investigate.

The *Leviathan*, with thousands of US servicemen on board, was a three-funnel liner, and at the time was the largest ship in the world – 54,282 tons gross, 950 feet long. She had a top speed of 26 knots. Formerly the German (Hamburg-America Line) SS *Vaterland,* she had been taken over by the United States Shipping Board in June of 1917 and, in September, renamed *Leviathan* by US President Woodrow Wilson. She eventually carried up to 14,000 troops at a time on each crossing.

Bayly said it was clear to him that if the *Leviathan* were torpedoed and sunk, so many of the troops would lose their lives at sea that American women would rise up and attempt to force a stop to American troops being sent overseas – at least until the waters of the Western Approaches were made absolutely safe. This was why he went out from Queenstown in his flagship, then commanded by Captain Gordon Campbell of Q-ship fame.

In filthy weather, with seas coming over their forecastles and sweeping their decks, the escorts at last picked up the *Leviathan* on 22 December near Tuskar Rock and escorted her to the Mersey. Bayly, furious with the *Leviathan*'s behaviour, requested Admiral Sims to investigate why the liner had failed to turn up at the first two rendezvous points. Sims' investigation revealed that *Leviathan*'s captain had, off his own bat, deliberately avoided the rendezvous points, considering them too dangerous. He was relieved of his command when the ship returned to the USA.

As the year drew towards its end, the Admiralty decided to lay a new deep mine barrier from the south coast of England to the coast of France to close off the English Channel to the U-boats. It would force them to take the long and time-consuming north-about route to reach the Atlantic. They selected the 20-mile stretch of water between Folkestone and Cap Gris Nez. Work began in November and continued into December. The mines were laid at depths of between 30 and 100 feet below low water. The minefield itself – 20 parallel lines of mines – was to be 6 miles wide. It was vividly illuminated along its length by night patrols using flares and searchlights to force any U-boats that might try to traverse the channel on the surface during the hours of darkness to dive into the mines. Before it was even completed, three U-boats sank in the Dover Barrage.

Another and even bigger minefield was planned to seal the northern exits of the North Sea to U-boats. It would extend 250 miles from the Orkneys to Hardanger Fjord south of Bergen in

Norway. But the laying of that gigantic barrage would have to wait until 1918.

But for the German navy, the number of U-boats lost during the last five months of 1917 made grim accounting – 37 of their submarines lost in action, many of them sunk by mines. Nevertheless in December of 1917, U-boats sank over 399,000 tons of Allied shipping. And, if that figure wasn't sobering enough, there was the bald and terrible fact that in the first six months of unrestricted U-boat warfare, 3,850,000 tons of shipping were destroyed. The shipbuilding industry was unable to keep pace with such a rate of loss.

Adding his contribution to the tonnage figures was Dohna-Schlodien in the commerce raider *Moewe*. On 2 December, 650 miles west by north from the Fastnet, the *Moewe* at last showed up in Admiral Bayly's area of command. She captured the British 8,618-ton *Voltaire*, outward bound to the United States, made prisoners of her entire crew of ninety, and sank her. The *Moewe* ended the war by being the most successful of all the German armed merchant ships, sinking thirty-eight vessels – almost 175,000 tons.

By the end of December 1917, nearly 180,000 American troops had landed in Europe, but the New Year was to see an astonishing increase in the numbers: 40,000 arrived in January; 104,000 in April; 317,000 in July. By November 1918 nearly 2,000,000 American servicemen had been brought safely across the North Atlantic and landed in France. Not one transport was sunk, not one life lost. American ships carried 44 per cent of the two million men sent to the battlefields of Europe and American warships escorted 62 per cent of them.

When the First Sea Lord of the Admiralty, Sir John Jellicoe, arrived at his office on Christmas Eve, 1917, he found a letter on his desk. It was from the administrative controller of the Royal Navy, the former railway manager who had become, in turn, British Army Inspector General (with an honorary rank of major general), and then First Lord of the Admiralty (with the honorary rank of vice-admiral) – Sir Eric Geddes. Geddes was a classic bureaucrat and as such was looked upon with disfavour by many senior officers of the Royal Navy. But he had shown himself to be a strong advocate of the convoy system from the outset, whereas Jellicoe had been reluctant about its adoption.

The letter from Geddes to Jellicoe was short and couched in bureaucratic officialese, saying that 'after very careful consideration' Geddes had come to conclusion that a change was desirable in the post of First Sea Lord. There was the obligatory claim of regret and reluctance, but essentially the letter was letting Jellicoe know that he was being fired.

26

NEAR END AND END
OF DESTROYERS

From his many trips up and down, in and out and around the harbour in his green barge with his long-time coxswain Chief Petty Officer Wade at the helm, Admiral Bayly knew well what Queenstown looked like from the water. He knew its shape, its outline, its silhouette, with its terraces rising one above the other from the waterfront up to the top of the ridge on which it was built. He was very familiar with the Deepwater Quay, and the low redbrick pile of the railway station behind it; the impressive high-gabled villas on the Low Road; the elegant bulk of the Italian-looking Royal Cork Yacht Club building with its round-topped windows, right on the water's edge; the plain and stately buildings of Westbourne Place; the Promenade with its massive Russian cannon pointing towards Spike; the Market House built by Smith-Barry, and the pack-of-cards rooftops of steep Barrack Hill climbing behind it; the grey bulk of St Colman's cathedral, the smaller brown bulk of the Protestant church, and the Scot's Presbyterian church at the bottom of Spy Hill; the splendid curved row of houses called the Crescent; the piers and wharves and Custom House, the Baths Quay with its soaring chimney, East Hill slanting upwards and eastwards, and the Holy Ground with its little boat harbour just off the shingle beach.

He knew the waters of the harbour, the mooring buoys in Cove Road and elsewhere, the anchorages, Spike Island and Rocky Island, Haulbowline with its Martello tower on the high end of the island,

and its big dockyard at the eastern end, Whitepoint and Black Point, Ringaskiddy, Monkstown, Glenbrook and Passage, and up past Rushbrooke, Carrigaloe and Marina Point, Lough Mahon with Little Island on its eastern shore, Douglas and Blackrock on its western shore, and then up the narrower stretch of the Lee to Cork City. He knew these things because it was important to him to know them, because he was the consummate professional seaman.

The American destroyers had generally come over six at a time. In each instance Bayly sent the new arrivals to sea for four days soon after they reached Queenstown. He wanted their officers and crews to study the weather conditions and the tides off the south coast, to learn certain points of land so that they would be better equipped to deal with thick and stormy weather. They soon became accustomed to the shuddering impacts on their destroyers' narrow hulls as they headed into steep seas at over 15 knots, with wind-whipped cold salt spray showering over the bridge and funnels. When the weather was particularly thick, leaving Cork Harbour could be a tricky and unpleasant experience, with the buoys hard to pick up. But the sound signals at the Spit and Roche's Point and on the Daunt Rock lightship were good guides.

Because the system of signalling used by the US Navy differed from that used by the Royal Navy, Bayly ensured that each American destroyer was given a Royal Navy signalman who stayed on board for the first month of service, so that good communication would come into effect without undue delay. The admiral laid down that every two hours each destroyer's position was to be passed to the wireless operator, so that in the event of the destroyer being shelled or torpedoed or rammed, and the navigator perhaps killed, the wireless operator would be able to send an SOS giving accurate co-ordinates.

Of the eighty-strong US destroyer force sent to Europe between 1917 and the end of 1918, Admiral Bayly listed forty-seven based at Queenstown. The *Jacob Jones,* one of Commander Taussig's Eighth Division, was among the first six to arrive. She was one of the 30-knot

Tucker Class ships – 1,090 tons displacement, twin-screw, with a crew of ninety-nine. She'd been commissioned on 10 February 1916. When she arrived in Queenstown Lieutenant-Commander David W. Bagley captained her. In July she rescued forty-four survivors from the British merchantman SS *Valetta*. Later in the same month a ship that the *Jacob Jones* was escorting, was sunk right in front of her. The destroyer picked twenty-five men out of the sea that time. Throughout August and September, and well into October, she escorted cargo vessels through the U-boat danger zone.

One of the destroyers that had come across the Atlantic with her on 7 May 1917 was the USS *Cassin*, captained by Lieutenant-Commander W. N. Vernou. On 15 October the *Cassin* had her stern blown off by a torpedo when she was 20 miles south of Mine Head, County Wexford. There was a heavy sea running and a strong south-west wind. The after part of the ship was wrecked; her rudder was blown off; a gun was blown overboard; one crew member was killed and nine were wounded.

The man who died was Gunner's Mate Osmond K. Ingram, and he would ultimately have a destroyer named after him, that ship becoming the first American naval vessel ever to be named after an enlisted man. Ingram had been one of those who had spotted the track of the torpedo as it raced towards the *Cassin*. He knew that if it struck the ship at the stern where the depth charges were stacked, they would explode and sink the destroyer. He ran aft from his station at his gun and started to try to heave the depth charges into the sea. He knew that he wouldn't have a chance of surviving if he was in the stern when and if the torpedo struck that part of the *Cassin*. It did strike the stern, blew 35 feet of it off and Osmond Ingram was blown to pieces. He gave his life to save his ship and its crew.

After the explosion the *Cassin* was a mass of tangled twisted girders and plates. Because of not having a rudder, she was moving in circles and drifting to within a mile of the jagged rocks of Hook Head. An attempt was made to steer her by use of her engines. But it didn't work because the starboard engine failed. Her radio antenna had been demolished, there hadn't been any chance to send out a distress signal or call for help. Her wireless operators contrived to assemble a temporary antenna, and only then could assistance be summoned.

When Admiral Bayly at Queenstown was alerted to the *Cassin*'s plight, he ordered all available ships to go to her aid. The first ship to arrive on the scene was one of Taussig's Eighth Division destroyers, the USS *Porter*. Later that evening two British vessels turned up, the special service ship HMS *Tamaris*k, and the sloop HMS *Jessamine*. By this time it was blowing half a gale, and several attempts to get a tow-line to the *Cassin* failed. But then a young Royal Naval Reserve officer from Australia, Lieutenant Dalziel, who was serving on the *Tamarisk*, volunteered to try to get a line to the *Cassin* by boat – despite the darkness and the high wind and waves. He was successful, and until morning came, the *Tamarisk* kept the *Cassin* from going onto the rocks. The wind dropped during the morning and shortly after half-past ten another Queenstown sloop, HMS *Snowdrop*, took the *Cassin* in tow. After Herculean efforts, she was eventually brought into Queenstown.

On 19 October the *Jacob Jones* again acted as a rescue ship when the British armed merchant cruiser *Orama* was torpedoed in convoy. Commander A. W. Johnson, captain of the USS *Conyngham*, had attacked and driven off a U-boat that was stalking the convoy. He then suggested to the commanding officer of HMS *Orama* that, because of the presence of a U-boat ahead of the convoy, the convoy should change course. His recommendation was turned down, and the convoy stuck to its original course. Just before 6 p.m. the *Orama* was torpedoed on the port side opposite No. 3 hold. Black smoke billowed up, and the *Orama* listed to port and started to sink.

The two destroyers USS *Conyngham* and USS *Jacob Jones* stayed close to the *Orama*, and though it was pitch dark by the time the ship finally went down, the two escort ships rescued every one of the 478 people who had been on board the armed merchant cruiser. The *Jacob*

Jones picked up 305 of them. But the destroyer's own time was running out.

On 6 December 1917, around half-past four in the afternoon, she was west of the Scilly Isles, on her way back to Queenstown from Brest. They were about 25 miles south-east of Bishop's Rock and 20 miles east of Start Point when one of her lookouts saw the track of a torpedo off the starboard bow running towards the destroyer. The helm was put hard over and the destroyer leaned in a sharp turn, trying to get out of the way of the torpedo, but it was too late. The explosion on the starboard side just abaft the engine-room and 3 feet below the water line tore a hole in the *Jacob Jones'* oil tank, and killed a number of men instantly. It also wrecked the wireless equipment. There was no time to send out any SOS.

Very quickly the destroyer began to sink by the stern and suddenly, when the stern went underwater, her depth charges exploded, killing anyone nearby and blowing the ship to pieces. The *Jacob Jones* sank eight minutes after being torpedoed. Sixty-two men died.

The sea where the destroyer went down on that December afternoon was bitingly cold. A few survivors who had jumped overboard swam towards the three rafts and the small boat that had managed to stay afloat. On the rafts and in the boat the men huddled together in an attempt to keep warm.

The U-boat that had sunk the *Jacob Jones* was U-53, commanded by Hans Rose. Rose was respected, brave, a highly successful and much decorated U-boat commander who had taken U-53 to Newport, Rhode Island in September of 1916 where he had invited various US naval personnel to visit and inspect the U-boat. But war was war, and after leaving Rhode Island, Rose had sunk a number of ships off Nantucket Island. He had earned a reputation for humanity and fairness, frequently putting his boat at risk when ensuring that the crews of ships he had sunk had more than a fair chance of being rescued.

The torpedo that struck the *Jacob Jones* had been fired from 3,000 yards. About twenty minutes after the destroyer went down, U-53 surfaced and approached the boat and rafts. Rose ordered that two Americans who were in the water be picked up and taken aboard the submarine. He then performed another of his chivalrous acts of mercy – he sent a wireless message to Queenstown, giving the position of the boat and rafts so that ships could be directed to the area to pick up the survivors.

Around eight o'clock that night the liner *Catalina* came across the boat with some of the *Jacob Jones'* crew in it, and took them on board. The other survivors were not so lucky. They spent a freezing night in darkness until, at around 8.30 in the morning, the sloop *Camellia*, thanks to the chivalry of Hans Rose, was able to rescue them. One man died of exposure and exhaustion, a young officer named Lieutenant Kalk. No other American destroyer was sunk by U-boat.

Later in December a gale nearly claimed another American destroyer of Bayly's navy. It happened in the Bay of Biscay when the ship's rudder became jammed at hard-a-starboard and couldn't be moved. The ship fell into a deep trough and massive waves battered her every time she rolled. All her boats were smashed to small pieces, and any equipment that wasn't bolted or lashed down was swept clear off the decks. The captain went aft with a group of men to try to fix the steering gear, and one of the seamen next to him was hurled overboard by a breaking wave. If he hadn't had a rope tied around his waist, the man would have been lost. Instead he was hauled back on board.

Objectively looking at their situation, the captain privately didn't expect his ship to stay afloat. They were steaming in a huge circle, exposed to the worst that Biscay's waves and wind could hurl at them. When after a desperate struggle they got the steering gear partially fixed, they were in danger of being thrust ashore on a rock strewn coast.

The captain gave an account of the incident in *Atlantic Monthly* in 1918. He said they were drifting to leeward at a rate he hated even to guess at. There was the certainty that 'unless matters mended' they would eventually pile up on the Spanish coast which they were now quite near. Because he hadn't been able to take any sun or star sightings for several days, he didn't know within 50 miles where they were. When he eventually brought the bow around to head into the seas, he found he could just about hold her, but without making much, if any, headway. 'You cannot drive a destroyer dead into a heavy sea at full speed without bursting her in two,' he said.

The ship was running low on oil. Her commanding officer reckoned he could do one of three things – (1) let the destroyer drift, though still using up his fuel in the hope that the gale would blow itself out; (2) run into a Spanish port, or (3) run for France, which was his destination anyway, and if he couldn't make it, call by wireless for help. He chose the third option and 'jammed her into the teeth of it for all I thought she could stand'. He increased speed half a knot at a time. 'I never thought any ship could stand the bludgeoning she got. It seemed as if every rivet must shear, every frame and stanchion crush under the impact of the juggernaut seas that hurtled into her … She reared and trembled, only to bury herself again in the roaring Niagara of water.'

Below decks some compartments were awash with a foot or more of oil and water swishing about. After seemingly endless hours of struggle and danger, the ship eventually made it to the coast of France, but 25 miles from where the captain's dead reckoning told him they were. They made it safely into harbour.

27

ELEVEN, ELEVEN, ELEVEN, EIGHTEEN

In February 1918 the Dover Barrage was completed, all the 9,600 mines in place in deep parallel rows. It was hoped that it would be a death trap for any U-boat trying to get through the Dover Straits. By mid-August it had accounted for twelve German submarines, most of them destroyed with the loss of everyone on board. Men who escaped from U-boats that sank gave horrifically graphic descriptions of what took place in submarines that went to the bottom of the sea never to rise again. They told of the spreading terror in the claustrophobic, machinery-packed hulls as water gushed in through the holes ripped in the metal; of what it was like when the air pressure suddenly increased unbearably, and the batteries leaked chlorine gas. They spoke of men in the doomed U-boats who tried to commit suicide and failed when the revolvers they put to their heads, or into their mouths, wouldn't fire because of the pervasive dampness. They told of the men who managed to get out of these iron coffins, but died before they reached the surface.

Far out at sea from Queenstown the continuing success of Bayly's destroyers working as convoy escorts saw the rate of shipping losses from U-boat attacks declining steadily. In April the merchant tonnage dropped to 296,558 tons, or 139 ships. Only once more in August before the end of the war did the tonnage figure exceed 300,000. Also in April, for the first time since the opening of the unrestricted U-boat warfare campaign, the shipbuilding tonnage exceeded that of the tonnage sunk. The death-knell for Germany was sounding in the war at sea.

On 4 May 1918, Admiral Bayly sent a memorandum to the American naval forces under his command:

> On the anniversary of the arrival of the first United States men-of-war at Queenstown I wish to express my deep gratitude to the United States officers and ratings for the skill, energy and unfailing good nature which they all have consistently shown, and which qualities have so materially assisted the War by enabling ships of the Allied powers to cross the ocean in comparative freedom.
>
> To command you is an honour, to work with you is a pleasure, and to know you is to know the best traits of the Anglo-Saxon race.
>
> Lewis Bayly
> Admiral
> Commander-in-Chief

Eight days later, four American destroyers – the USS *Conyngham*, the USS *Davis*, the USS *Porter* and the USS *O'Brien* – sent out into the Atlantic from Queenstown by Admiral Bayly, met and formed an escort for an incoming convoy that included the troopship *Olympic*, laden with American servicemen. The destroyers' orders were to escort the troopship as far as the Lizard (the southernmost point of Britain). The *Olympic* was the former White Star liner that had come to the aid of HMS *Audacious* when that battleship struck a mine off Tory Island early in the war – the battleship Admiral Bayly had boarded and done his damnedest to save.

At four o'clock in the morning, with the convoy steaming through a slight sea in a light wind from the north-east, the *Olympic* suddenly came upon the U-103 on the surface about 500 yards off the starboard bow. The troopship fired three shots at the submarine, changed course, and ran at her at full speed, intending to ram. The U-boat tried to get out of the way of the huge ship, couldn't manage it, tried to submerge, but couldn't get down quickly enough. The *Olympic* slammed into her, and ripped open the U-boat's hull along the port side abaft the conning tower. The submarine remained afloat for a little over a quarter of an hour before plunging to the bottom. The survivors were rescued by the USS *Davis* and were eventually taken to Milford Haven, handed over to the military, and taken away to a prison camp for internment.

By the end of May, 650,000 American servicemen had been safely transported across the Atlantic to France. In that same month German U-boat chief Michelsen belatedly attempted to put into operation a version of his predecessor's proposal that U-boats try to attack convoys in numbers rather than singly. In some ways there could hardly have been a more suitable time to test the tactic as there was then a profusion of incoming and outward-bound convoys in the Western Approaches, thirty in all.

Michelsen ordered six U-boats to gather off the approaches to the English Channel. Between 10 and 25 May, the six U-boats were in position, with *Kapitanleutnant* Rucker in U-103 in charge. Michelsen hoped that they would decimate the convoys. They didn't.

For a start the U-boats were too widely dispersed, and only two of them managed even to sight any of the convoys. Claus Rucker's U-103 was one of them and, as already described, she was rammed and sunk by the *Olympic* on 12 May. The second submarine to make contact with a convoy – thirty-five ships with a protective screen of eight destroyers and three sloops – was U-70. All she managed to do was fire two torpedoes at one of the ships at the back of the convoy. Both missed, and the U-boat gave up.

A combination of first class intelligence from Room 40, far too much use of giveaway wireless traffic by the U-boat commanders, and general ineptitude, caused the U-boat experiment to fail – 183 ships made it safely through the danger zone. May 1918 turned out to be a black month for the U-boats. Fourteen of them were lost, a bigger total than for any other single month. But as Admiral

Sims said later, 'Until it was possible ... to find the enemy that was constantly assailing our commerce, and destroy him, it was useless to maintain that we had discovered the antisubmarine tactics which would drive this pest from the ocean for all time. Though the convoy, the mine-fields, the mystery ships, the airplane, and several other methods of fighting the under-water boat had been developed, the submarine could still utilise that one great quality of invisibility which made any one final method of attacking it such a difficult problem.'

Sims accurately called the Allied effort to destroy the submarine 'still largely a game of blind man's buff', because the Allies, in this instance, 'were deprived of one of the senses which for ages had been absolutely necessary to military operation – that of sight'. They were attempting to destroy an enemy they could not see. It is worth pointing out that the U-boat – indeed any submarine – was also blind when under the water at anything lower than periscope depth.

Even before America officially came into the war, work had begun in Europe on trying to develop a listening/detection device that would allow vessels on the surface to 'hear' a submerged submarine, to pick up its distinctive sounds. The American scientists were given copies of the hydrophone research results achieved by Allied scientists to study and work on. The upshot was that the Americans produced devices that could not alone pick up the underwater sounds, but also indicate the direction from which the sounds were coming. The British Admiralty, impressed by the superiority of the American devices, ordered quantities of them for the Royal Navy.

In America construction had begun on the building of 60-ton, 110-feet-long, wooden, 16-knot, gasoline-engined submarine chasers, known by their shortened name, subchasers. Assistant Secretary of the Navy Franklin D. Roosevelt had strongly advocated them, and their construction was a pet project of his. They were the smallest commissioned warships in the United States navy, and were soon given the nickname 'The Splinter Fleet'. They were also frequently referred to by Americans as 'The Cinderellas of the Fleet'.

Albert Loring Swasey, a naval architect, had come up with a design for a long, narrow, triple-screw craft with a flat flush deck, a bow flare like a whaleboat's, a beam of between 14½ and 15 feet, and a maximum draft of 5 foot 8 inches. Steel was scarce, so the boats were made of timber (white oak). They were built in small boatyards by people who were experienced at constructing launches, motorboats, sailing craft, fishing smacks and the like.

Each subchaser was equipped with three 220-horse-power engines that, at full speed, guzzled 50 gallons of gasoline hourly. With a fuel tank capacity of 2,400 gallons, the vessels had a cruising radius of around 1,000 nautical miles at 12 knots. They proved to have excellent sea-keeping qualities, but were cramped and gruellingly uncomfortable, and more than one man who served in them said they were just like corks in the sea, incessantly tossed and rolled about by the waves.

Four hundred and forty-eight of the craft were ordered, of which well over a hundred were sent under their own power to Europe. These boats didn't have the fuel capacity for a straight-across-the-Atlantic voyage, and so had to make the 3,000-mile trip in three separate stages – from the east coast of the USA to Bermuda, from Bermuda to the Azores, and from the Azores to Europe. Accompanied by ocean-going tugs, a tanker, and at least one warship, they had to refuel a few times, usually on the leg between Bermuda and the Azores.

They were manned in the main by amateur sailors, young men who had had little or no nautical training and suffered the miseries of the seasickness induced by the shallow-draft, narrow boats' corkscrewing motion in heavy seas. Ventilation on the craft was practically non-existent, and water sloshed around the forecastle floor and occasionally left puddles in the middle of bunks. There were fumes from the petrol engines, and the stink from the bilges caused nausea and headaches. And there was the ever-present danger of fire.

Each subchaser was crewed by two commissioned officers, a chief petty officer, and twenty-one ratings. As well as a 3-inch deck gun, the subchasers were equipped with depth charge launchers, depth charge racks and machine guns. And, significantly, with the new detection devices – the SC-type C-Tube hydrophones, and the K-Tube hydrophones. The men who operated the detection devices were known as Listeners, and they learned how to tell not only where a submarine was but how far away, and the direction in which it was travelling.

Admiral Sims, the officially designated American member, asked the Allied Naval Council to consider the question of where the subchasers should go to be of most value to the Allies. In March they discussed it and agreed that the first two squadrons (a total of 36 boats) should be sent to the Adriatic for patrol duties. The rest were to be used around the various coasts of Ireland and the British Isles.

It was a summer of bitter attrition, with the U-boats attempting to sink everything Allied that floated. For example, at half-past nine on the calm dark night of 27 June *Oberleutnant zur See* (Lieutenant) Helmut Patzig from Danzig, the captain of U-86, was 116 miles south-west of the Fastnet Rock when he fired a torpedo at the 11,423-ton *Llandovery Castle*. She was a hospital ship, and Patzig knew it.

A four-year-old former Union-Castle liner, the *Llandovery Castle* was returning to England from her fifth transatlantic voyage as a hospital ship. On those voyages she had carried a total of 3,223 wounded and sick Canadian soldiers back home from the European theatre of war. Some of the sick men were tubercular cases; some were suffering from mental disorders. When Patzig lined her up to be torpedoed, the ship was returning from Halifax, Nova Scotia, to Liverpool and was running at 14 knots on a zig-zag course. She was fully lighted, had big red crosses on her funnels. Powerful lamps brilliantly illuminated her hull. She bore all the distinguishing marks that the Tenth Hague Convention required in the case of naval hospital ships. There was no mistaking what she was.

The *Llandovery Castle* was carrying 258 people – her crew of 164; eighty officers (including doctors) and other ranks of the Canadian army Medical Corps, and fourteen female nurses. The master, Captain R. A. Sylvester, was on the bridge when the torpedo struck the ship's port side, causing a terrific explosion and blasting a huge hole in the hull. A number of the port side lifeboats were destroyed, and the ship's Marconi wireless equipment was put out of action when the top-hamper came tumbling down. The hospital ship could not send an SOS.

All the lights on the ship went out, massive damage having been caused in the engine room, and No. 4 hold blown in. Captain Sylvester rang the engine room telegraph for STOP, then for FULL ASTERN. There was no response. The *Llandovery Castle* continued her forward movement through the water, slowing gradually when she was forced down by the head as water poured in through the hole in the hull. Shouting through a megaphone from the bridge, Captain Sylvester ordered that the lifeboats not be lowered until the way was off the ship. A few minutes later he shouted for the boats to be lowered away, and gave the order: 'Abandon Ship'.

The *Llandovery Castle*'s boilers blew up with a deafening explosion when the sea surged into the engine room, and her funnel crashed down. Then her bow stood right up out of the water and she began a sucking swirling slide into the depths. In ten minutes the 517-foot long ship was gone, but not before those on board were able to scramble into lifeboats, climb onto rafts or jump overboard. Everyone other than those who had been killed when the torpedo exploded got off the ship.

An NCO of the Canadian Army Medical Corps, Sergeant A. Knight, who took charge of Lifeboat No. 5, placed the fourteen nursing sisters in it. Two of the women were wearing their nightdresses; the others were in uniform. The boat was quickly loaded and lowered to the surface but had great difficulty in getting away from the side of the sinking ship. Sergeant Knight tried with a hatchet to sever the ropes that were holding the boat hard against the side of the ship, but he failed. Trying to fend her off from continually crashing against the ship, the boat's small complement broke the oars, making them useless. Eventually, high over their heads, the ropes became loose and the lifeboat began to drift clear – but she went backwards in the darkness towards the ship's stern.

Apart from the matron, Nursing Sister M. M. Fraser, asking Knight, 'Sergeant, do you think there is any hope for us?' – to which he answered, 'No' – there was silence in the boat. No complaints from anyone, no cries for help, no screams of fear.

Knight reckoned they were in the boat for about eight minutes in all. 'Suddenly,' he said, 'the poop-deck [of the *Llandovery Castle*] seemed to break away and sink. The suction drew us quickly into the vacuum … into the whirlpool of the submerged after-deck.' The lifeboat 'tipped over sideways, and every occupant went under'. The last he saw of the nursing sisters was 'as they were thrown over the side of the boat. It was doubtful if any of them came to the surface again.' Knight himself surfaced three times, on the last of which he grabbed hold of a piece of floating wreckage, wrapped his arms around it, and was eventually rescued by the men in the captain's boat.

Twenty-eight-year-old Helmut Patzig, standing in the conning tower of U-86, ordered the lifeboat carrying the *Llandovery Castle's* master, Captain Sylvester, to come alongside the submarine. The men in the lifeboat were trying to haul a drowning man out of the water. The hospital ship's second officer, Mr Chapman, stood up in the boat and yelled to the U-boat, 'We are picking up a man from the water.'

'Come alongside!' Patzig roared. 'NOW!'

When the lifeboat was slow to respond, he fired two shots at it from his revolver, shouted the order again, and added, 'I will shoot with my big gun.'

The men in the lifeboat believed him, knew for a certainty that he was capable of doing it. So they left the drowning man where he was in the water and rowed the boat towards the submarine and lay alongside.

Captain Sylvester and Major Lyon of the Canadian Army Medical Service, were ordered on board. They were manhandled roughly along the deck and up into to the confined space of the conning tower where there was an unmistakeable atmosphere of hostility towards them. Patzig, flanked by his *Erster Wachoffizier* (First Watch Officer) Ludwig Dittmar and Second Watch Officer John Boldt, asked, 'What ship is that?'

'The hospital ship *Llandovery Castle*,' Sylvester said.

'Yes,' Patzig said, 'but you were carrying eight American flight officers.'

Strenuously Sylvester denied it, said he had had no Americans on board – just the ship's crew and Canadian medical staff. He told Patzig that the ship had been chartered by the Canadian government to carry sick and wounded Canadians from England to Canada. 'I have been running to Canada for six months with wounded,' he said.

'You have been carrying American [pilots],' Patzig insisted.

'We have carried no one other than patients, medical staff, nursing sisters, and the crew,' Sylvester said.

Major Lyon, who was so violently handled when being hauled on board the U-boat that he broke a bone in his foot, was accused of being an American flying officer. Lyon said that he was Canadian and a medical officer. The two men were then told to get back into the lifeboat, which was cast off and allowed to row away from the side of U-86.

People in the water were crying out for help. Those in the captain's boat could hear shouts, pleadings and screams close by and away out in the dark. The men in the lifeboat managed to drag eleven survivors over the gunwales. Sylvester got a sail rigged and when it was up he set a course that should eventually get them close to the faraway Irish coast. But Helmut Patzig wasn't finished with them yet.

The U-boat began to circle the wreckage, its speed increasing as its diesels hammered away faster and faster until, to men familiar with ships' speeds, she appeared to be doing at least 15 knots. The

U-boat captain cold-bloodedly drove U-86 at full speed at the lifeboat, obviously intent on ramming it and killing all those on board. The submarine missed the boat by less than 2 feet.

The lifeboat continued to endeavour to sail and row in the direction of the coast of Ireland. They hadn't travelled very far when the occupants of the boat heard gunfire coming from the U-boat. In the darkness they saw the flashes from the mouth of the U-boat's deck gun, and then, almost immediately after, the flashes as the shells exploded. Clearly they had been firing at close range at something or things near the U-boat – lifeboats? Rafts? People in the water? Two shells passed over the captain's boat.

Then the U-boat changed the direction and trajectory of its shells, firing anywhere from fourteen to twenty shells in all. Major Lyon said afterwards, 'The submarine did everything in its power to destroy every trace of the ship, its personnel and its crew.' Sergeant Knight spoke of the persistent efforts of the U-boat to obliterate all evidence of its crime by zig-zagging at speed through the area filled with lifeboats and wreckage, and then shelling the area.

At a war crimes trial in Leipzig in July 1921 when the German authorities on their own initiative arrested *Erster Wachoffizier* Dittmar and Second Watch Officer Boldt, the two officers were charged with murder in the first degree, and complicity in the action taken by Patzig in firing on the lifeboats. Britain had demanded the trial of only Patzig, but he had fled the country. Members of the U-boat's crew gave evidence that made it abundantly clear that the firing from the U-boat was directed against the people in the lifeboats. Both of the accused refused to give evidence.

The state attorney said he was convinced that the object of the U-boat's firing was to exterminate the survivors. The court decided that the lifeboats of the *Llandovery Castle* were fired on in order to sink them, that lifeboats were hit and their occupants killed by gunfire. It found 'the act of Patzig is homicide'. The two watch officers were sentenced to four years in prison. They never served them. They escaped, unlike the people from the *Llandovery Castle* who had been brutally denied the chance to escape. The U-boat captain and his two officers got off scot-free in the end.

The captain's lifeboat with its twenty-four occupants was the only lifeboat to survive of the nineteen on the *Llandovery Castle* when she sailed from Halifax on 20 June 1918. By a combination of sailing and rowing, the men in the boat had covered about 70 miles when the Royal Navy destroyer HMS *Lysander*, returning to Queenstown at the end of a patrol, sighted the lifeboat at 9.30 on the Saturday morning, and rescued the twenty-four occupants. Their empty lifeboat was cast adrift.

The captain of the *Lysander*, Commander F. W. D. Twigg, RN, notified Admiralty House by wireless and suggested that a search be made for any other survivors who might be adrift in the ocean. He took the twenty-four survivors into Queenstown where, once again, Admiral Bayly met them. He sat with them and listened to their accounts of what had taken place. Angered and appalled by what he learned of the sinking of the hospital ship, he immediately despatched four American destroyers and the sloop HMS *Snowdrop* on yet another mission of mercy, a systematic search of the entire area. The weather was fine, visibility perfect. But other than the empty boat cast adrift by the *Lysander*, they found nothing and nobody – no more lifeboats, no more survivors. Only twenty-four of the 258 people who had been on board the *Llandovery Castle* survived. The search was finally called off on the evening of 1 July.

The U-boats continued their campaign, but whereas in the spring of 1917 they had been sending to the bottom one ship for every two days spent on patrol, by the summer of 1918 the rate had dropped to one ship for every fourteen days at sea. Yet Admiral Scheer said, 'We must, and we will, succeed.' Having been thwarted in the ocean by the convoy system, the U-boats began operating in St George's Channel, the Irish Sea, the North Channel (between Ireland and Scotland) and the English Channel. They picked off ships that had come successfully through the danger zone guarded by their protecting screens of escorts, but then had to disperse, in most cases unescorted, to their individual ports. The Allied Naval Council recommended that a squadron of subchasers be based in Plymouth, and another in Queenstown. By the end of June 1918, thirty-six subchasers had arrived and begun operating out of Plymouth, hunting in groups numbering not less than three craft.

The following month, America's Assistant Secretary of the Navy, Franklin D. Roosevelt, who had been granted his wish to visit Europe, arrived at Queenstown in the company of Britain's First Lord of the Admiralty, Sir Eric Geddes. That was the visit on which Roosevelt found Admiral Bayly 'had the qualities which inspired the imagination of every man who served with him or under him', and was why he said, 'I shall always think of my visit to Queenstown in July 1918 as the high-spot of my round of inspections of American naval activities in European waters during the World War.' Admiral Bayly made his green barge available to ferry Roosevelt and Geddes around the harbour and to visit various ships.

The thirty-six subchasers that came to Ireland in September operated out of Bearhaven, Wexford, Holyhead and Queenstown itself. Admiral Bayly, acknowledging that they had arrived from America late in the war, said of them that the officers and crews had had to learn the appearance of the coast, and the navigational necessities such as tides, currents, the appearance of headlands and so on but that they would soon have become a great asset.

By the end of June, there were almost 7,500 officers and men of the United States Navy in European waters. More than half of them belonged to the destroyers, mother ships and tugs. There were five air stations in Ireland by then – at Queenstown, Castletownbear, Whiddy Island in Bantry Bay, Wexford and Lough Foyle. The pilots for the Irish air stations were trained at Queenstown.

In the third week of August a division of six American battleships arrived at Bearhaven, because it was feared that the German High Fleet might try to break out into the Atlantic in a great final effort to stop the escorted convoys. It never happened. What did happen was that seven U-boats were sent to lurk off Brest.

When U-boats crossed the Atlantic and began to operate in American waters off its east coast in the summer of 1918, and sank 100,000 tons of merchant shipping, the US Navy Department and Secretary of the Navy Josephus Daniels were decidedly alarmed. And they still weren't seeing eye to eye with Admiral Sims, their Commander, United States Naval Forces Operating in European Waters. Daniels kept harping away at Sims about the necessity of putting more emphasis on destroyers being used to escort troop convoys. The secretary also wanted the escorting destroyers to be used over greater distances out in the Atlantic. Daniels told Sims that, if necessary, in order to ensure the safe landing of troops, fewer destroyers were to be assigned to the protection of ships carrying *merchandise*.

Sims, while he admitted to recognising the importance of protecting the troop transports, said that the safety of vessels carrying merchandise to Europe was hardly less essential to the successful prosecution of the war than was the safety of troop transports. He said the war might be lost 'through making excessive demands upon our escort forces for the protection of troops'.

On 31 May, the American troopship *President Lincoln* was sunk while on its return westward voyage to the United States. She was 500 miles out in the ocean when three torpedoes, all fired from the U-90, struck her. Of the 715 people on board the troopship, three officers and twenty-three other ranks were lost when the ship sank twenty-five minutes after being torpedoed. Seven of those who died were killed by explosion, or drowned on board the ship; the sixteen others were on a life raft that was dragged under by the suction as the ship surged to the ocean floor. From then on, the stationing of warships at Brest resulted in there being more destroyers at Brest than at Queenstown.

A promise by the senior German naval officers that the U-boats would choke off the seemingly endless supply of American personnel being ferried into France was never fulfilled. The U-boats were thwarted by the presence of the intimidating escort screens, and the fact that most troop transports steamed at between 15 and 20 knots, a speed far in excess of the speed a submarine could travel when submerged. Two other factors militated against the U-boats: (1) the troop transports travelled through the danger zone in darkness, which made them extremely difficult to pick up visually, and (2) their routes were being constantly changed in order to cause confusion among the U-boats.

Secretary of the Navy Daniels claimed that American naval forces operated in forty-seven different localities extending from the Arctic Ocean to the Adriatic. Among the principal ones were: Brest, Queenstown, Bearhaven, Gibraltar, Cardiff and Plymouth. There were thirty aviation bases, including the two at Queenstown (seaplane) for assembly and repair, and others in Ireland, England, France, Italy and the Azores. Daniels held that the US naval forces in Europe didn't operate together as one fleet, but constituted a 'task force'.

In his book *Our Navy at War* he wrote:

No navies in all history ever worked together in such close cooperation as did ours with the British, French and Italians. The cordial relations between the civilian populations, as well as the naval personnel, will be a lasting tie. I wish it were possible to put on record the sentiments expressed, the appreciation felt by all Americans in the navy for the gracious courtesies and friendly offices shown to our men serving a common cause far from their homes.

The one regrettable incident at Cork, where an unruly element attacked some of our sailors, was recognised as an exception. It was confined to the few engaged in the trouble, the people of that city and country having no relation to it and not affected by it in their feeling of friendship for our sailors and our country. It left no resentment towards the great Irish people, who received us with open arms and showed hospitality and cordiality towards our forces domiciled in that country.

The Kingstown (Dún Laoghaire)/Holyhead mail boat RMS *Leinster* was torpedoed 4 miles east of the Kish lightship by a U-boat at 9.50 on the morning of 14 October 1918. She was bound for Holyhead. That morning she was carrying 694 passengers. Her crew numbered seventy-seven. The Kish is 3 miles offshore at the entrance to Dublin Bay.

The U-boat that sank the mail boat was UB-123, whose commander was twenty-seven-year-old *Oberleutnant zur See* Robert Ramm. He was responsible that day for the deaths of 501 people. Neither he nor his crew lived for very long afterwards – the U-boat never reached her home port. She was lost with all hands. Ramm fired three torpedoes at the *Leinster*, missing with the first, hitting her with the next two. President Wilson, deeply shocked and angered at the wanton loss of life, sent another note to Berlin, this one decrying their 'acts of inhumanity, spoliation and desolation'.

On 20 October Admiral Scheer abandoned the campaign against shipping by recalling all the U-boats at sea. The close of October 1918 saw the Germans losing everywhere, on land and at sea.

Deep trouble was brewing in the German navy. Mutinies erupted in the High Fleet as sailors rebelled. Stokers deliberately extinguished fires in ships' stokeholds so that there was no steam to power the engines; at one stage a thousand mutineers were arrested. The navy situation worsened on 4 November when at Kiel thousands more sailors mutinied, and the malaise spread during the next couple of days to Hamburg, Wilhelmshaven, Bremen and Cuxhaven. Revolution was rampant. Germany's position was hopeless. Morale was lower than ever, resentment and fury were dangerously high, and there was a powerful movement to ditch the Kaiser. The troops knew that they were being forced to retreat even if those at the top spoke about withdrawals. On 9 November the Kaiser was forced to abdicate. He slipped into neutral Holland and took refuge there.

On the same day, the UB-50, commanded by Heinrich Kukat, fired three torpedoes at the 16,000-ton pre-dreadnaught battleship

HMS *Britannia* off Cape Trafalgar. His first two torpedoes missed. The third caused a cordite explosion on board the old battleship, and though every effort was made to prevent her from sinking, she went down three hours after being hit. Another forty men died. The UB-50 completed seven patrols from the time she was commissioned in 1916, and sank thirty-eight merchant ships for a total of 97,284 tons.

But also on that day in the Straits of Gibraltar Germany's fourth most successful U-boat of the war, U-34 (she accounted for 121 merchant ships, 262,886 tons) was hunted down by two British motor-launches and the former Q-ship *Privet* as she tried to get through the Straits. They successfully depth-charged and destroyed her. She was never seen or heard from again. Nobody on board her survived.

On 11 November 1918, Queenstown had twenty-four US destroyers, thirty subchasers, two tenders, and three tugs. Bearhaven on the same day had three battleships, seven submarines, one tender, one tug and one oiler.

At 5 o'clock on the morning of 11 November 1918, in a railway coach in the Forest of Compiegne, north-east of Paris near the Franco-German front line, the final armistice was signed. The principal signatories were the Allied Commander-in-Chief, Marshal Ferdinand Foch of France, and the leader of the German delegation, Matthias Erzberger, a civilian politician. The cessation of hostilities, the Armistice, was to come into effect at 11 a.m. that same morning – the eleventh hour of the eleventh day of the eleventh month.

But at two minutes to eleven a Canadian soldier, Private George Lawrence Price, who had been living in Moose Jaw, Saskatchewan, when he was conscripted in 1917, was picked off and shot through the heart and killed by a German sniper in the town of Ville-sur-Haine. He was twenty-two years old and was the last soldier killed in the First World War. His grave is in a military cemetery south-west of Mons.

The day the war ended was the 1,586th day since it had started. Now 'the war to end wars' was officially over. At the spot in the forest where the Armistice was signed there is a large granite block with lettering cut into it saying: 'Here on 11 November 1918 the criminal pride of the German Empire was brought low, vanquished by the free people whom it had sought to enslave.'

Thomas Hardy wrote:

> Calm fell. From heaven distilled a clemency;
> There was peace on earth, and silence in the sky;
> Some could, some could not shake off misery ...

The U-boat, as somebody said, had turned most of the civilised world against Germany. Instead of bringing her victory, it had been the cause of her doom. The U-boat arm of the German navy had sunk 5,708 ships, a total of 11,018,865 tons. Well over six and half million tons of that shipping was British. The total number of civilian men, women, and children who died on the ships sent to the bottom of the sea by the U-boats came to 13,333. When the war ended, 176 U-boats were surrendered to the Allies and associated powers.

And the surface ships of the German navy? Eleven battleships, five battle cruisers, eight light cruisers and fifty destroyers were sent to Britain to be impounded. The majority of them went to Scapa Flow where, on 21 June 1919 at 1.00 p.m., they were scuttled by their officers and crews.

The Great War had caused the battle deaths of 4,888,891 mobilised individuals among the Allies – 908,371 of them from the British Empire, 50,585 Americans. Approximately 350,000 Irishmen served in the British forces during the war; at least 35,000 of them were killed.

The Central Powers lost 8,020,780 people. Of those, 1,808,546 were German.

The British Empire's total of war-related civilian deaths was 40,000 out of an overall figure of 6,642,633.

But the salient fact is that every single individual of all the millions killed had had a body, a brain, a heart and feelings. Each one of them was a *person*, a human being.

May they rest in peace.

They shall grow not old, as we that are left grow old,
Age shall not weary them, nor the years condemn.
At the going down of the sun and in the morning
We will remember them.
From *For the Fallen* by Laurence Binyon

Look up, and swear by the green
of the spring that you'll never forget.
From *Aftermath* by Siegfried Sassoon

28

LAST GOODBYES

In December of 1918, Sims was made a full four-star admiral. He had mixed feelings about it – glad to be given it, regretful that he hadn't had the use of the rank while the war was on. His promotion came just in time to relinquish it – which he was required to do on being detached from his position as Force Commander of the United States Navy in European Waters – because there was no permanent grade in the US navy higher than rear-admiral. So though Sims left England with four stars on his collar, when he arrived in America he was entitled to wear only two. It was in effect a demotion.

After a series of farewell celebrations in London, he went back to America on the *Mauritania* in April 1919. 'Rousing Welcome To Admiral Sims Home From The War' said a headline in *The New York Times* on 18 April. The famous stormy petrel of the US Navy was home. Mrs Sims and their five children – Margaret, Adelaide, William, Anne and Ethan – had been waiting since eight o'clock in the morning on the day of ship's expected arrival, but the liner was delayed by fog outside New York harbour. It was well into the afternoon before the Sims family was reunited.

Steaming into the harbour, the big Cunarder was escorted by a flotilla of six destroyers, as well as subchasers and other welcoming vessels. These included the police patrol boat which had the mayor of New York and his welcoming committee on board. Planes and dirigibles circled the liner. The Secretary of the Navy was represented by a rear-admiral sent specially from Washington. Whistles were blown, hooters and sirens were sounded, flags were raised and flapped and fluttered in the breeze. People cheered, bands played and speeches were made. Admiral Sims' arrival back in America brought a showy, impressive, raucous welcome for an outstanding officer who had served with distinction overseas.

He experienced the intense joy of being reunited with his family. 'His heart went out to little children,' his biographer wrote. 'It was their innocence, their helplessness, their utter freshness that appealed to him.' And all he wanted to do was get back to the Naval War College at Newport, Rhode Island. But he had to try to cope with his simmering anger – anger over the performance of the Navy Department, especially during the nightmare months in 1917. He felt that the Navy Department had seriously compromised the navy, and he felt personally alienated from the department.

He resumed as president of the Naval War College on 11 April 1919. Having fulfilled a series of speaking engagements (mainly in the mid-west), and having been approached by a number of publishers to write a book about his experiences as force commander of the US Naval Forces Operating in European Waters, he eventually signed a lucrative contract with Doubleday Page & Company, and set about the preparation of *The Victory at Sea*. He wrote the book in collaboration with Burton J. Hendrick, and it was awarded the Pulitzer Prize for American History.

That same year, at a University of Pennsylvania celebration of George Washington's birthday, Sims was given an honorary doctorate of law and he used the occasion to speak about what he considered the unkindest things that had been said about him over the course of his life. He told the assembled audience that his father was 'a native Pennsylvanian', that his mother was 'a Canadian who happened to be in Canada when I was born', and added, 'Perhaps you may be kind enough to consider me also an American, notwithstanding the title that has been given me by certain unfriendly critics – "The leading British admiral in the American navy".' He intimated that Admiral

Benson, the Chief of Naval Operations, had adopted the view that Anglophilism rather than patriotism had motivated Sims.

His retirement in 1922 was overshadowed by the controversy that surrounded the accusations he made during an acrimonious congressional hearing on naval affairs that Secretary of the Navy Josephus Daniels had been obstructive and inefficient during the war. Sims also claimed that the Navy Department 'failed for at least six months to throw full weight against the enemy'. Further, that for the first six months of American involvement in the war, the Navy Department had 'cost the Allied cause two and a half million tons of shipping, 500,000 lives, and $15 billion'.

Some senior officers tried to get Daniels to relieve Sims of the presidency of the Naval War College, and to court martial him. But no action was taken against him. The admiral, however, failed to prove that his accusations were justified.

He retired on 15 October 1922. He died of a heart attack at his Back Bay home in September 1936. He was almost seventy-eight. When President Roosevelt was informed, he said he was 'deeply grieved' and that it 'marks the closing of a brilliant and colourful career in the navy, the end of a remarkable period of service to his country. Dynamic and forceful, he was admired and respected by friend and foe alike.'

His remains were taken to Arlington National Cemetery in Washington DC on a rainy Thursday. The coffin was placed on a caisson for its passage through the roads of the burial ground. The caisson was hauled by six white horses. Muffled drums and mournful music accompanied it, and a seventeen-gun salute boomed in the damp air. And then, with full military honours, he was put into the ground and laid to rest.

Bayly had things to attend to at Queenstown before leaving. Typical of the man, on the evening of 11 November when the vessels based at Queenstown were ordered to cease hostilities, he sent a signal to all the ships:

> The Commander-in-Chief congratulates all British and United States officers and crews under his command on the splendid victory achieved which their loyalty, ability, and ever-ready energies have so greatly assisted. It will always be a source of great pride to him to have been so closely associated with them in this great war.

American and Royal Navy officers with whom he had forged a close relationship based on respect and affection, went up the hill to Admiralty House for the last time. They wanted to say goodbye, and they did so with full hearts. About forty of the young American commanding officers clubbed together and subscribed for a handsome silver half-model of an American four-funnel destroyer. They named her USS *Pulltogether*, and presented the model to the admiral. Their signatures were engraved on the small plate attached to the mounting.

On the last day of the year Admiral Bayly sent a memorandum from Commander-in-Chief's Office, Queenstown, to the Admiralty in London. He wanted the Admiralty to send a copy to the Navy Department in Washington, through Admiral Sims. In his memoirs *Pull Together* (which, incidentally, he wrote at the request of his niece, and asked her not to publish it during his lifetime), the text of the memorandum is reproduced, in order, he said, to 'explain my feelings towards these [American] officers'.

The fighting units of the USA stationed on the coast of Ireland, having completed their work and been withdrawn, he thought it opportune for him to make some remarks 'as a record of what is probably a unique situation – United States Navy Forces operating entirely under a British admiral in British waters'. The Americans had been 'faced by an unprecedented kind of warfare and new methods of attack, and found themselves operating in waters which were strange to them, and in unfamiliar types of weather'. But they had at once set to work 'with all their energies, to learn the new methods; there was no foreign feeling about them, not a sign of jealousy, no impatience at receiving their orders from a foreign admiral'.

They were 'single-minded in their endeavours to do their utmost for the common cause ... and [they] assisted magnificently to save a very dangerous situation ... It is hard to express in words the singleness of purpose which animated them, the eagerness with which they set themselves to learn all the methods which had been tried, and to improve these methods so as not to lose any chance of possible success.' He went on to say that 'it should be remembered that success in this submarine war is not only measured by the number of submarines sunk ... but by the number of ships, crews and cargoes preserved from an attack, and in this they have every reason to be most proud of their success'.

He pointed out that frequently the American destroyers were under the orders of British officers – when the senior officer of an escort was a British commander or lieutenant-commander – but that frequently the American officers had British officers under them, but 'there never was a question, a doubt, or any sign of anything put perfect cooperation'.

In a paragraph devoted to the repair ships, he said that without them the work could never have been done. 'Working complete twenty-four hours in three shifts of eight hours each; sleeping among the noise of the machinery; always ready for extra work when an unexpected accident happened, or an unforeseen call was made that was being dealt with – they never failed me. Captain J. R. P. Pringle of the *Melville*, and Captain H. B. Price of the *Dixie*, were not only always ready to do the unexpected, but used their utmost endeavours to be prepared for the unforeseen, and the result was such as their country has reason to be proud of.' The behaviour of 'the men on shore' was 'excellent'.

He ended by acknowledging 'the generous, broadminded help' which he had always received from Admiral W. S. Sims. 'From first to last he has worked with me for the Allied cause in a way which has compelled the admiration of all concerned.'

In his book Bayly said, 'If before the US destroyers arrived there had been a certain number of destroyers sent to Queenstown from the

Grand Fleet and Harwich, or other places, a great deal of our [overall] losses would not have occurred.'

Between the arrival of the first six US destroyers in 1917 and the signing of the Armistice in November 1918, Admiral Bayly had had ninety-two different American ships under his command. Now the ships of the Queenstown fleet left the harbour. The American vessels went back to their own country across the Atlantic. The British ships dispersed to ports all around Britain. The great stretches of water in the harbour took on an empty look again, and Queenstown slipped back into quiet inactivity.

Admiral Bayly had controlled the second largest naval command in the war – only Brest, to which the majority of the 2,000,000 troops sent across the Atlantic from the United States were despatched by convoy, was bigger. When the sums were done, the records checked, and the statistics made available, the picture that emerged was truly remarkable. In the nineteen months the American naval forces were based on Queenstown, 360 convoys were escorted, and 91 per cent of the escorts were Queenstown-based ships.

Before he left the town in 1919, Admiral Bayly invited Bishop Browne to Admiralty House for tea. The admiral himself best described what took place at the end of the visit: 'As [Bishop Browne] was leaving, he put his hands on our heads and said, "Although you belong to a different religion, I feel sure you will not refuse an old man's blessing for what you have done for my people." ... He was a really great man.'

Among the people who committed to paper their appreciation of Bayly's work at Queenstown was the Assistant Secretary of the US Navy, Franklin D. Roosevelt. In May 1919 he wrote to the Force Commander, US Naval Forces Operating in European Waters, saying:

The [Navy] Department believes that without exception the feeling toward Admiral Bayly of all United States Naval Officers who have served during the War, either ashore or afloat, from the Queenstown base is not only unusual, but unprecedented in the Allied warfare.

United States naval officers who have operated under Admiral Bayly's orders admired him particularly for his ability, his efficiency, and his consideration for their comfort and welfare. In his requirements as to the performance of duty he was as exacting of the United States naval officers as he was of British officers, but he invariably backed them in all matters in which they were obliged to exercise independent judgment, and so arranged the details of duty that every vessel knew exactly what would be required of it.

The department is pleased to acknowledge the tact and courtesy with which Admiral Bayly administered his command as regards United States naval officers, and desires here to express its high appreciation for the consideration which guided Admiral Bayly in his exercise of authority over the United States naval officers acting under his command. The department is of the opinion that the thorough co-ordination of effort which prevailed under this command is due entirely to Admiral Bayly's tact and courtesy.

Bayly wrote to Roosevelt saying how proud he was to have received so kind and courteous a letter, and how honoured he felt at Roosevelt's appreciation of the results of the combined work on the Queenstown station:

The fact that you permitted your ships to be put under the command of a British admiral was a very high honour to our navy, but the unity, excellent good feeling and the success of our two navies working together could never have existed had it not been for the determination of the United States officers who were stationed there to make it a success, and for the ability they brought with them which enabled them to do so …

I have commanded many ships and squadrons, and have spent the greater part of my life at sea, and can truly and honestly say that a finer lot of seamen and gentlemen I have never commanded …

It is with deepest regret that I shall never again have the chance of working with a force which no one is more proud of than I am.

Back in England in 1919, Bayly was offered the position of Commander-in-Chief at Portsmouth. He declined it. At sixty-two years of age, he had nearly fifty years of service in the navy under his belt. Over forty-seven of those years were spent at sea. His career had encompassed the Royal Navy's transition from canvas sails and wooden hulls to steam turbines and steel. It was time to come ashore.

In March he went down to South Devonshire, to Plymouth Hoe, the place where Drake played his famous game of bowls while waiting for the wind and tide to change as the Spanish Armada came up the Channel. Above the rocky seafront, looking down on Plymouth Sound and Drake's Island, Admiral Bayly said goodbye to his beloved Royal Navy.

His return to England had been a far more low-key affair than Sims' return to the United States, not that that would have bothered Lewis Bayly. He had an abiding abhorrence of the limelight, hated publicity and remained innately shy. But he still had things he wanted to do, things he wanted to say.

Later in the year a development took place in America that Bayly could never have envisaged. A former United States Navy lieutenant named Junius S. Morgan, who had served at Queenstown, conceived the idea of setting up a Queenstown Association. It should be, Morgan felt, an informal, non-dues-paying organisation made up of American naval officers who had served under Admiral Bayly. Morgan discussed the idea with a few colleagues. They were fully in favour of it. They mailed 750 letters to former colleagues setting out their ideas. They received 400 positive, supportive replies, as a result of which the fledgling association held its first meeting and dinner on 3 January 1920 at the Ritz Carlton Hotel in Philadelphia. Ninety-three people attended it.

Admiral Sims and Admiral Bayly were unanimously elected honorary presidents, and Captain Poinsett Pringle was elected president. Junius Morgan became the association's secretary/treasurer, a position he held until he died. Miss Voysey was elected an honorary member. The menu for that first dinner included Bantry Bay Oysters, Potage Haulbowline, Sea Bass Ballycotton, Roast Chicken Dixie, Peas Poinsett, and Bombe Fanning. The *Dixie*, it will be remembered, was one of the mother ships at Queenstown; the *Fanning* was the only US destroyer to sink a U-boat, the U-58.

Late in 1920, Admiral Bayly and his niece set off on a Blue Funnel liner on a trip to Japan. The Queenstown Association contacted him and invited him to return via the United States, and said that he and his niece would be the association's guests. Bayly accepted the invitation, and after a short sojourn in the Far East, he and 'the only niece' (as Admiral Sims called her) crossed the Pacific to San Francisco, arriving there in January 1921. To Bayly's astonishment, six US destroyers had been detailed to meet their ship and escort it into the bay.

There followed three days of lavish entertainment in the San Francisco area – all of it laid on and financially covered by the Queenstown Association. Bayly was treated as an honoured guest; he dined on board the USS *New York*, and attended a lunch in his honour hosted by 800 businessmen. Then it was south by train to San Diego and a meeting with many officers who had served under him at Queenstown. After a trip down America's west coast on the SS *San Juan*, Bayly and his niece travelled along the Panama Canal, and then finally up the east coast to New York on the SS *Toloa*. They arrived off New York harbour on the morning of 14 February, and once again their ship was escorted into harbour, this time by seaplanes and a dirigible. Admiral Sims was on the quayside to meet them when they stepped ashore.

In Washington on the following day Admiral Bayly had a meeting with Secretary of the Navy Josephus Daniels, who later hosted an official dinner. The admiral was also taken on a visit to the US Naval Academy at Annapolis where he was greeted by a brass band and a seventeen gun salute. He made a speech to the Academy's 2,000 cadets on the subject of traditions.

A suite of rooms in the Vanderbilt Hotel in New York was reserved for him and his niece for the duration of their stay, the Queenstown

Association again taking care of the cost. Admiral Bayly and Miss Voysey were guests at the association's dinner in the Biltmore Hotel on the 19 February when the association presented Bayly with a large silver rose-bowl that bore the inscription:

> From the Queenstown Association, composed of Officers
> of the United States navy who served under his command
> during the World War,
> To Admiral Sir Lewis Bayly, RN,
> an Honorary President of that Association,
> and a Master of his Profession.
> Presented to him upon the occasion of the Association's
> Dinner given in his honour in New York City
> on February the nineteenth, nineteen hundred and twenty-one
> as a testimonial of loyalty and affection

In his acceptance speech Bayly spoke emotionally, saying at one stage, 'Let the US Navy be proud ... of the days when you worked in Queenstown with an Allied country, with the greatest possible success, and the admiration of everybody who watched you work.'

The admiral and 'the only niece' spent the following three days as the Sims' guests at Newport, Rhode Island, and eventually sailed for home on 26 February on the White Star liner *Celtic*.

Bayly was clearly moved by the generosity of the Queenstown Association, and by all the honours bestowed upon him at the association's behest. He wrote to the association:

> On leaving the USA I wish to tell you how deeply grateful I am to you
> all for your most kind and generous hospitality to my niece and me.
> It has been the most wonderful proof of true and lasting friendship
> that I have ever met, and, I believe, that has ever before been shown by
> a great navy to a naval officer of a foreign country. The real affection
> that exists between us requires no explanation and defies analysis; it is
> to me too sacred to attempt to analyse. To me the American flag on

the sea represents a welcome. I leave you with a deep affection, and I take away with me a proud recollection of the wonderful honour you have accorded to us both.

Lewis Bayly

The association, knowing that Bayly was, if not in exactly straitened circumstances, barely financially comfortable, set up what they called the Bayly Fund. Subscriptions were sought and gladly given, with a view to the money being used by Bayly to purchase a home where he could live out his last years of life. Junius Morgan, the Queenstown Association's secretary/treasurer, wrote to Bayly early in May 1930. By then the Bayly Fund had reached a total of $15,000. The admiral was seventy-three, and it was decided that the time was right to send the money to England for his use. Morgan's letter was short and heartfelt:

> My Dear Admiral
>
> Long before you receive this letter you will have been advised by the Manager of Lloyd's Bank, Portsmouth, of the receipt of a sum for your credit. There is little that any of us here can add to what has been said before in regard to this, and we all hope that you will accept this evidence of the affection and regard of your American officers in the spirit in which it is meant. Many have contributed to it and all with the greatest pleasure in being able to do something to show their affection for their former chief. In writing you I am acting as a messenger from all your associates at Queenstown in 1917–19.
>
> With best regards to Miss Voysey and yourself,
>
> I am
>
> Very sincerely yours
>
> Junius S. Morgan Jr.

When Bayly replied to Morgan with what he described as 'a very deep sense of gratitude for the most real affection shown by your letter', he said that the wonderful gift 'touches us both very deeply, and we are both overwhelmed …' He found it, he said, 'very difficult to express in writing my real feelings … but you may be assured that when we have been able to find a house, its value to us will be greatly increased by the knowledge that it has been given by those who came over to help us in the war, and have honoured us with their affection through the years that have passed since it was over.'

He ended his letter with these words: 'There are many guiding forces in the world, but none has a greater power and rests on a more secure foundation than true friendship, and it is that which binds us together, and when I pass on, the gift will remain with Miss Voysey, reminding her of happy days when the US officers did all they could to show her how they valued all her friendship and kindness.'

He bought a house in Virginia Waters in Surrey, and he and his niece lived there until failing health and advancing age took their tolls on him. In September 1932, the death took place of one of his greatest friends, Vice-Admiral J. R. Poinsett Pringle, who had been Bayly's American chief-of-staff at Queenstown, and the first foreign naval officer to appear on the English navy list as serving under a British admiral in time of war. Pringle's death greatly saddened Bayly, and he had a commemorative brass plaque made as a memorial to a man he held in such high esteem. Curiously, he submitted the wording for the plaque to King George V, who approved it. The wording was:

IN MEMORY OF
VICE-ADMIRAL JOEL ROBERT POINSETT PRINGLE
UNITED STATES NAVY •
CLASS OF 1892 •
BORN FEBRUARY FOURTH
1873 •
DIED AT HIS DUTY SEPTEMBER TWENTY-SIXTH 1932 •
AN
OFFICER OF EXCEPTIONAL ABILITY WHO WAS RE-
SPECTED AND
LOVED BY ALL WHO SERVED WITH HIM •

DURING THE WAR 1917-1918
HE SERVED WITH THE UNITED STATES NAVAL FORC-
ES OPERATING
FROM QUEENSTOWN AS UNITED STATES CHIEF OF
STAFF TO
ADMIRAL SIR LEWIS BAYLY K.C.B., K.C.M.G., C.V.O., HIS
COMMANDER-
IN-CHIEF WHO PLACES THIS TABLET TO HIS MEMO-
RY AND WHO
WILL EVER REMEMBER HIM WITH GREAT PRIDE
AND AFFECTION

To tread the path of death he stood prepared
And what he greatly thought he nobly dared

Bayly obtained permission from the US Secretary of the Navy, Claude Swanson, to have the plaque placed in the US Naval Academy's Memorial Hall at Annapolis.

In 1934 the Queenstown Association invited Admiral Bayly and his niece to New York to mark the occasion of the visit of the Fleet to that city. A realist, Bayly knew that his life was ending. Time was winding down for him, but there were still things he needed to say, and wanted to say in his straightforward manner, as he had done all through his career; still some things he wanted to experience before it was too late. Besides, it was a chance to take the brass tablet across the Atlantic, his personal memorial to Pringle. The admiral and his niece travelled over on the Cunard liner *Aquitania*, arriving on 18 May.

Among the messages and greetings awaiting Bayly was one from 'We're-ready-now-sir' Taussig, who was by then an admiral holding the position of Assistant Chief of Naval Operations. Taussig's message said, 'Your comrades of the Queenstown Association, who had the honour and privilege of serving under your command in 1917–18, and who retain always for you a great respect for your friendship, are glad to welcome you to the United States and to offer recognition of your mission in coming to do honour to the memory of the past president of the Association.' That past president was, of course, the late Admiral Pringle. The commemorative plaque was handed over to an air force officer and flown to Annapolis. The officer was given orders, according to Bayly's account, 'if for any reason he failed to do so, he was to disappear and never to be seen again'.

A schedule had been prepared, giving details of what had been laid on for every day from Bayly's arrival to his departure on 9 June. A full round of engagements began almost as soon as he and his niece stepped off the liner's gangway. There was a luncheon with President Roosevelt, a stay with Admiral Sims and his family, a dinner with Admiral Taussig, visits to Philadelphia, Washington, Annapolis, Boston, Newport and Jamestown. Also arranged were calls on the British ambassador, the British naval attaché, the Secretary of the Navy, the navy yard at Philadelphia, and the Naval War College. And he was taken up in the whistling lifts to the top of New York's Empire State Building.

At Annapolis, the unveiling of the Pringle memorial plaque was a formal affair. Bayly heard Admiral Hart, the Superintendent of the Naval Academy, say to the assembled crowd that the death of Admiral Pringle, whose memory they had gathered to honour, had brought pain that still throbbed. Hart said the occasion also commemorated 'a period which is unique in history, a time when the forces of two allies served side by side in a spirit of full brotherhood, and without one instance of criticism or recrimination directed at each other'.

Having dwelled briefly on the years 1917 and 1918, when the naval forces of the USA and Britain commingled as one unit, he said their commander was a British admiral who 'did not work too much with papers. He commanded most actively, and dealt with a large number of subordinates face to face. Therefore large numbers of us came to know him personally, and we carried out of the war a feeling toward that commander of respect and affection, which will last throughout our lives.

'He has now come out of his retirement and well-earned rest to cross the Atlantic and present a tablet, which we are to unveil and receive. I present to you Admiral Sir Lewis Bayly of the Royal Navy.'

In his short reply Bayly referred to 'the exceptional characteristics' of Admiral Pringle, 'a great seaman, a thorough gentleman, and a wonderful leader of men'. He ended by saying, 'I have spent my whole life at sea, and have been thrown in contact with all sorts and conditions of men all over the world, and I have lost one of the greatest friends I have ever had.'

The brass tablet, with the Stars and Stripes draped over its right-hand side and the white ensign draped over its left-hand side, was then unveiled by the academy's two youngest cadets.

On 31 May, at the personal invitation of President Roosevelt, Bayly went out from New York to Sandy Hook on the USS *Indianapolis* to watch the review of the United States fleet – a massive gathering of ships that included destroyers, light and heavy cruisers, battleships and aircraft carriers. He stood at Roosevelt's side during the review. Before disembarking, the president gave him a message for the King.

At the Queenstown Association's dinner at the Harvard Club on 8 June, Bayly again spoke of 'an affectionate friendship' which bound all its members together. 'It is even more than that,' he said, 'for though love is a word rarely used between men, the feeling between us can only be expressed by a word of similar meaning, and this feeling is the result of the knowledge of each other that was gained by working together for eighteen months during the war.' He said that seventeen years earlier most of them were coming across the Atlantic wondering what fighting against submarines would be like, what kind of weather would be found off the south coast of Ireland, 'and what it would be like to serve under a British admiral'. At Queenstown, he said, the British wondered how they would get on with the United States Navy, 'but on the arrival of the United States ships, both navies did their utmost to make the working together a success – and splendidly they succeeded'. He closed with his 'most heartfelt gratitude for the wonderful affectionate friendship that you have honoured me with, which is my most valuable possession, and which I cordially return. Goodbye; good fortune to you all.'

It sounded and felt like a last farewell. He must have known he had only a few years of life left. He was seventy-seven years old, tired, and beginning to fail. He sailed for home the following day.

A leader in the *Times* on 30 July 1934 concluded with this passage: 'In the world at this moment there is only too much evidence that hatred and savagery are quick to spread. Friendship and goodwill also, it seems, will spread and will endure; and Admiral Bayly's visit to the United States will turn many a gaze upward towards one of the serenest gleams in a wild and stormy sky.'

Towards the end of March 1935, the admiral felt a deep sadness at the news that one of his cherished friends in Queenstown (it had reverted to its old name Cove/Cobh by then), the Catholic Bishop of Cloyne, Dr Robert Browne, had died on the 23 March at the age of ninety-one.

In 1937, Admiral Bayly had to sell the house that he had purchased with the money sent to him by the Queenstown Association. He and his niece moved to a flat in London. He was frail now and his health was failing. But his mind was as lively as ever, and his memory largely unimpaired. He could remember with clarity passing out of the training ship *Britannia* in June 1872 when he and three colleagues were the only navigating cadets out of a total of forty-two. He had clear recollections of HMS *Ariadne*, the first Royal Navy ship to which he was posted, and of the year-long cruise to such faraway places as Lisbon, Cadiz, Gibraltar and the Mediterranean; the island of Madeira off the west coast of Morocco; the Azores, 900 miles west of Lisbon, and across the Atlantic to Halifax, the capital of Nova Scotia. He remembered two sailors being flogged on the *Ariadne* as a punishment for mutiny, and he guessed that that was the last flogging carried out in the Royal Navy. He could recall going to Greenwich College in 1883 to do a nine-month course to qualify as a torpedo lieutenant. And he could name all the ships he served in, all the places he went to, all his promotions and what they entailed.

And then of course there were his most recent memories – the memories of his time at Queenstown as Commander-in-Chief. Particularly sharp were the memories of the men, the sloop captains and the trawler skippers and the skippers of the drifters. And the Americans who came over and fought the sea war alongside the Royal Navy. Who could forget the Americans? Their names were imprinted on his brain and in his heart – Sims and Poinsett Pringle and Taussig and Hanrahan and Berrien and Fairfield and Zogbaum and Poteet and Carpender and Johnson and Blakely and Williams – and Bagley, poor Bagley of the *Jacob Jones*. And so many more.

He remembered Commander Williams, USN, when his destroyer's steering gear was out of action and he had come into Queenstown to get it repaired, turning the USS *Duncan* by her propellers, and taking her backwards out the harbour to look for a U-boat he'd been told was operating there! Bayly was very proud of him.

He remembered going to sea several times on American destroyers (twice with Hanrahan on the *Cushing*) so that he could observe how the ships behaved and how the Americans worked them. He had been duly impressed. And each time he'd gone to sea with them, the Americans had honoured him by flying his admiral's flag. He remembered, too, the day he had taken Admiral Sims and Captain Pringle out to sea with him on his flagship to watch depth charge exercises, and how he had ribbed them about the headlines that would result if the flagship was sunk by a torpedo, and how the Germans would gloat over the coup of getting the Commander, US Naval Forces Operating in European Waters, the Commander-in-Chief of the Western Approaches, the chief-of-staff to both of them – all in the one day!

Lewis Bayly's niece persisted in trying to get her uncle to write his memoirs, and he finally but reluctantly agreed, but on the condition that she did not publish the book while he was alive. Then in May 1938, two days after completing the memoirs, he became ill. He died on 16 May. He was eighty-one.

Miss Voysey – his constant companion for thirty-one years – turned down the offer by the Admiralty to give her Uncle Lewis a full naval funeral. Her reason – 'It was so unlike him.' The sun was shining when his coffin was taken to the chapel. After a simple ceremony, the remains of Admiral Sir Lewis Bayly were cremated, and Violet Voysey later scattered the ashes in a Garden of Remembrance in London. She sent all the flowers, other than one single wreath, to the Cenotaph. She placed that lone wreath on her uncle's ashes. It was the one sent by the Queenstown Association.

Five months after Lewis Bayly died, President Roosevelt wrote in a foreword to *Pull Together* that the admiral, under whose command had been ninety-two different American ships, had been able to inspire in the officers and men of the American ships 'a feeling that went beyond mere confidence ... a spirit of personal affection for the admiral sprang up, and within a year he had become almost a household word in both the American and British navies'. Roosevelt, who had been Assistant Secretary of the Navy during the American ships' time at Queenstown, revealed that before they left for overseas duty 'many young officers came to me in the Navy Department and pleaded, almost with tears in their eyes, for assignment to new destroyers that were about to go into commission for duty under the Queenstown Command'.

Along with Britain's First Lord of the Admiralty, Sir Eric Geddes, Roosevelt had visited Queenstown in July 1918 on a tour of inspection. At the time he had told an Associated Press man in Queenstown that he had been greatly impressed with the pulling together of the British and American naval units into one efficient antisubmarine operating force, without either losing any feature of its identity. 'All are working together under a British admiral [Bayly], who has the admiration of every officer of the fleet,' he had said.

In a press release, Roosevelt said that he had found in Queenstown frictionless and efficient unity. 'The entire absence on both sides of any national or professional jealousy,' his statement said, 'and the ease and simplicity with which the principles of a single command had established itself' had impressed him as 'one of the soundest guarantees for eventual victory'. He considered that 'only by the unifying of command had it become possible to systematise the methods of war at sea'. He also referred to the naval forces being used as a single weapon.

'Admiral Bayly and Miss Voysey's house on the hill,' he said, 'was not only the centre for the planning of major operations, but was also a haven where the young American officers were made to feel at home … The memory of Admiral Bayly will live for all time in the tender affection of the navy of the United States.'

AFTERWORD

And what of Admiralty House, built in 1886, Admiral Bayly's nerve centre for the war against the U-boats?

On 10 August 1922 *The New York Times* ran a story under the headline: 'Free State Lands 1,500 Near Cork; Queenstown Afire'. It had a sub-head that said: 'Steamship Captain Notes Five Fires in Queenstown – Admiralty House Ablaze'. The steamship SS *Orlock Head* arrived at Queenstown from Antwerp with a cargo intended for Cork, but had to turn back at Blackrock because sunken barges blocked the channel. 'Further down [the captain] noticed five distinct fires in Queenstown, including the Admiralty House, which is the former British Naval headquarters in South Ireland, and a military hospital,' the story said. 'The building is known to thousands of the personnel of the American naval units which served in these waters during the war.' Republican forces had set the house alight.

The Catholic Church later bought the gutted shell and refurbished it. For a time it was used as a noviciate for the Sisters of Mercy. The Benedictine Order of nuns purchased it in 1993 and, at the time of this writing, they use it as a contemplative monastery. Its name now is St Benedict's priory.

BIBLIOGRAPHY

Ansted, A. *A Dictionary of Sea Terms*. (Revised by Peter Clissold) Browne, Son & Ferguson Ltd, Glasgow 1991

Bayly, Admiral Sir Lewis. *Pull Together!* George Harrap & Co. Ltd, London 1939

Beesly, Patrick. *Room 40*. Hamish Hamilton, London 1982

Broderick, Mary. *History of Cobh*. Mary Broderick, 1989

Carr, John. *The Stranger in Ireland*. London 1806

Chatterton, E. Keble. *Danger Zone*. Rich & Cowan Ltd., London 1934

Corbett, Julian S. *Some Principles of Maritime Strategy*. Naval & Military Press, Uckfield 2003

Daniels, Josephus. *Our Navy at War*. Pictorial Bureau, Washington 1922

Delany, Vice-Admiral Walter S., United States Navy (Retd). *Bayly's Navy* (pamphlet). Naval Historical Foundation, 1980

Elleton, D. H. *Roosevelt and Wilson. A comparative study*. John Murray, London 1965

Eyewitness to History, *U-boat Attack, 1916*. John Murray, London 1905

Frost, Wesley. *Letter to Secretary of State, 24 May 1917*. Wesley Frost Papers (RG 30/30) Oberlin College Archives

Frost, Wesley. *German Submarine Warfare*. D. Appleton & Co., 1918

Gibbons, Edward. *Floyd Gibbons – Your Headline Hunter*. Exposition Press, New York 1953

Gilbert, Martin. *First World War.* Weidenfeld & Nicholson, 1994

Gray, Edward A. *The Killing Time.* Seeley, Service & Co. Ltd, 1972

Gregory, Mackenzie J. *Marauders of the Sea.* The Naval Historical Society of Australia, 1984–2008

Hart, B. S. Liddell. *History of the First World War 1914–1918.* Cassell & Co., 1970

Hawkins, Nigel. *The Starvation Blockades.* Leo Cooper, 2002

Hendrick, Burton J. *The Life and Letters of Walter H. Page.* Doubleday, Page & Company, New York 1922

History of the Office of Naval Intelligence. Office of Naval Intelligence, Washington D.C, 1993

H.M. Stationery Office 1943. *His Majesty's Minesweepers.*

Ireland, Bernard. *War At Sea.* Cassell, London 2002

Jellicoe, John Rushworth. *The Crisis of the Naval War.* Cassell, London 1920

Keegan, John. *The First World War.* Hutchinson, London 1998

Kemp, Peter (ed.). *The Oxford Companion to Ships and the Sea.* Oxford University Press, 1976

Kittredge, Tracy Barrett. *Naval Lessons of the Great War.* Doubleday, Page & Co., 1921

Knight, E. F. *The Union-Castle and the War.* The Union-Castle Mail Steamship Co. Ltd, London 1920

Knox, Dudley W. A. *History of the United States Navy.* Putnam, New York 1936

Lauriat, Charles E. *The Lusitania's Last Voyage.* Houghton Mifflin, Boston 1915

Lewis, Samuel. *Lewis' Cork.* 1837

Messimer, Dwight R. *Find and Destroy.* Naval Institute Press, Annapolis 2001

Morison, Elting E. *Admiral Sims and the Modern American Navy.* Houghton Mifflin, Boston 1942

Mullins, Claud. *The Leipzig Trials.* H. F. & G. Witherby, 1921

Naval Doctrine Publication 1. Department of the Navy, Washington D.C. 1994

Pope, Stephen and Wheal, Elizabeth-Anne (eds). *The First World War* (Dictionary). Macmillan, 1995

Port Alberni Public Library, British Columbia. *The Sinking of H.M.H.S. Llandovery Castle.*

Preston, Diana. *Wilful Murder.* Doubleday, 2002

Ramsay, David. *Lusitania.* Chatham Publishing, London 2001

Shermer, David. *World War I.* Octopus Books Ltd, London 1975

Simpson, Colin. *Lusitania.* Longman, London 1972

Sims, Rear Admiral William Sowden. *The Victory at Sea.* Doubleday, Page & Co., 1920

Tarrant, V. E. *The U-boat Offensive 1914-1945.* Arms and Armour, 1989

Terraine, John. *Business in Great Waters.* Leo Cooper Ltd, London 1989

Thompson, Julian. *The War at Sea 1914-1918.* Sidgwick & Jackson, 2005

Trask, David F. *Captains and Cabinets.* University of Missouri Press, 1972

Taussig, Commander Joseph Knefler. *The Queenstown Patrol, 1917.* Naval War College, Newport R.I. 1996

Tuchman, Barbara. *The Guns of August.* Random House, 1962

— *The Zimmerman Telegram.* Constable, London 1958

Venzon, Anne Cipriano (ed.). *The United States in the First World War.* Garland Publishing Inc., New York 1995

Weddigen, Otto. *The First Submarine Blow is Struck.* The American Legion, Indianapolis 1931

Woodham-Smith, Cecil. *The Great Hunger.* Hamish Hamilton, 1962

www.uboat.net

INDEX

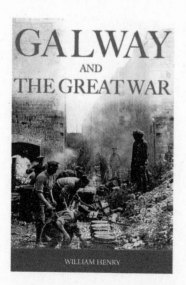